The Legal Environment of Insurance

Volume I

The Legal Environment of Insurance

Volume I

JAMES J. LORIMER, J.D., CPCU
Retired Vice President, Government Relations
Nationwide Mutual Insurance Company

HARRY F. PERLET, JR., J.D.
Retired Assistant General Counsel
Insurance Services Office

FREDERICK G. KEMPIN, JR., J.D., LL.B.
Retired Professor and Chairman
The Wharton School Legal Studies Department
University of Pennsylvania

FREDERICK R. HODOSH, Ph.D., J.D., CPCU
Retired Vice President and General Counsel
Director of Legal and Claims Education
American Institute for CPCU

Coordinating Author
KAREN K. PORTER, J.D.
Assistant Director of Curriculum
American Institute for CPCU

Fourth Edition • 1993

AMERICAN INSTITUTE FOR
CHARTERED PROPERTY CASUALTY UNDERWRITERS
720 Providence Road, Malvern, Pennsylvania 19355-0716

Fourth Edition • July 1993

Library of Congress Catalog Number 93-071085
International Standard Book Number 0-89463-064-4

Printed in the United States of America

Dedication

The American Institute for Chartered Property Casualty Underwriters dedicates this edition of *The Legal Environment of Insurance* to the memory of Dr. Clyde M. Kahler, CLU.

Born in 1901, Dr. Kahler was educated at the Wharton School of the University of Pennsylvania, earning a bachelor of science degree in economics in 1922, a master's degree in 1925, and a Ph.D. in 1930. He began his teaching career at the Wharton School in 1922, encouraged to join the faculty by his teachers, especially Dr. Solomon S. Huebner and Dr. Harry J. Loman, who were pioneers in the movement toward professionalism in insurance.

When Dr. Loman became the first dean of the American Institute, he turned to Dr. Kahler to help develop and grade the Institute's examinations. He officially joined the CPCU examination committee in 1954, chaired the committee from 1964 until 1977, and continued to serve on the committee until 1981. He also served as corporate secretary of the Institute's board of trustees and, on his retirement, was elected secretary emeritus and life trustee.

Dr. Kahler's work on the early CPCU examinations did much to help establish the standards that earned for the CPCU designation the respect and reputation it now enjoys throughout the property and casualty insurance business. Because of his all-encompassing command of all disciplines related to insurance, including insurance and business law, this dedication is intended as a most appropriate tribute to his memory.

Foreword

The American Institute for Chartered Property Casualty Underwriters and the Insurance Institute of America are independent, non-profit, educational organizations serving the needs of the property and liability insurance business. The Institutes develop a wide range of programs—curricula, study materials, and examinations—in response to the educational requirements of various elements of the business.

The American Institute confers the Chartered Property Casualty Underwriter (CPCU®) professional designation on those who meet the Institute's experience, ethics, and examination requirements.

The Insurance Institute of America offers associate designations and certificate programs in the following technical and managerial disciplines:

Accredited Adviser in Insurance (AAI®)
Associate in Claims (AIC)
Associate in Underwriting (AU)
Associate in Risk Management (ARM)
Associate in Loss Control Management (ALCM®)
Associate in Premium Auditing (APA®)
Associate in Management (AIM)
Associate in Research and Planning (ARP®)
Associate in Insurance Accounting and Finance (AIAF)
Associate in Automation Management (AAM®)
Associate in Marine Insurance Management (AMIM®)
Associate in Reinsurance (ARe)
Associate in Fidelity and Surety Bonding (AFSB)
Certificate in General Insurance
Certificate in Supervisory Management
Certificate in Introduction to Claims
Certificate in Introduction to Property and Liability Insurance

The Institutes began publishing textbooks in 1976 to help students meet the national examination standards. Since that time, we have produced more than seventy-five individual textbook volumes. Despite the vast differences in the subjects and purposes of these volumes, they all have much in common. First, each book is specifically designed to increase knowledge and develop skills that can improve job performance and help students achieve the educational objectives of the course for which it is assigned. Second, all of the manuscripts of our texts are widely reviewed prior to publication, by both insurance business practitioners and members of the academic community. In addition, all of our texts and course guides reflect the work of Institute staff members. These writing or editing duties are seen as an integral part of their professional responsibilities, and no one earns a royalty based on the sale of our texts. We have proceeded in this way to avoid even the appearance of any conflict of interests. Finally, the revisions of our texts often incorporate improvements suggested by students and course leaders.

We welcome criticisms of and suggestions for improving our publications. It is only with such constructive comments that we can hope to improve the quality of our study materials. Please direct any comments you may have on this text to the Curriculum Department of the Institutes.

Norman A. Baglini, Ph.D., CPCU, CLU
President and Chief Executive Officer

Preface

Professionals today must know about the law relating to their areas of expertise, but they also must be familiar with many general legal concepts. CPCU 6 fills this need for insurance professionals. Although some areas of law discussed in CPCU 6 do not have an obvious direct relationship to insurance, they are still necessary for the insurance professional in his or her career, as well as in everyday life.

The fourth edition of the *Legal Environment of Insurance* is a revision of the textbook for the business law part of the CPCU program. The original text was written by James J. Lorimer, J.D., CPCU; Harry F. Perlet, Jr., J.D.; Frederick G. Kempin, Jr., J.D., LL.B.; and Frederick R. Hodosh, Ph.D., J.D., CPCU. These authors completed a monumental task in summarizing a substantial part of the law school course of study.

In some areas of law, there have been few changes since publication of this book's third edition in 1987. However, in other areas there have been significant changes in the law and in legal emphases. This edition not only reflects changes and shifts emphases but also attempts to present legal concepts more clearly.

All chapters have been reviewed closely and then rewritten. Significant amounts of material have been rearranged, deleted, or added. For example, the new Chapter 1 presents a clear and comprehensive introduction to American law and the American legal system and now includes a summary treatment of the material formerly in Chapter 15 on administrative law.

This edition contains significant new contributions by the following authors:

Sheryl S. Chernoff, J.D.

John D. Cross
Claim Consultant
State Farm Mutual Automobile Insurance Co.

Andrew C. Jacobson, J.D.
Mound, Cotton & Wollan

Patrick F. O'Keefe, J.D.
Vice President and Associate General Counsel
Fireman's Fund Insurance Co.

Editing these authors' contributions was a very pleasing experience because, without exception, their manuscripts were comprehensive, clear, accurate, and well written.

Another rewarding aspect of revising CPCU 6 was working with its many consultants, reviewers, and contributing authors. In addition to the authors' uniformly excellent contributions, many of the reviewers contributed a substantial amount of time and work toward making CPCU 6 an even better course. Mary Ellen Maatman, J.D., Legal Writing Instructor at Widener University School of Law, deserves special mention for her meticulous review of the entire text. We are most indebted to the following reviewers, whose constructive criticism and suggestions have contributed greatly to efforts to make the new edition technically accurate, up-to-date, more comprehensive, and more readable:

Christopher P. Barr, J.D.
Barr, Weinraub, & Litman/Harleysville Insurance Companies

R. Michael Cass, J.D., CPCU
President and Principal Consultant
R.M. Cass Associates

David G. Condon, J.D., CPCU
Executive Vice President, Secretary and General Counsel
SMIS, Inc.

Christian C. Day, J.D.
Professor of Law, College of Law
Syracuse University

Richard C. Giles, LL.B.
Casualty Claim Manager
Allstate Insurance

Bruce D. Haarmann, J.D., CPCU
Assistant General Counsel
Wausau Insurance Companies

Barbara Reid Hartung, J.D.
Greenebaum, Doll and McDonald

Greg R. Hawkins, J.D.

Joseph M. Inwald, J.D., CPCU
Inwald Consulting Services

Edward M. Kopanski, J.D.
Counselor at Law

Irwin Lengel, CPCU, AAM
Master Underwriter
CIGNA Property and Casualty Companies

Peter M. Lencsis, J.D.
Assistant Vice President-Legal
Greater New York Mutual Insurance Companies

Kevin P. McKernan, J.D.
McKernan & Gatins

Charles Morgan, J.D., CPCU
Risk Engineering Manager
Zurich-American Insurance Group

Gerald D. Seidl, J.D., CPCU, CLU
General Counsel
United Fire and Casualty Company/United Life Insurance
    Company

Douglas R. Smith, CPCU
Personal Lines Underwriting Manager
Union Insurance Co.

Finally, special thanks are due to the following course leaders for their consultation for the new edition: Donald M. Grimes, J.D., CPCU, Kelly, Grimes, Pietrangelo, and Vakil; James I. Keenan, Jr., J.D., CPCU, Vice President, General Counsel and Corporate Secretary, The F&D Companies; and John J. O'Brien, J.D. Many other course leaders from all parts of the United States gave essential advice on questionnaires mailed early in the revision process. They, in a very important way, gave direction to the fourth edition of CPCU 6 and deserve all our thanks.

Your comments regarding this edition are not only welcome, but needed. In preparation for the next edition, we need any corrections, comments, or advice you may have to offer and ask that you call or write to give your input.

Karen K. Porter, J.D.

Table of Contents

xvi—Contents

CHAPTER 1

Introduction to American Law

The modern professional must be familiar with the law relating to his or her field, as well as with many other general legal concepts. Just as the business world constantly increases in complexity, so does the law relating to any particular business. This course is entitled "The Legal Environment of Insurance" rather than "Insurance Law" because insurance law is a very specific area within the whole of American law and is too limited in scope to provide the insurance professional with the background he or she needs.

This course, however, examines general law within the insurance context and gives students an overview of many legal subjects that the insurance professional may meet in the course of business. The topics in the course do not always have an obvious direct relationship to insurance but are topics an insurance professional needs to know about and can encounter at any point in his or her career. Knowledge of these areas of law may also be helpful in everyday life.

THE NEED TO STUDY LAW

The insurance business depends on agreements between insurance companies and individuals or business entities, which are formal contracts that create legal relationships. The provisions of an insurance contract govern the rights and obligations of the parties to the contract. The language of insurance contracts, however, is not always clear to all parties. In many cases, the insurer and insured have different beliefs about the rights and obligations that an insurance policy has created. As a result, courts must often interpret insurance policy terms.

Over the centuries, general contractual interpretations have developed into rules that are also applicable to the insurance contract. Although it is unnecessary for every insurance professional to understand all facets of the law relating to insurance, those who work in insurance should have some understanding of general legal principles as they relate to insurance.

Insurance policies cover many types of losses. Some losses arise from one person wronging another, and the law calls these acts "torts." Chapters 8, 9, and 10 examine torts, a major classification of law. A tort can be intentional, such as an assault and battery, or unintentional negligence, such as an automobile accident. When a question arises as to the meaning of the insurance contract with regard to a wrongful act, not only may the law of contracts apply, but also the law of torts.

A specific case may present no question about insurance coverage at all, but may instead introduce a question involving only tort law. A lawsuit may also raise questions under some other body of law, such as employment law. An employer may insure against claims for alleged employment discrimination, for example, or for unfair labor practices, both of which federal statutes prohibit, while other employment-related lawsuits are based entirely on torts.

The question in many lawsuits involving wrongs by one person to another is not whether the insurance contract covers a wrong, but whether it covers a particular wrong as the law defines it. People often do wrong things to each other, but not all wrongs are legal wrongs. If one person merely teases another, it is probably not a legal wrong. A threat to do bodily harm, however, may be a legal wrong.

Even if a legal wrong occurred, the question still may be whether the wrongdoer is liable. When the insured has liability coverage for negligence, for example, the first legal question may be whether negligence, as tort law defines it, actually occurred. The second question may be whether the wrongdoer had any duty to the complaining party. When the insured has liability coverage for alleged age discrimination, as another example, the first question may be whether illegal age discrimination occurred. The second question may be whether the act forbidding discrimination covered the employer in question.

Another body of law, agency law, may decide whether an insurance company employee can bind the insurer to cover an insured's loss although the written policy did not create coverage. Agency law may also decide whether an insurance company must cover a loss incurred because of an insured's negligent hiring of an employee. Still another body of law, property law, applies to real estate title disputes in which most, if not all, claimants have title insurance.

THE AMERICAN LEGAL SYSTEM

When people first gathered in groups, they adopted rules to govern their relations with one another. In early times, generations handed these rules down to succeeding generations by word of mouth. As people developed the ability to record their thoughts, they began to write their laws.

Hammurabi, a Babylonian ruler, developed his famous code of 300 laws circa 1792-1750 B.C. These laws dealt with business and family relationships. A main principle of Hammurabi's Code was that "the strong shall not injure the weak," a principle that modern law also attempts to observe. A well-developed legal system was one of the great contributions of the Roman Empire to western civilization. Today, concepts of the Roman law form the basis of civil law in several continental European and Latin American countries.

Civil Law System

The civil law and common law systems differ significantly in origin and in form. Both systems exist in the United States. The *common law system,* deriving from English law, is the foundation of the American legal system. The *civil law system,* deriving from Roman law, was not only the origin of law in several continental European and Latin American countries but also became the basis of the law in parts of the United States that were at one time under French or Spanish rule, such as Louisiana and California.

Countries using the civil law system have comprehensive codes of written laws, such as the Code of Napoleon, to cover all legal questions. They rely on scholarly interpretations of their codes, rather than on court cases, for interpretations of the law. The English common law system, on the other hand, relies heavily not only on written laws but to a great extent on written court decisions about actual cases. The most complete vestige of the civil law system in the United States today is the law of Louisiana, which retains many aspects of the French civil law that formed its foundation.

Common Law System

Nonlawyers often refer to "the law" with a belief that there are written laws to answer all legal questions. American law, however, is not so simple. Written laws, or *statutes,* form much of the law, but "the law" in this country also includes thousands of actual cases in which courts analyze sets of facts and then apply rulings from prior cases.

Many cases involve no statutory law at all. This system differs greatly from the civil law system, which depends on statutory law. One term people often use is *black-letter law,* implying that one can find a very clearly enunciated "law" in a lawbook. American law contains more case analysis than black-letter law.

At the basis of both English and American law is the common law. Beginning as unwritten customs that local courts recognized and enforced, the common law system arose in England after the Norman conquest in 1066 A.D. The "law common to all England" developed out of a constantly expanding number of cases involving actual disputes that the English royal courts and tribunals decided. English and American courts still cite English cases dating back to the fifteenth century.

When English colonists settled in North America, they brought with them the English common law. By then, the common law had become a well-developed body of principles, and it became the foundation for American law. The common law, however, is not just an ancient set of principles forming the foundation of modern law. The decisions American courts make today are part of the constantly evolving common law. When lawyers speak of the common law, they refer not only to historical law, but also to rules that are undergoing revision every day.

The foundation of the common law system is the adherence by American courts to prior case rulings, or *precedents.* Once a court has decided a dispute, that decision serves as authority for the solution of similar cases in the future. This method of legal analysis is the *doctrine of stare decisis,* which means "to stand as decided."

The following example illustrates how the common law grows from day to day in courts all over the country. If an insured and an insurance company disagree as to the meaning of a policy provision and go to a state court because of this dispute, the court may examine prior cases in which courts determined the meaning of the same or similar provisions. The court looks first for similar cases in the same state. If there are none, or if the court needs additional guidance, it looks for similar cases in other states. If the court finds no similar cases, it may draw upon general contractual principles and court rulings in somewhat similar cases to analyze the "case at bar," or current case. The court also scrutinizes the facts of the current case very carefully to determine distinctions and similarities between that case and prior cases.

Synthesis is the process of reviewing prior cases, along with statutes, if any, and applying previous law to a new fact situation. Facts, however, vary greatly as thousands of new cases arrive in courts each year. At times courts can find little or no guidance in previous law. They often call unprecedented situations *threshold cases* because they present new questions. When they encounter threshold cases, judges summon all applicable law in an attempt to arrive at fair decisions. The judicial thought process involves some subjectivity, as well as objective synthesis of law.

Judicial Influence on Common Law

Although most court decisions have sound objective rationales, individual judges' biases can affect decisions. The legal system, however, has built-in controls for arriving at fair outcomes in disputes. For example, if a party loses in trial court and appeals that decision, the appeals court may view the situation differently. People holding judicial positions change from time to time, either by election, appointment, or attrition. One political party may succeed in getting certain judges with that party's views on the bench. When the political party in power changes, however, the composition of a court may also change. On the other hand, some judicial positions, notably at the federal level, are lifelong, so a political view can extend for the life of a judge.

The method of selecting judges varies from state to state. In some states voters elect most judges, while in other states voters elect people who either appoint judges or who choose other officials to appoint judges. In a system where voters elect judges, the electorate can select new judges when terms expire if it perceives a need for changes in the directions the courts are taking. In a system in which public officials appoint judges, often called *merit selection of judges,* voters elect new officials who appoint judges either directly or indirectly.

The United States Supreme Court ("Supreme Court" in this course) is a good example of how changing political climates affect law, particularly the threshold legal questions that are not easy to solve and for which there is little precedential guidance. The political party in power at the presidential level can "stack" the Supreme Court with justices reflecting party views. Later, another political party can stack the court with justices having different viewpoints. Because Supreme Court justices hold their judicial positions for life, a president can affect the law for many years to come through appointments that reflect a certain political view. The Supreme Court usually has nine justices, and every judicial retirement, resignation, or death gives the incumbent president an opportunity to appoint a new justice reflecting that president's own philosophy.

Individual views and values, therefore, can influence Supreme Court decisions, particularly when justices must go beyond prior case law to decide novel questions. The common law doctrine of *stare decisis* gives a degree of certainty to the law. People should be able to rely on definite law and conduct their affairs accordingly. This does not mean that courts must decide all similar cases exactly the same way, but only very strong reasons should persuade a court to depart from the rulings in precedents.

Common Law Not Absolute. The law is not an absolute but is part of the evolution of society. What many considered good law in the United States a century ago would, in many instances, be considered bad law today.

In the 1880s, in most jurisdictions, there were few restrictions on the use or abuse of child labor. Less than half the population had the right to vote, with women and many blacks denied that right. Married women did not have full legal rights because the law merged their identities with those of their husbands. The rule of the marketplace was *caveat emptor,* or "let the buyer beware," with little legal protection for consumers. Labor unions were just beginning, and workers were at the mercy of employers. Industries had no restrictions in their efforts to crush or wipe out competitors. In the uncontrolled insurance industry of the nineteenth century, some policies contained so many conditions and exceptions that payment of benefits would occur only under the most unusual circumstances.

The common law reliance on precedent gives American law great flexibility. A court can find that a prior decision was clearly wrong and thus decide not to follow the law of that decision. Courts generally do not follow precedent when the earlier rule of law has lost its usefulness or when the original reasons for the rule no longer exist. Both legislatures and courts are subject to changing times. A legislature can change the law by new legislation, and courts can also change the law from time to time by overruling prior decisions.

Landmark decisions are historically important court rulings that change or add to prior law significantly and that have far-reaching effects upon society. One of the most well-known examples is the United States Supreme Court decision in Brown v. Board of Education,[1] overruling previous cases condoning racial segregation in schools. Another example well known to the public is Miranda v. Arizona,[2] which required that police give certain warnings to suspects in criminal cases before questioning them. The rulings in Brown and Miranda drastically changed practices in two areas.

Although courts may overrule prior decisions, the common law system permits courts to do so only when there are sound judicial reasons to do so. The common law system is designed to remove capriciousness from the law and to give stability to society and business. In many areas the law has evolved to a position clearly different, if not completely opposite, from the law that previously existed. Most fields of the law have experienced such an evolution.

Law of the Future. The law of the twenty-first century may make much of today's law as obsolete as much of nineteenth-century law is now. It is likely that major changes will continue in the field of human rights. For example, the Americans With Disabilities Act of 1990 (ADA) granted numerous new rights and protections to approximately forty-three million Americans.[3] Case interpretations of that act will continue for many years. As people live longer, a rapidly growing specialized field of law is developing around the special problems of an older population.

In the early 1970s, American environmental law was in its embryonic stages, but it since has developed rapidly in its importance and impact nationally and globally. In the 1970s, only a few lawyers specialized in health care law, which has grown into yet another major legal specialty and which appears destined to grow still more in the future. The widespread use of computers has resulted in another new field, computer law, which is now in its early stages. Many scientific and technological discoveries and advances in various fields, such as genetic engineering and reproductive medicine, pose and will continue to pose novel legal questions and are thus developing into new legal specialties.

The accelerated development of the global economy has resulted in an emphasis on international law and on international aspects of legal areas such as tax and corporate law. The development of the European Community is an example of change in the political organization of the globe. European countries in the future may not be as distinct politically, socially, and economically as they once were. One goal of unification is to eliminate most trade barriers among European countries. The dissolution of the former Soviet-dominated bloc of countries in Eastern Europe, territorial disputes in the Middle East, and instability in many developing countries present additional global concerns, contributing to the importance of international law today and in the future.

Certainty Necessary. Certainty is as crucial in the law as flexibility. Citizens and businesses need a degree of assurance about what the law prescribes. In business law, for example, the requirements of economic life dictate that commercial activities have definite legal meaning.

Certainty about what constitutes a binding agreement and the conditions under which courts enforce an agreement is essential to the success of an advanced economy in which people finalize millions of business transactions daily. In countries like the United States, where ownership of private property is a basic characteristic of the economy, the certain and effective transfer and inheritance of property are of great importance. In nations such as China, where the institution of private property has been less significant in this century, laws relating to private ownership of property are less important.

Whatever a society's philosophy and values, certainty in the law is necessary for general stability. American law provides a balance between flexibility to meet changing times and certainty to provide a sense of security for citizens.

Classifications of American Law

American law is capable of several methods of classification:

- As civil and criminal
- According to subject matter
- As substantive and procedural
- According to court or remedy

Each classification overlaps with and includes law from the other classifications.

Criminal and Civil. *Criminal law* applies to acts that society deems so harmful to the public welfare that government takes the responsibility for prosecuting and punishing the perpetrators. *Civil law* applies to all other legal matters. Civil law in this context is not the same as the civil law system discussed previously.

Criminal Law. Using criminal law, society prescribes a standard of conduct to which all inhabitants must adhere. A crime may be major, such as murder, or minor, such as a traffic violation. A major crime is called a *felony.* A minor crime, or *misdemeanor,* has historically been a crime punishable by fine or by imprisonment for a short period of time.

Misdemeanors are generally any crimes that are not felonies under state or federal law. *Summary offenses* are any crimes that are not felonies or misdemeanors under state law. Summary offenses usually do not carry jail sentences, but only monetary fines, while misdemeanors can result in inprisonment or fines. An example of a summary offense is a speeding ticket. An example of a misdemeanor is driving under the influence of drugs or alcohol. Written laws, such as statutes and *ordinances,* specify the nature of crimes and their punishments, whether imprisonment or fines or both.

The government controls the criminal law process and is the *prosecutor,* taking charge of the case on behalf of the public, whether or not a victim can or will come forward. The government decides that it is in society's best interests to press charges and then prosecutes in society's behalf. However, it is difficult to prove that a crime occurred without a complaining victim.

The prosecution in a criminal case must establish guilt beyond a reasonable doubt, while in civil actions the injured party must establish a case only by a preponderance of the evidence. The evidence in a civil case need only tip the imaginary scales of justice to one side or the other.

Civil Law. Civil law protects rights and provides remedies for breaches of duties. In a civil action, the injured party generally requests payment of damages as reimbursement for harm. The court can also direct the wrongdoer to perform in a certain manner, such as to transfer real estate that was the subject of a contract to sell. Failure to abide by a court order can result in a finding of *contempt of court,* or hindering a court's administration of justice. Contempt is quasi-criminal in nature.

One act can be both a criminal and a civil wrong. In such a case, an injured party can bring a civil suit requesting damages, while the government may prosecute the wrongdoer in a criminal case. An example of this occurs when one person unjustifiably hits another. This action, the commission of a battery, or unlawful touching, can be both a civil wrong and a crime. The one act results in separate civil and criminal trials.

In the civil trial the *plaintiff,* or complaining party, must establish the *defendant's,* or alleged wrongdoer's, wrongdoing only by a preponderance of the evidence. In a criminal case, however, the government must establish the defendant's guilt beyond a reasonable doubt to justify a punishment of imprisonment or fine.

Subject Matter. American law falls into many subject matter classifications. The major areas have their own rules and precedents. Examples of subject-matter classification of law are admiralty, contracts, torts, and property law.

Substantive and Procedural. Another way to classify American law is to call certain laws either substantive or procedural. Substantive law includes all the subject-area classifications discussed above, as well as other specialized areas. Procedural law governs the processes involved in determining rights and liabilities. These two classifications are intertwined and are often very difficult to distinguish.

Substantive Law. *Substantive law* defines citizens' rights and liabilities. It results from legislative and judicial case law, which defines legal relationships, such as those between individuals and between the state and individuals. It includes rules of law that specify what constitutes an enforceable contract, who may own and transfer property, and what forms of conduct are criminal or tortious. When nonlawyers refer to "the law," they usually mean substantive law.

Procedural Law. *Procedural law* specifies the methods used to enforce substantive law. Substantive rights must have procedures that provide a means for enforcing those rights, and practicing lawyers must have expertise in the procedural means for enforcing rights. Criminal and civil actions require different procedures, called *civil procedure* and *criminal procedure.*

In civil actions, such as breach of contract, the procedural law may be specific about what steps one must follow. A plaintiff must file certain *pleadings,* or legal papers, in the appropriate court and must serve the defendant properly with a summons or court order and a copy of the original complaint.

Procedural law not only governs the form and method for filing papers with a court but also tells courts the means by which they may apply substantive law. A state may, for example, set a maximum period of time within which a criminal defendant must come to trial. This is a procedural rule that enforces a criminal defendant's Sixth Amendment right to a speedy trial.

Law and Equity. Finally, another major way to classify American law is to divide it into *law* and *equity*. This division has ancient roots in England. Courts of law determine legal rights and remedies and can award money damages. Courts of equity supplement law courts and recognize many rights that common law courts do not recognize.

The term "equity" is unique to English and American law, and courts of equity arose in England long ago because of the failure of law courts to give adequate remedies in some cases. For example, in a contract for the sale of a unique item such as a one-of-a-kind antique, the usual legal remedy for breach of the contract would be money damages. A court of equity would consider the inadequacy of money damages as a remedy because the more important question is the right to possess the antique. A court of equity might direct specific performance of the contract by requiring a transfer of the antique to the new owner from the original owner.

A few jurisdictions still have law and equity courts. In most states, however, the courts now are in a single system, although one court may sit as a court of equity on one occasion and as a court of law on another. In the federal system and some state systems, law and equity are merged and the same court provides both equitable and legal remedies. An American citizen is entitled to a trial by jury on questions of law, but jury trials are not a part of equity court practice.

SOURCES OF AMERICAN LAW

There are fifty-one separate and distinct legal systems in the United States:

1. The federal legal system of the United States
2. The legal systems of each of the fifty states

Within each of the fifty-one legal systems, there are five sources of law:

1. The *constitutions* of the federal government and of each of the fifty states
2. The federal and state *legislative bodies,* which enact statutes
3. The *courts,* including the federal court system and the fifty state court systems, which report case law
4. The federal and state *executive branches,* which are not strictly sources of law, but which greatly influence law
5. *Federal and state administrative agencies,* which are responsible for considerable lawmaking and enforcement

The sources of American law are numerous, and it is not easy to understand the complex web of legal systems, each with its own statutory, case, and regulatory law. The insurance professional, however, should be acquainted with the general framework of the American legal system.

Constitutions

The United States Constitution ("Constitution" in this course) defines itself as the "supreme Law of the Land."[4] Each state has its own *constitution,* which is the supreme law of that state, subject only to the Constitution, which is supreme over all state constitutions. In the case of a conflict, the Constitution always prevails over a state constitution. A copy of the Constitution is appended to the end of this volume.

Since its adoption in 1789, the Constitution has survived the most significant social and economic developments in history to become the oldest constitution in the world today. The full text of the Constitution is printed in the Appendix to this volume.

An American constitution, whether federal or state, sets forth basic principles about a government's powers and limitations and the way that government may exercise those powers. Not all countries, however, have constitutions. For example, the United Kingdom and Israel do not have constitutions. Ghana had four civilian constitutions in a thirty-three-year period and several military regimes ruling under proclamations only.

In democratic countries, constitutions not only define governmental powers but also specify individual rights. The Constitution has served as a model for many countries in stating those individual rights. On the other hand, the Republic of South Africa has a constitution, but no bill of rights for individuals. Its parliament has an exclusive right to pass any law it wishes, and no court can declare legislation void.

In over 200 years of American history, the Constitution has experienced few changes. Generally, the first ten amendments place limitations upon the federal government's power, while the Fourteenth Amendment imposes many of the same limitations on state governments.

State Constitutions. Each of the fifty states has its own constitution. The Constitution is dominant, and any law that violates that Constitution, whether state or federal, is void. A state, however, may grant broader rights to its citizens than federal law or the Constitution as long as it does not violate the federal Constitution. For example, the Constitution does not contain an amendment explicitly prohibiting gender-based discrimination. Some states, such as Alaska, Colorado, Pennsylvania, Texas, and Virginia, do have equal rights amendments, which grant broader rights in this regard than the federal Constitution.

Constitution. Few lawyers study all fifty state constitutions. To do so would be a mammoth task. A lawyer usually studies a state constitution if necessary to analyze a legal question. It is necessary, however, not only for lawyers, but for insurance and other business professionals, to have some knowledge of the following provisions of the Constitution that most affect their businesses:

1. Congressional powers
2. Commerce Clause
3. Due Process Clause
4. Equal Protection Clause

Congressional Powers. The Constitution sets forth the *express powers of Congress,* which are to regulate commerce, levy and collect taxes, borrow money, and establish uniform laws on bankruptcy, as well as other powers.[5] The Constitution also provides for the *implied powers of Congress* to pass laws necessary to carry out all of Congress's express powers.[6] If the Constitution does not specify that the federal government has a particular power, and if it does not forbid state exercise of that power, then the states may exercise that power.

Commerce Clause. The *Commerce Clause* of the Constitution gives Congress the power to regulate commerce with foreign nations and among the states. *Commerce* includes any commercial activity, whether interstate or intrastate, if it has any appreciable effect upon interstate commerce, whether that effect is direct or indirect.

Trade or commerce includes, for example, the distribution of movies, real estate, gathering of news, professional sports, and insurance underwriting. The Supreme Court has upheld antitrust laws as a valid exercise of the commerce power. The *Affectation Doctrine* applies the clause to any commercial activity that affects interstate commerce.[7]

Due Process Clause. The Fifth Amendment *Due Process Clause,* one of the most important clauses of the Constitution, provides, among other things, that no one may be deprived of life, liberty, or property without "due process of law."[8] The Fifth Amendment provides this right with regard to actions by the federal government, and the Fourteenth Amendment provides the same right with regard to actions by state governments.

Most cases in which plaintiffs make due process claims involve procedural questions. An insurance company, for example, might protest a state insurance department's actions on the grounds that those actions affected the insurer adversely without a procedure providing the insurer enough opportunity to protect its interests.

Equal Protection Clause. The *Equal Protection Clause* of the Fourteenth Amendment provides that no state shall deny any person within its jurisdiction the equal protection of the law.[9] This clause prohibits laws that discriminate unfairly or arbitrarily and provides protection to both individuals and to corporations. This clause assures equal treatment to all persons under like circumstances and conditions, in terms of both privileges and liabilities. Many state constitutions also have equal protection clauses.

State automobile *guest statutes* are a good example of how equal protection clauses can work. A guest statute normally requires that the guest passenger in a vehicle establish that an accident resulted from the driver's gross negligence rather than just from ordinary negligence, in order to recover damages from the driver. Proof of willful misconduct or gross negligence in court is much more difficult for a guest to prove than ordinary negligence. Many courts have stricken these requirements as unconstitutional under equal protection clauses because they impose special burdens of proof on guest passengers.

Legislative Bodies

At practically every level of American government there are lawmakers, or *legislative bodies,* who enact *statutes,* or written laws. The two major legislative classifications in the United States are Congress and the fifty state legislatures.

Federal Congress. The federal legislative body is *Congress,* which is *bicameral.* That is, there are two chambers of Congress, the Senate and the House of Representatives. Each state has two representatives in the Senate and a number of representatives in the House, based on that state's population.

If the Constitution has granted powers exclusively to the federal government, only Congress may act. In the areas that are primarily the concern of the individual states, only the legislatures of the respective states may enact legislation.

State and Local Legislative Bodies. Most states have bicameral legislatures, or assemblies, mirroring the federal Congressional structure. At the city, township, and village levels, thousands of legislative bodies also enact various written laws called *ordinances* governing their citizens. Ordinances are the laws passed by local government, usually municipal corporations. A state or local legislative body can clarify or change common law and can proscribe unacceptable conduct as long as the laws it passes do not violate either the United States Constitution or the state constitution.

If there is a question of whether Congress or a state legislative body has the power to enact a law, a court must determine the answer. Frequently, courts must also interpret statutes and ordinances.

Uniform Laws. With the federal government and each of fifty states, as well as thousands of local governments enacting laws, confusion can result. Business law can be confusing when it varies from state to state and from local government to local government. To minimize these difficulties, many states have adopted *uniform laws,* which are essentially the same from state to state. For example, the *Uniform Commercial Code (UCC),* which all states except Louisiana have adopted, regulates the sale of goods and other commercial transactions. The UCC has resulted in much uniformity in commercial transactions throughout the country.

Another example of attempts to promote more uniformity among state laws occurs in insurance law. Insurance companies are subject to a multitude of statutes, rules, and regulations among the various states. As early as 1871 states recognized the need to establish an organization among the states to promote uniformity in regulation between the states and to exchange regulatory information, resulting in the creation of the *National Association of Insurance Commissioners (NAIC).* The NAIC's unique role in the insurance regulatory system is to assist state regulators through NAIC resources and services. This pooling of information enables regulators to coordinate responses to changing conditions in the insurance marketplace. The NAIC de-

Exhibit 1-1
Federal Court System

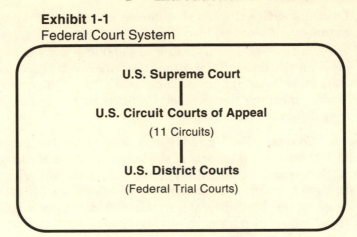

velops model acts and regulations with respect to state insurance department functions and intends to encourage uniformity in insurance regulation.

Courts

The federal government has its own federal court system, and each of the fifty state governments has its own court system. All fifty-one of these systems are separate and unrelated in most respects. A party may appeal from a state to a federal court, but only if that party alleges a violation of the Constitution or of a federal statute.

Federal Court System.   The Constitution provides that "the judicial power of the United States shall be vested in one Supreme Court, and in such inferior courts as Congress may from time to time ordain and establish."[10] Thus, the Constitution provides specifically only for the Supreme Court, but Congress has provided for courts of appeal in eleven judicial circuits and for many United States district courts. Exhibit 1-1 summarizes the federal court system structure.

Jurisdiction.   There are also special courts that hear particular kinds of cases, such as the United States Customs Court, Bankruptcy Courts, Patent Appeals Court, and the Court of Military Appeals. Federal courts handle cases raising federal questions, such as those that involve the Constitution, federal laws, and cases in which the United States is either a plaintiff or defendant. Original jurisdiction also rests with federal courts in cases involving the following:

•   Admiralty and maritime jurisdiction.

- Lawsuits where citizens of different states claim land under grants by different states.
- Cases with disputes amounting to $50,000 or more in damages between citizens of different states or between citizens of one state and of a foreign state. These cases involve *diversity jurisdiction,* meaning that a diversity of citizenship, or of parties from different states, exists.

District Courts.   The United States District Courts (mentioned in Exhibit 1-1) are the trial courts of the federal system. If the government has, for example, charged a person with a federal crime, that defendant stands trial in a United States District Court, If there is a suit for damages involving federal law, the trial may occur in a district court. District courts also try cases involving diversity jurisdiction.

There may be one federal district court sitting in a state, as in Maine, or more than one. In Washington, for example, there are two federal district courts, one each for the eastern and western districts. In California there are four federal district courts, one each for the central, eastern, northern, and southern districts. Louisiana has eastern, middle, and western district courts, as does Pennsylvania.

Circuit Courts of Appeal.   The losing party in a case before a federal district court may appeal to the appropriate United States Circuit Court of Appeals. There are eleven circuits, each covering more than one state or territory. In early American history, judges "rode the circuits" over a large area, holding court in different places within that area. This practice resulted in naming the federal appeals courts "circuit courts."

An appeals court of any kind, in either the federal or a state system, is called an *appellate court.* If, for example, a party loses a lawsuit in the United States District Court in Maine, that party may appeal to the United States Circuit Court of Appeals for the First Circuit, which serves as the federal appellate court for Maine, Massachusetts, New Hampshire, Puerto Rico, and Rhode Island. If a party loses a lawsuit in a federal district court in Colorado, that party may appeal to the Circuit Court of Appeals for the Tenth Circuit, which is the federal appellate court for Colorado, Kansas, New Mexico, Oklahoma, Utah, and Wyoming.

The Supreme Court.   The losing party on appeal in a circuit court of appeals may take the case to the Supreme Court. The Supreme Court, however, has the discretion to choose which cases it will hear. The party asking the Supreme Court to consider a case files a petition for a writ of *certiorari.* The Supreme Court grants review solely within its discretion, and it need not explain to anyone the reasons it grants or denies a petition for a writ of *certiorari*. Each year the Supreme Court receives over 5,000 requests to decide cases.[11]

The Supreme Court does not agree to consider most of these cases, and therefore the Circuit Courts' decisions usually stand as the law. Whether or not the Supreme Court decides to consider a case, it is the final avenue of appeal in the American legal system for the parties involved.

State Court Systems.   The state court systems are somewhat similar to the federal court system, but the names of the various courts can result in great confusion. There is no conformity in the use of court names at various levels among the fifty states, and lawyers must learn the court system in each state in which they might practice.

The highest appellate court in each state usually bears the name "supreme court," but there are exceptions. For example, the highest court of Massachusetts is the Supreme Judicial Court; the highest court of New York is the New York Court of Appeals, and the trial court of general jurisdiction is the Supreme Court.

Some states have an "intermediate appellate" level court, which hears appeals from trial courts before they can go on appeal to the state's highest court. In Pennsylvania, for example, there are two intermediate appellate courts, the Commonwealth Court, which hears all appeals involving the state, and the Superior Court, which hears everything else. Therefore, in Pennsylvania a party can appeal a case from the trial court to either the Commonwealth or Superior Court, then ultimately to the Pennsylvania Supreme Court.

Another designation for the trial court system of a state is the "court of general jurisdiction," and these courts have various names, including courts of common pleas, superior court, and district court. A "superior court" is a trial court in some states but can be the name of an appellate court in others. These are the basic trial courts, and most litigation starts there.

The trial court system of a given state also includes *courts of limited jurisdiction,* which means that these courts hear cases in only very specific and limited situations. Examples are probate courts, county courts, or municipal courts. A probate court hears primarily estate cases, while a municipal court may hear cases involving only limited amounts of money. Finally, the lowest-level judges having limited jurisdiction in a state may be called justices of the peace or magistrates, and the lowest courts may be called municipal, small claims, or mayors' courts, depending on local custom and resources for the court system. Exhibit 1-2 shows the general structure of most state courts. It would be useless to attempt to list or to know the names of all court levels in all states.

Exhibit 1-2
State Court Systems

STATE COURT SYSTEMS

Highest Appellate Court

(Court of final resort)

(Varied names: Supreme Court, Supreme Judicial Court, etc.)

|

Intermediate Appellate Courts

(Parties appeal here from trial courts before
going to highest appellate court)

(Varied names: Appeals Court, Superior Court)

|

Trial Courts

(Courts of general jurisdiction)

(Varied names: Court of Common Pleas, District Court, Supreme Court
in New York, etc.)

|

Courts of Limited Jurisdiction

(Probate Court, County Court, Municipal Court, etc.)

|

Lowest Courts

(Varied names: Justice of the Peace, District Justices, Magistrates,
Mayors' Courts, etc.)

Conflict of Laws. Because there are fifty state court systems in the United States, as well as the federal court system, questions arise concerning which law should apply in given cases. The body of law known as *conflict of laws* answers these questions by resolving questions when the laws of more than one state come into conflict.

Questions about insurance contracts often involve people living or traveling in different states. A person living in Ohio might obtain insurance with a company in Connecticut to cover property located in Oregon. The laws of each state may vary. Which state's law would apply in the event of loss to the property? Different conflict of laws rules govern tort and contract cases. The state at which a party commences an action, or the *forum state,* applies its own procedural rules; but what state's substantive law applies?

Tort Cases. *Tort cases* are those involving wrongs between people. A person may purchase automobile insurance, while living in Mississippi, that follows one law pertaining to accidents. While driving in Michigan, which has another form of law applicable to automobile accidents, the policyholder may be involved in an accident that results in injury to another person. The two states' laws vary considerably in application to this kind of case. Which state's law applies? The general rule is that the substantive law in force where the injury occurred would apply. If the injured person sued the policyholder in Mississippi, where he or she resides, Mississippi courts would apply Michigan law with regard to the accident itself. Mississippi courts would, however, apply their own procedural law.

Contract Cases. If the plaintiff, who is the complaining party, files suit in his or her state of residence, the local court may apply the law of that state. This practice is the *center of gravity rule,* which courts apply more often in contract cases than in accident cases. Under the center of gravity doctrine, courts apply the law of the state with the most significant relationship to or contact with the event, parties, and issues. Although courts often apply the center of gravity rule to contract cases, there is not so much uniformity in conflict of law rules among the various states in contract cases as there is in tort cases. In these cases, courts consider the following:

1. Where the parties to a contract live
2. Where the parties entered into the contract
3. Where the parties are to perform the contract
4. Other, similar matters

With this information, courts determine which state has the greatest contact with the agreement and apply that state's law. The parties to a contract may also agree, in advance, in their contract, as to which state's laws will apply if a dispute arises.

Federal-State Conflict Problems. Conflict of laws problems also arise between the federal and state court systems. When parties start lawsuits in federal courts, they apply their own procedural law in every case and also apply federal substantive law in matters involving a federal law dispute.

Substantive law is the law governing the *merits* of the case, which are based on the factual issues giving rise to the lawsuit. *Procedural law* involves the rules of procedure, or mechanics, of court processes. In a diversity of citizenship case, where the parties reside in different states, a federal court may apply the substantive law of the state in which the court is located, including that state's conflicts of law rule.

Executive Branches

Federal and state constitutions, along with the charters of most municipalities, provide for a *chief executive* who shares the responsibilities of government equally with the legislative and judicial branches. Inherent in the American system is the concept of *checks and balances,* which assures that no one branch of government can become too powerful. The legislative branches of governments, such as Congress and state legislatures, pass laws; the court systems interpret those laws; and the executive branch enforces or vetoes those laws.

An executive officer who is the President of the United States, a governor, or a mayor must either recommend and approve or veto laws after the legislative body enacts them but before they become effective. The executive branch can also appoint the heads of administrative agencies to assist in carrying out the laws.

The executive branch can influence the numerous rules and regulations that administrative agencies issue. For example, the president appoints the head of the Securities and Exchange Commission (SEC). Through this appointment power, a president can influence SEC activities. Sometimes executive appointments, however, require legislative branch approval.

Administrative Agencies

The legislative and executive branches cannot perform all functions necessary to administer government. The legislative branch, whether Congress or state legislatures, creates, by statute, administrative agencies to carry out governmental functions. At the federal level, more than sixty regulatory agencies administer laws affecting thousands of companies and all individuals.

The federal regulatory system began by regulating certain large and powerful industries, such as railroads, banks, utilities, communications companies, and airlines. More recently, the federal government has created agencies that regulate particular functions across all industries, such as equal employment opportunity, financial disclosure, worker health and safety, and environmental concerns.

Administrative agencies regulate specific areas, such as tax, health, and labor. They vary in the scope of their functions, purposes, and powers, but they all generally have in common the rights to make rules and to determine the rights of parties to behave in certain ways in areas falling within their jurisdictions.

Agency rules, regulations, and rulings have the full force of law and comprise the body of *administrative law.* Federal agencies *promulgate* thousands of rules every year, which means to put formal rules into effect by making a formal public announcement. The legislative delegation of rule-making power to an administrative agency is constitutional so long as the following conditions exist:

1. The scope of the delegated power is carefully defined.
2. The agency exercises the rule-making power within the scope of that delegation.
3. The rules are subject to court review.

Business Regulation. Few businesses, if any, escape administrative agency supervision. Regulation of business is valid so long as the regulations apply uniformly to all members within the same class. The federal government may impose any regulations upon any phase of business necessary for the nation's economic needs. The states, by virtue of their *police power,* which is the power to protect public health, safety, and morals, can regulate business as long as they do not impose unreasonable burdens on interstate commerce or on any federal government activity.

Insurance Regulation. Insurance is a highly regulated area and is subject to both state and federal regulation. As a large industry, insurance remains unique in that it is subject more to state than to federal regulation. An insurance company doing business in more than one state must carefully comply with insurance department rules and regulations in each state, as well as with federal regulations. Additionally, many other state and federal agencies oversee various aspects of the insurance business, such as employment practices, unfair competition, postal regulations, tax matters, and the issuance of securities.

LEGAL PROCEDURE

Legal procedures are complex and vary from court system to court system, from court level to court level, from state to state, from county to county within a state, and from federal courts to state courts. Each system has its own set of rules to which parties must strictly adhere. A party can lose a case entirely for failure to adhere to procedural rules. This section examines procedures for trial courts and administrative agencies, which are the primary forums in the United States for settling disputes. *Alternative dispute resolution (ADR)* is a rapidly developing alternative to court settlement of disputes, and this section also summarizes the various forms of ADR.

Court Procedure

Most disputes between people never go to court, yet thousands of cases do reach the courts each year. When individuals or businesses cannot resolve their differences privately and question whether legal obligations exist between them, they may go to court. Many of these cases involve insured interests, and many lawsuits result in insurance payments.

At any point in *litigation,* or a lawsuit, parties may settle a case by agreeing to terms and taking the dispute out of the court's domain. The legal system encourages settlements. Litigation is extremely costly and time-consuming, and it is often desirable that parties reach agreement rather than "battle it out" in court for what can take several years.

Many people who have never been involved in litigation believe that the process is much like what they see on television or in the movies. They expect drama, surprises in court, and flamboyant, eloquent lawyers. In most cases, each party to a lawsuit believes that justice is on his or her side and that "I must win—I can't lose." Parties are often totally unaware of the labyrinthine process of the law: meticulous pretrial preparation by lawyers on both sides, carefully contrived trial tactics, and procedural "boobytraps" each step of the way.

Substantive law governs the merits of the case. For example, was Mary's careless driving that resulted in her car hitting Joe an assault and battery against Joe for which she must pay damages? The procedural law of the court in which the plaintiff sues governs all procedure, and it is the lawyer's role to guide the case carefully through the proper procedures to obtain a decision on the merits. While there is some variation in terminology in each jurisdiction, the following discussion gives a general picture of pretrial, trial, and post-trial procedures in most courts, whether federal or state.

Pretrial Procedure. While surprises can occur in the midst of trial, lawyers do substantial pretrial preparation and will, in most cases, know before trial all allegations and evidence the parties may present. *Allegations* are claims that a party asserts are true and expects to prove.

Pleadings. An individual or business starts a lawsuit by filing a *complaint* with the court having jurisdiction over the dispute. The complaining person or business is the *plaintiff,* and the party against whom the complaint was made is the *defendant.* The complaint is the first *pleading,* or legal paper, filed with the court. The complaint "pleads" the plaintiff's case and tells the court, as well as the defendant, why the plaintiff is suing and what remedy the plaintiff requests. The complaint also tells the court why it has jurisdiction over the matter and why the plaintiff has a *cause of action* against, or legal grounds to sue, the defendant.

In a small claims or municipal court, which hears cases involving smaller amounts of money or values, a person can usually file a complaint without a lawyer's assistance. In a court of general jurisdiction, however, a lawyer usually has responsibility for filing all pleadings. Pleadings usually follow prescribed forms, which have developed over many years. Lawyers usually have files of pleading forms that they can adapt to individual cases. For example, if a party alleges negligence by a defendant, a lawyer will most likely have sample negligence complaints on file and will convert a sample to fit the new client's case.

When a plaintiff files a complaint, a court issues a *summons* to the defendant, informing that person of the lawsuit, along with a copy of the complaint. This notice to the defendant also specifies a period of time within which the defendant must file an *answer* to the complaint. The answer is the defendant's own first pleading and tells the court why the defendant believes the plaintiff cannot prevail in the case. The defendant may also have complaints against the plaintiff, which take the form of *counterclaims* in the answer. Alternatively, the defendant may simply file an *entry of appearance* in the case, which does not admit or deny anything in the complaint but states only that the defendant will appear in court.

The plaintiff, after receiving the defendant's answer, may then file a *reply* to that answer. All of these pleadings—the complaint, the answer, and the reply—form a written dialogue between the parties that informs the court about the substance of the dispute.

The parties may also make various *motions* before trial that "move" that the court do something. A motion is a party's formal request that a court take a particular action. For example, the defendant may admit that the facts are true as the plaintiff states but that they are not enough to justify a legal action. To say this to the court, the defendant files a *motion to dismiss* the action for failure to state a claim for which the court can grant relief. An older name for the motion to dismiss is "demurrer," a term that some courts still use. A trial is necessary only when the facts are in dispute. One party may believe that the other party has stated the facts accurately but may question whether the law provides a remedy. In this case, the party holding that belief files a *motion for judgment on the pleadings* or a *motion for summary judgment.* Either motion essentially says, "I admit all the facts, but the law is on my side." Many cases end at this stage and never go to trial.

A party may also request a *pretrial conference* with the judge, where the plaintiff and defendant agree to some of the facts, or *stipulate* (agree) as to the truth of some matters, weeding out the matters in dispute. Courts use pretrial conferences to encourage settlements when possible.

Discovery. The pretrial stage also includes *discovery,* the often lengthy and involved process in which each party "discovers" the other party's evidence. In a case involving complex business questions, such as antitrust litigation, for example, discovery can take a very long time and can involve what is often tedious examination of thousands of documents and records. Discovery alone in complex cases can take years.

There are three basic discovery tools:

1. *Depositions*—oral examinations of witnesses, transcribed by a stenographer to produce a written verbatim record
2. *Interrogatories*—written questions requiring written *answers to interrogatories*
3. *Motions to produce*—requests to produce documents or physical evidence in a case, as a contract or an allegedly defective product

Parties must provide everything requested, unless the court decides otherwise because of the other party's objection. The information enables the parties to know as much as possible before trial and to help avoid surprises to the extent possible. For example, testimony at trial may contradict an earlier deposition or an answer to a written interrogatory. The intended result, however, is that the parties know all the facts and may settle before trial when they realize all the facts. Trial, however, provides the opportunity for a judge or jury to see witnesses' expressions, to hear subjective arguments, and to judge more than just written or other tangible evidence.

Trial Procedure. Though the legal system encourages settlement of disputes at each step of litigation, many cases still go to trial. Trials are costly but often provide the best means for obtaining justice.

Juries. Initially, the parties choose whether to have a jury trial, which is unique to the Anglo-American justice system and is unknown in civil law and other legal systems. A *jury* is a group of people who consider the evidence in a case and decide what facts are true. If a jury trial occurs, the jury decides all questions of fact, and the judge decides all questions of law. Judges do not make factual determinations in jury trial cases, and juries do not answer legal questions. A *question of law* in a negligence case, for example, may be whether a defendant owed a plaintiff any duty. A *question of fact* in the same case may be whether the plaintiff actually suffered any harm.

The parties may decide not to have a jury trial. In that case, the judge makes all decisions, whether they pertain to the facts or the law. Many factors go into the decision of whether to have a jury trial. For example, a large corporation involved in a lawsuit against an individual may not want a jury trial because some juries do not empathize with big businesses. Juries often empathize with the "little guy," who may want a jury trial for this reason. This is not always true, however, because juries can be sophisticated when it comes to determining fairness. Geography may be an important factor in the decision of whether to have a jury trial. For example, in an area with a strong work ethic, juries may not like to see plaintiffs get "windfall" judgments, perceiving them as making big profits without working for them.

If there is to be a jury trial, each party can eliminate jurors from service. They can exclude any number of jurors by use of a *challenge for cause* when those jurors appear to be biased. The parties also have a specified number of *peremptory challenges,* which they can use to eliminate jurors for no stated cause.

Opening Statement. After the selection and swearing-in of the jury, or in a trial before a judge only, the plaintiff's lawyer makes an *opening statement* to the jury, telling jury members the facts of the case and the reasons the plaintiff should prevail. The defendant's lawyer also can make an opening statement. The most important part of the trial, however, is the presentation of evidence.

Evidence. It often takes years of experience for a lawyer to use the *rules of evidence* effectively. The rules governing the proof of facts and examination of witnesses form evidence, a major classification of substantive law. Many trial lawyers, during their first trials, have no idea why the other side is objecting at times, why the court rules the way it does on those objections, or when or why they should object in their clients' behalf. Some object to "practically everything," then grapple for reasons to give the judge later.

Although lawyers acquire textbook knowledge about evidence in law school, it is often difficult to recall all the evidentiary rules in the heat of courtroom battle because they are complex and require quick, "on-your-feet" reasoning. To be admissible, evidence must be relevant, material, and competent.

Relevance. Generally, parties may present only relevant evidence. *Relevance* has to do with the relationship to the matter at issue, and a trial court excludes irrelevant evidence. A simplistic example is that the model of a car may be irrelevant in a case in which a car hit a person when there is no dispute as to which car caused the accident. The limits of a defendant's liability insurance, or the existence of insurance, is irrelevant to the determination of the defendant's negligence, which is why these acts are inadmissible as evidence.

Materiality. Evidence must also be material, a concept very close to relevance. *Materiality* means that the evidence has significance and consequence in the case. A fact may be relevant but of no importance, rendering it *immaterial.* Although materiality is very close to relevance, testimony may be relevant but so minor that it is not material. For example, testimony that the car in the accident was a 1990 model is immaterial unless, say, there is evidence that the 1990 model had some defect relevant to the accident.

Hearsay. Evidence must also be *competent,* which means that it must be of a proper nature. The usual argument against admission of evidence on the basis of incompetence is the *hearsay rule.* Basically, a party offers *hearsay evidence* to prove the truth of an allegation by a witness who has no personal knowledge of the facts about which he or she is testifying. Usually, it is an out-of-court statement offered through someone who heard it (someone other than the person who made the statement) or a written paper or document offered to establish the facts alleged in the statement. For example, Wilma testifies about figures on a chart that someone else prepared and about which Wilma has no personal knowledge. This is hearsay.

At common law, courts excluded all hearsay. Over the years, however, so many exceptions to the hearsay rule have developed that the exceptions constitute a large portion of evidence law. When a lawyer perceives hearsay testimony during the course of a trial, the lawyer must object and give a sound reason for the objection in order for the court to rule on the objection. This is a good example of the quick, "on-your-feet" thinking a lawyer must call up at trial.

Opinion. *Opinion evidence* is another important tool for making a case in court. Witnesses generally may not give opinion evidence. If, however, a witness is an expert in a particular area, then opinion testimony is admissible. Proving a witness an expert usually involves detailed questioning at trial about the witness's background and qualifications. An expert in statistics, for example, may testify as to statistical evidence about many subjects, or a physician may testify as to medical matters.

Examination of Witnesses. The plaintiff presents a case against the defendant first by calling and examining witnesses, and the rules for examination of witnesses are also part of the law of evidence. *Direct examination* is questioning one's own witnesses. For example, a plaintiff's lawyer questions witnesses testifying for the plaintiff. The other side can conduct a *cross-examination* of these witnesses, as when the defendant's lawyer questions the plaintiff's witnesses.

The rules applying to allowable questions vary with regard to whose witness is testifying. Cross-examination of opposing witnesses involves more latitude because, presumably, those witnesses are not as cooperative as one's own witnesses. For instance, the lawyers conducting cross-examination of an opponent's witness may ask *leading questions,* which are questions that suggest an answer, such as: "You got into the car, didn't you?" The court would not allow such a question of one's own witness, but would require something like this: "What did you do next?"

Burden of Proof.   The *burden of proof* is a party's duty to prove the acts he or she claims to be true. In the end, the plaintiff must establish a case against the defendant by a *preponderance of the evidence,* which is merely by evidence that outweighs the apparent truth of the other party's evidence. That is, the party shows that his or her story is probably true. This burden of proof in a civil case is not as onerous as that in a criminal case, where the prosecution must establish guilt *beyond a reasonable doubt.*

Closing Arguments.   After the lawyers have introduced all evidence, each lawyer may summarize it and make a closing argument to the jury. The judge then instructs the jury concerning the law applicable to the case, and the jury retires to reach its verdict. The court may decide to take the case from the jury at any time by *directing a verdict* in favor of one party, by declaring a *mistrial,* or by declaring a *nonsuit* if the plaintiff failed to present a sufficient case.

"Directing a verdict" means that the court tells the jury what verdict it must give. A mistrial is a trial terminated because of some egregious errors, an extraordinary event, or a jury that cannot reach a conclusion. A nonsuit generally occurs when a party cannot prove his or her case or in some way does not comply with court orders. Any of these actions by the judge is subject to review by an appellate court.

Many jurisdictions provide for two kinds of verdict: general and special. A *general verdict* is one in which the jury makes a complete finding and a single conclusion on all issues presented. In a *special verdict* the jury makes only findings of fact by answering specific questions. When a jury makes only findings of fact, the judge must apply the law to the facts as found by the jury.

Appeals.   Either the plaintiff or defendant may allege errors at the trial that constitute grounds for appeal to a higher court. The person who appeals is the *appellant* and the other party is the *appellee.* An appeal must be made to the appropriate court and be made within the prescribed time period. A transcript of the lower court proceedings must be filed with the appeals court, which will rely on the transcript, along with additional briefs and arguments made by counsel, in reaching its decision as to whether the trial court's decision was correct.

Res Judicata and Collateral Estoppel.   Under the doctrine of *res judicata* a final judgment in a suit is conclusive on the parties in all future actions brought on the matters in issue. Parties are entitled to their full day in court. However, once a court of competent jurisdiction has finally settled the matter, it may not be relitigated. The rule applies when the same parties desire to litigate the same issues that a court of competent jurisdiction has already decided. If any of these three elements—that is, identity of persons and issues and final adjudication—is missing, the rule does not apply. All of these essential elements must be present for *res judicata* to apply. *Collateral estoppel,* on the other hand, means that the determination of an issue by litigation between two parties is binding in a later lawsuit involving the same parties.

Appellate Procedure. The appeal of a case to a higher court does not mean that the higher court will hold a new trial. An appellate court reviews only questions of law, and it takes as true all findings of fact. A party may make numerous objections before, during, and after a trial. When the trial court overrules those objections, each one of them is a potential ground for appeal. The appellant can claim that the trial court made a legal error in each instance.

In an appellate court, lawyers for the appellant and appellee present legal *briefs* that present and argue their viewpoints and make oral arguments to the court concerning only these legal points. Briefs are written statements presenting the issues, facts, and legal arguments in a case. Each party files a brief. On appeal, briefs are mandatory and courts prescribe their format and content. Some appellate courts render decisions on the basis of written briefs only and hear oral arguments in only a limited number of cases. Lawyers on appeal do not argue that their clients are innocent or not liable because of the facts of the case, but, rather, they argue that the lower court applied the law improperly to the facts.

Even though a trial court erred, the error may not have been important to the outcome of the case. For example, the trial court may have admitted or refused to admit evidence in error. An appellate court may determine that the evidence, although improperly admitted or improperly refused admission, was insignificant and did not harm the appellant in any way.

An appellate court may affirm the trial court outcome, may reverse it, or may send the case back to the trial court for a new trial. If, for example, the trial court improperly admitted evidence, the appellate court may find that the evidence was so *prejudicial* to the appellant's case that a new trial is the only appropriate way to rectify the error.

"Prejudice" means that the evidence substantially affected the outcome of the case. Again, appellate courts do not hold new trials, and "winning on appeal" does not always bring ultimate victory. The appellee may win the case again at a second trial, or a new trial may have the same result as the first trial. The time involved in the appeal process may also jeopardize the appellant's case because time can make testimony stale. Losing parties in lawsuits often decide not to appeal after they weigh the probability of an ultimate victory against the costs of appeal.

Alternative Dispute Resolution

As the number of lawsuits filed in the United States continues to increase, congesting court dockets (calendars), long delays, and additional costs result. As a result, fair, less expensive, and less time-consuming methods of settling disputes are evolving. *Alternative dispute resolution (ADR)* techniques include, but are not limited to, arbitration, mediation, and negotiation.

Arbitration. While the judicial system handles many thousands of disputes, parties resolve the greatest number of controversies by compromise or settlement agreements. Out-of-court settlements have the advantages of economy, greater speed of resolution, less hostility between the parties, and some degree of privacy.

Although legislation and court rules in some states mandate non-binding, court-administered arbitration for some cases, *arbitration* is also an important method of resolving disputes without resorting to courts or administrative agencies. Arbitration involves the submission of a controversy to a private body for a decision the parties agree will be final and binding. It has become a major means of dealing with controversies in contract disputes, labor-management relations, and insurance settlements.

The decision to seek arbitration most frequently results from an agreement between the parties. Either as part of a preexisting contract or upon confronting a dispute, parties may agree to submit the matter to an arbiter or to an arbitration panel. In some instances, state statutes may require submission of controversies to binding arbitration.

Most states have enacted general arbitration laws that cover all aspects of arbitration procedures. At common law, agreements to arbitrate future disputes were contrary to law because they appeared to be attempts to evade the jurisdiction of the courts. Even under common law rules, however, parties could agree that, after a dispute arose, the matter would go to arbitration. In most states, statutes have modified this common law view by making contracts to arbitrate valid and enforceable. Even in those states that have comprehensive arbitration statutes, parties can still pursue common law arbitration procedures. In most states, the parties to a contract can revoke the agreement to arbitrate. Where statutes are involved, arbitration agreements are irrevocable.

While procedures vary under arbitration statutes, they generally involve submission of an existing dispute to arbitration and an arbitrator's making an award or decision. Both the Uniform Arbitration Act and the Federal Arbitration Act provide specific remedies if one of the parties refuses to arbitrate or denies the existence of an arbitration agreement.

The parties may provide for selection of an arbitrator according to rules from the *American Arbitration Association.* Under those rules, each party receives a list of proposed arbitrators and has ten days to cross off any objectionable names and to list the arbitrators according to preference. The association then appoints an arbitrator acceptable to both parties. An alternative method of selecting an arbitrator is to require each party to appoint an arbitrator and have those arbitrators in turn appoint a third arbitrator.

Arbitration proceedings do not generally require strict adherence to rules of evidence and procedure. The power to subpoena witnesses exists under most statutes. Once the award or judgment of the arbitrator has been rendered, it is filed with a clerk of court. There are very few grounds for appealing an arbitrator's award. If a party does not appeal within the period prescribed by law, the arbitrator's finding is treated the same as a judgment of a court and may be carried out like any other court judgment.

Arbitration as a means of settling insurance disputes is increasingly frequent. Many insurance policies specifically provide for arbitration. Uninsured motorist coverages in automobile policies uniformly include an arbitration provision in the event of dispute under the policy.

Over 1,000 insurance companies participate in programs of the Insurance Arbitrations Forums, Inc., an industry-sponsored arbitration system. The Nationwide Inter-Company Arbitration Agreement, for example, binds the companies to arbitrate automobile physical damage claims not exceeding a certain dollar amount. A special arbitration agreement is widely used to allocate costs of settlements when coinsurers are involved and for resolving difficulties of overlapping coverages. Increased use of arbitration has also resulted from provisions in various no-fault statutes, which about half the states have adopted. Under these acts, persons involved in automobile accidents look to their own insurance carriers for payment of benefits.

When disputes arise as to payment of first-party benefits, or when subrogation problems arise between insurers, some no-fault laws provide for submission to arbitration. As an effective method of settling disputes in all types of commercial undertakings, arbitration will be even more frequent in the future.

Mediation.   Another private ADR procedure is *mediation.* A mediator has no binding authority but serves as a catalyst to help parties analyze their dispute, consider possible solutions, and perhaps devise a formula for compromise. Although a judge may attempt to mediate in court during a settlement conference, this ADR procedure generally involves submission of a dispute to an outside mediator. Through this process the mediator, an impartial third party who is generally an experienced trial lawyer or retired judge, tries to encourage a satisfactory compromise to a dispute.

Negotiation. *Negotiation* can provide the most direct route to the settlement of a dispute. Because negotiations can terminate at any time, they do not limit opportunities to pursue other methods to resolve disputes. As the name implies, negotiation involves discussing all issues and arriving at a mutually satisfactory disposition of the case. Private *mini-trials* and court-sponsored mock *summary jury trials* are sophisticated devices used to encourage negotiation of major disputes.

Mini-Trials. The mini-trial permits lawyers or others familiar with the case to present evidence and arguments to a panel, which may be composed of executives or others. A neutral party, a retired judge, or another expert may act as a mediator or issue an advisory opinion following the presentations. The mini-trial serves as an aid to negotiation following the hearing.

Summary Jury Trials. Summary jury trials available in some courts involve mock trials before juries. The parties may accept the jury's advisory verdict, following a brief one-day trial, or the verdict may provide the basis for further negotiations toward settlement.

Administrative Agency Procedure

Administrative law affects a wide variety of the activities of people and organizations, from obtaining a dog license to building a nuclear power plant. The legislative output of administrative agencies exceeds by many times that of legislatures, and the number of administrative decisions far exceeds the numerous decisions courts make.

When government furnished few services, in keeping with the *laissez-faire* and *caveat emptor* doctrines, the need for agencies was small. The *laissez-faire*, or "hands-off," doctrine allowed businesses to operate freely to maximize profits, and the *caveat emptor*, or "let the buyer beware," doctrine placed total responsibility on consumers for their purchases. As American society became more complex and required increased regulation of everyday affairs, administrative agencies grew in number and power.

Legislative Delegation of Powers. Legislators at the federal and state levels delegate responsibilities to administrative agencies in much the same way that a supervisor in a company delegates responsibilities to an employee. Legislators have neither the time to pass all the rules and regulations necessary to implement legislation nor the time to develop expertise in every area of regulation. Nor can they settle disputes that arise from legislation, rules, and regulations.

For example, a state government may pass a law prohibiting excessive insurance rates in general language with no details. An insurance department then uses its considerable insurance expertise to set standards for and examine insurance rates. Legislators have neither the time nor the expertise to do all the follow-up that legislation requires.

Courts have generally upheld the legislative delegation to administrative agencies. Although legislators cannot delegate their ultimate power and responsibility, they can delegate to agencies the duty to fill in the details of legislation by allowing them to make rules and regulations and to resolve disputes that may arise. *Enabling legislation* creates an administrative agency and states its purpose. An example of this is a state legislature establishing an insurance department.

Agency Composition.   The appointment of agency officials may appear to be simple, but it is complex for several reasons. Frequently, the enabling act specifies that only a certain number of members (a majority) can be members of the same political party, and this is occasionally a problem. Another problem involves whether an agency's officials may be composed of members chosen from regulated interests. Staffing professional licensing boards demonstrates the problem of balancing conflicts of interest with the desire to obtain knowledgeable people.

Investigatory Powers.   Agencies need to obtain information and evidence in connection with administrative proceedings. The use of subpoenas is primarily a judicial function, and the general rule at one time was that subpoenas were enforceable only if there was probable cause to believe there had been a violation of law.

Subpoenas.   It is common for Congress and state legislatures to include provisions authorizing agency investigations in laws creating agencies. Agency investigations may relate to rule making, ratemaking, adjudication, licensing, prosecution, establishment of general policy, or recommendation of legislation.

A *subpoena* is a legal command to appear at a certain place and time and to testify or produce documents. A legislative grant of subpoena power to an agency is necessary because an agency has no inherent right to issue subpoenas. Today there is no question about a legislative body's ability to delegate subpoena power to an agency to assist it in acquiring information, if the agency issues the subpoena in connection with an otherwise lawful investigation.

Agencies may issue subpoenas in adjudicatory proceedings or contested cases. Many states limit the use of subpoenas to these proceedings. There is a question with respect to rule-making proceedings, unless they include a formal investigation. An agency may issue a subpoena not only on its own behalf, but also at a party's request. For example, a party in an insurance case may request the insurance department to subpoena records of another party in the case.

In contested cases, a party's right to present testimony includes the right not only to testify personally, but also to obtain relevant testimony and records from others. If the other parties refuse to cooperate, then due process requires compelling them to do so by subpoena. A subpoena to compel a witness to testify is a *subpoena ad testificandum* (command to testify), but is usually referred to merely as a subpoena. A subpoena to compel production of documents or records is a *subpoena duces tecum* (command to bring things "with you").

Constitutional Limitations. The constitutional limitations on agency investigations include the following:

- Fourth Amendment protection against unreasonable searches and seizures
- Fifth Amendment protection against self-incrimination

The Constitution invokes strict standards in these areas, and violations of constitutional rights can defeat an investigation.

Unreasonable Searches and Seizures. In administrative law, the Fourth Amendment prohibition against unreasonable searches and seizures principally applies to the inspection of books and records. Although today there is practically no limit on a governmental agency's right to obtain books and records, there are some qualifications.

First, the requested material must be relevant to the investigation. However, if there is the slightest connection between the requested records and the subject of the investigation, the courts usually find them relevant and require that they be provided.

The second qualification concerns the "breadth" or spread of the records required. For example, a governmental agency may request from an insurer all records in connection with automobile insurance for the past twenty years. Sometimes the records requested fill several rooms and take years to reproduce. The courts usually compel production except in flagrant cases where the agency demonstrates no possible need.

Some courts have held that when record retrieval and production are very expensive, the burden is on the agency to establish the relevance of the records. A variation is the so-called "fishing expedition," when the regulatory agency has no specific purpose in mind but is looking through the records for a possible violation of law. For a long time courts disfavored "fishing expeditions," but this view has been altered.

To aid agencies in spotting violations of law, Congress gave some administrative agencies, such as the Occupational Safety and Health Administration (OSHA), the power to make unannounced investigations. The theory was that an announced investigation would enable the investigated party to hide the violation, undergo the inspection, and then proceed to violate the law again. The Supreme Court, however, has guaranteed court control of the scope and breadth of investigations by these agencies and has ruled that the investigated party need not be forewarned of an investigation. Requirements for search warrants apply to both business and residential premises. Unannounced inspections, however, are permissible for firms engaged in traditionally regulated businesses, such as the alcoholic beverage and firearm industries.

Self-Incrimination. The Fifth Amendment states that no person "shall be compelled in any criminal case to be a witness against himself." Court decisions have broadened the word "criminal" to mean almost any type of investigation or proceeding in which legal sanctions may arise. The term "witness" includes not only oral testimony but also the production of records and documents.

Record-Keeping Requirements. A legislative body can require that certain records be kept, and it can delegate this power to an agency. Inspection power is not limited to records the law requires but extends to other relevant records. This does not create a general unlimited right to investigate beyond what is necessary, and any agency request must be reasonably relevant to proper investigatory purposes.

Agency Functions. Administrative agencies have two primary functions: *rule making* and *adjudication.* Rule making is similar to legislation and is the process by which agencies promulgate rules to implement legislative policies. Adjudication is the process by which agencies decide actual cases. Rule making affects larger numbers of people and is the implementation or prescription of law or policy for the future. Adjudication, the evaluation of past conduct, affects only the parties involved.

When a state legislature passes a law prohibiting excessive insurance rates, the state insurance department can then make rules regarding insurance rate review and guidelines for determining whether rates are excessive. The insurance commissioner, a private citizen, or a group of citizens may contest a rate as excessive. The insurance department then holds a hearing on the matter to decide about the rate in question. This is an adjudication. It affects only the insurance company involved and insureds who would have had to pay the new rate, and it affects past conduct (the rate set).

Rule-Making Procedure. There are three classes of rules:

1. Legislative, or substantive, rules
2. Interpretative rules
3. Procedural rules

Legislative rules emanate from a statutory delegation of authority and have the same force as a law that Congress enacts. Legislative rules require adherence to rule-making procedures. An agency makes *interpretative rules* to interpret a statute. These rules (1) exist for the guidance of the agency staff or the regulated parties, (2) do not have the force and effect of law, and, thus, (3) are not binding upon individuals. *Procedural rules* are primarily internal and describe agency operations, requirements for legislative rule making, and adjudication proceedings. Like interpretative rules, procedural rules need not conform to the notice and comment requirements of rule-making procedures.

The *Administrative Procedure Act (APA)* prescribes the procedure for administrative agency rule making at the federal level. Most states follow the rule-making procedures of the *Model State Administrative Procedure Act (MSAPA),* which requires strict adherence to these three basic steps:

1. Publication of a notice of intent to adopt a regulation
2. Opportunity for public comment
3. Publication of the final regulation

Notice. Federal agencies publish notices in a weekly publication called the *Federal Register,* and states usually have their own similar publications for state agency notices. In Pennsylvania, for example, a weekly publication called the *Pennsylvania Bulletin* contains all administrative agency notices. Notice in one of these official publications usually suffices as official notice to all interested parties that the agency contemplates an action that will affect them. If, for example, a state insurance department plans to adopt a regulation concerning an aspect of the insurance business, the department publishes a notice in the state's official publication for agency notices. Insurance companies and consumers must watch for these notices.

Opportunity for Public Comment. Typically, an agency publishes the text of a proposed regulation in an official publication and invites comments by a certain date, usually within two to three weeks. Agencies need not hold public hearings for every proposed rule making, but, at times, legislation requires public hearings. If a hearing is not necessary, interested businesses and individuals may submit written comments on a proposed regulation. The MSAPA requires a public hearing if either a governmental agency or twenty-five interested individuals request it.

If an agency holds a hearing, a *hearing examiner* presides. The hearing examiner usually has discretion as to who testifies. If large groups of people attend, the examiner may require that only their chosen representatives testify. If the proposed rule is controversial, the examiner may require advance registration of speakers.

Publication of Final Rule.   After the agency has reviewed all comments about the proposed rule, it may adopt the originally proposed rule, make minimal or extensive changes, or nullify it. If the agency decides to finalize the rule, it must publish the final version. A rule usually becomes effective thirty days after publication. This period gives affected parties time to conform with the new rule or, if they wish, to challenge the legality of the rule. Agencies can publish emergency rules with immediate effective dates when it is necessary for the public health and welfare.

Adjudicatory Procedure.   Adjudicatory proceedings are similar to court cases and affect the rights of an individual or a limited number of people. As in court, an individual or group in an agency adjudicatory process has a constitutional right to due process of law. The specific requirements for due process may vary by the nature of the proceeding.

The Due Process Clause of the Constitution demands the right to an opportunity to be heard in most adjudicatory hearings. There is no right to a hearing in every case, but a party involved in an administrative matter has the opportunity for a hearing unless he or she waives the right in some way. A hearing includes reasonable notice, opportunity for a fair hearing, and a decision supported by the evidence. Denial of due process may be grounds for reversal of a decision if the denial harmed a party.

The adjudicatory procedure includes the following necessary elements:

- Notice of a hearing
- Hearing of the case
- Adjudication of the case

Notice.   Appropriate notice is essential to due process, and improper notice can result in nullification of an entire proceeding. Appropriate notice requires the following:

- Statement of the time, place, and nature of the hearing
- Statement of the legal authority and jurisdiction of the hearing
- Reference to the particular statute or rule involved
- A short, plain statement of the matters asserted

The test of appropriate notice is whether there is sufficient information in the notice to apprise the interested party fairly about the case so that he or she can respond adequately and not claim surprise at the hearing.

Hearing. As in rule making, formal adjudication, complete with a full hearing, is necessary only where the law specifically requires it. Thus, many matters, such as pension or social security claims, do not warrant full hearings and, in fact, are too numerous to make formal proceedings practical.

An agency may use an *informal hearing* when time, the nature of the proceedings, and the public interest permit. The right to informal proceedings, however, is not absolute. Either party may demand a *formal hearing* at which a hearing examiner, or administrative law judge, presides. That person is usually both an agency employee and a lawyer.

Generally, any person compelled to appear before an agency has the right to counsel, and every party to a dispute has the right to counsel. Counsel need not be a lawyer, but may be a qualified representative, which is, practically, any trusted person. The government does not have to provide free counsel for an administrative hearing.

In general, the rules governing witnesses in court proceedings apply in agency hearings, but the rules are not as strict. For example, there are no absolute rules governing the competency of witnesses, and the hearing examiner makes decisions about testimony and other evidence. As in court proceedings, expert witnesses may also testify and, in fact, do testify in many agency cases.

Unlike court cases, agency cases do not have juries. Many of the rules of evidence developed in the court system are designed to prevent jurors, as lay people, from hearing incompetent evidence. The hearing examiner in an agency case, who decides matters of both fact and law, is usually a lawyer and does not need this protection. The rules of evidence, therefore, do not apply strictly in agency proceedings. Generally, evidence in an agency hearing must be relevant, although competence is not always an important criterion.

With regard to hearsay evidence, the general rule appears to be that any hearsay that has probative value is admissible unless there is better evidence available or unless the hearsay evidence will waste time or prejudice a party unduly. Unless the hearsay is remote, such as "double hearsay" like, "I heard that he said that she said that he committed the act," hearsay is admissible "for what it is worth" in the typical administrative hearing.

Counsel in an adjudicatory hearing can make arguments, and there are no rigid rules about them. Most arguments are relatively short and are often written instead of oral. There is no inherent right or duty to present formal written briefs arguing the law.

Adjudication. A final order of an administrative agency, *adjudication,* must include findings of fact and conclusions of law. Parties may propose findings of fact or conclusions of law. The hearing examiner considers these proposals and may accept, reject, or modify them.

An example of a hearing examiner's findings in an insurance rate case could be as follows:

- The insurance company kept statistics properly.
- The company interpreted those statistics properly.
- The statistics indicated a loss ratio of 35 percent.
- Insurance companies can make a profit with a loss ratio of 50 percent.

From these facts, the hearing officer could conclude that the 35 percent loss ratio was too low and the proper loss ratio should be 50 percent. The hearing officer's decision, based on a statute prohibiting excessive rates, would be to lower rates by a stated percentage to produce a 50 percent loss ratio. The Appendix to this chapter is a sample rate hearing.

Appeal Rights. Agencies can grant different forms of relief, including imposing fines or granting, revoking, or suspending licenses. Enabling legislation for an agency usually determines appeal rights, whether they are to a court or within the agency. Most agencies have at least one, and sometimes three or four, tiers of appeal within the agency. Once a case has gone through all levels of the agency adjudication and appeals process, the party has exhausted all administrative remedies and can seek judicial review in a court of law.

Unlike courts, administrative agencies can give advisory opinions. In the American legal system, courts, with very limited exceptions, do not indicate informally and in advance how they would decide a case based upon a given set of facts, but agencies have done this for years. Although these advisory opinions are not binding either on the agency or on any parties, a recipient of an advisory opinion can usually rely upon it.

Judicial Review. As a general rule, federal courts review actions of federal agencies, and state courts review actions of state agencies. As the actions of agencies increasingly affect personal interests, the courts protect those interests more vigorously by insisting on strict judicial scrutiny of agency action. Judicial review is available as long as no statute precludes it, or the action is not one the law leaves solely to administrative agency discretion. Judicial review is not limited to agency adjudications but may also apply to agency rule making.

Standing. In order to bring an action for judicial review, a plaintiff must have *standing to sue.* That is, the plaintiff must be the right person to challenge the agency action. The person seeking the review must be suffering a legal wrong or adverse effect from the agency action. A party who seeks judicial review of a rule-making procedure must show that the rule or its application impairs or interferes with his or her legal rights or privileges. If it is an adjudicatory hearing, the person must usually be "aggrieved," which means that the order affects the plaintiff's personal rights in a substantial manner.

Exhaustion of Administrative Remedies. Another prerequisite to the right of judicial review is that the party must have exhausted all available administrative remedies, or review procedures. Cases generally fall into two categories:

1. When a court determines that the agency has not issued a final order
2. When the party wishes to raise a constitutional or jurisdictional question before the agency has issued a final order or before it has held a hearing

In the first category, a party can appeal only a final order of an agency. A *final order* is one that substantially concludes or disposes of any material private right of a party, and it must terminate the proceeding at the agency level.

The second class of cases involves application of the doctrine called *exhaustion of administrative remedies.* This doctrine holds that there can be an immediate appeal to the courts only when the party who wishes to appeal has taken the case through all possible administrative appeals. A court will except a case from this doctrine only when the available administrative remedy is inadequate and requiring the party to exhaust administrative remedies would be a futile gesture. Otherwise, a party must go through all administrative procedures before ever reaching court review, even though in reality that process may be a waste of time and resources.

Standard for Review. A court will set aside an agency action only in the following situations, which form the standards for review:

*   The agency action was arbitrary and capricious, an abuse of discretion, or otherwise unlawful.

- The agency action was unconstitutional.
- The agency action exceeded statutory authority.
- The agency action was the result of illegal procedures, or the agency failed to follow its own procedural rules.
- The agency action was unsupported by substantial evidence in the record.

A court may review the law fully and substitute its own judgment about the law for the agency's judgment, just as courts may review lower court decisions for incorrect interpretation of the law. A court will review facts only to determine whether *substantial evidence* supports an agency's action and will not set aside agency action unless it is *clearly erroneous.*

On appeal, parties often allege that an administrative agency's action was *arbitrary and capricious,* or an abuse of discretion. An agency's action is arbitrary or capricious if it is so clearly erroneous that it has no rational basis or if it is willful and unreasonable. Generally, courts give great deference to agency conclusions on questions of fact because of their assumed special knowledge and expertise. In cases in which reviewing courts believe that they need more facts to make judgments, they usually remand cases back to agencies for additional hearings.

Privacy and Freedom of Information Acts. Two pieces of federal legislation address issues concerning privacy and citizen access to information held by government agencies and also affect the insurance industry, which accumulates massive amounts of information about individuals.

Privacy Act. The federal *Privacy Act* of 1974[12] responded to a growing concern over the increasing invasion of individual privacy in the name of information collection. It does not apply to all government documents, but only to those in a system of records maintained by an agency from which information about an individual is retrievable by some identifying mark or number.

The record can contain only information relevant to the agency's purpose. The individual has the right of access to the records concerning himself or herself. The act prescribes requirements about how to maintain the system of records and the methods of collecting the information. There are exceptions for CIA and law enforcement agency records, as well as to certain other records.

Disclosure of the records without the individual's permission is prohibited, but there are numerous exceptions. An agency may issue compilations of statistics or records in its possession as long as it does not reveal information pertaining to a single company or individual.

Freedom of Information Act (FOIA).   The *Freedom of Information Act (FOIA)*[13] of 1966 established for the first time a statutory right of access to agency information. Its purposes were to ensure an informed citizenry, to check corruption, and to hold government accountable to the governed.

These goals sometimes conflict with other vital goals, such as the right of privacy, national security, and criminal investigations. Therefore, the act contains nine exceptions, including properly classified security information, law enforcement investigation records, trade secrets, confidential commercial or financial information, and the records of financial institutions.

Any person may request agency records for a fee. The person need not give a reason for the request. If the agency denies the request for any reason, the person may ask for agency review and ultimately for court review of the denial.

SUMMARY

Insurance professionals need to study law not only to prepare for problems directly related to insurance, but also to enhance their general business knowledge. Insurers bear the ultimate financial responsibility for many legal problems their insureds face, and insurance professionals must understand their insureds' legal disputes.

Insurance law is a very specialized and limited subject. This course covers American law generally because the insurance professional needs a much broader knowledge of law than that contained in the subject of insurance law. This course first introduces the common law subjects of most value to the insurance professional, then examines areas of law based on either statutes alone or both statutes and common law.

The American legal system had its origins in the English common law. The foundation of the common law system is the doctrine of *stare decisis,* which is the application of precedents to current cases. The common law system differs from the European civil law system, which is founded exclusively on codified laws rather than case law. American law falls into several classifications: criminal and civil, subject matter classifications, substantive and procedural law, and law and equity.

Sources of American law include the federal and state constitutions, legislative bodies, courts, executive branches, and administrative agencies. A system of checks and balances for the executive, legislative, and judicial branches of government attempts to prevent any one branch from becoming too powerful.

The fifty-one court systems in the United States, including the federal and fifty state systems, all include both trial and appellate courts. The names and methods of operation of each of the fifty-one court systems vary widely. Special rules govern conflicts of law between states and between the state and the federal systems.

Court procedures fall into different phases: pretrial, trial, post-trial, and appellate procedures. Alternative dispute resolution (ADR) methods, such as arbitration, mediation, and negotiation, are ways to resolve disputes more efficiently than through the overloaded court system. Administrative agency duties consist of rule-making and adjudicatory functions. A party also may appeal from an agency decision both within the agency and to a court.

The Privacy and Freedom of Information Acts protect the public from agency misuse of the vast amounts of data they collect. The Privacy Act protects people from use of data that would violate individual privacy, and the Freedom of Information Act guarantees public access to data to prevent abuse of data collection.

APPENDIX TO CHAPTER 1

Administrative Agency: Sample Rate Hearing

The following sets forth, in capsulized form, the proceedings before an insurance commissioner for a review of homeowners policy premium rates. The names, the state, and the statutory references are all fictitious.

The commissioner may institute the hearing on his or her own motion, or it may be at an aggrieved party's request. This case presupposes the latter situation.

REQUEST FOR HEARING

June 1, 199X

Hon. H. Smith, Commissioner of Insurance
State of X
Capitol Building
Capital City, X 10000

Dear Commissioner Smith:

Pursuant to the provisions of the insurance statutes of the State of X, and particularly Section 1803(a)(4) requiring that rates not be excessive, I wish to enter a formal objection to the Homeowners Rate Filing you approved on April 1, 199X.

I have been damaged by the approval of these increased rates and object to them on the following grounds, among others:

(1) They are producing an unconscionable profit for the insurers.

(2) The underlying statistics, the trend factors, and other procedures used to justify this increase were defective and improper.

I hereby request a formal hearing on this filing in accordance with
the applicable law and request the assistance of your office to subpoena
witnesses and documents.

> Yours very truly,
>
> H. Jones
>
> President
> Local Taxpayers Association

NOTICE OF HEARING

Following receipt of the request, and if it appears in order, the
commissioner issues a Notice of Hearing as follows:

State of X

Department of Insurance

Before the Commissioner of Insurance

In the Matter of
Homeowner Rate Filing   No. 93-301
of April 1, 199X

To: The ABC Rating Bureau
       Gotham City, State of X

Notice of Hearing

Please take notice that a hearing will be held under the authority
and jurisdiction granted the Commissioner of Insurance by Section
1600 of the Insurance Code and the Administrative Procedure Act
(Section 5011 et seq.).

The hearing will be held at 10:00 A.M. on July 15, 199X, in the
office of the Commissioner in the Capitol Building, Capital City, X.

The matters to be considered at the hearing are set forth in the
allegations contained in a letter of June 1, 199X, from H. Jones, President, Local Taxpayers Association, as follows:

"I have been damaged by the approval of these increased rates
and object to them on the following grounds, among others:

"(1) They are producing an unconscionable profit for insurers.

"(2) The underlying statistics, the trend factors, and other procedures used to justify this increase were defective and improper."

At the conclusion of the hearing the commissioner may affirm his or her prior action or may issue an order specifying in what respect the filing fails to meet the requirement of the statute.

PRELIMINARY PROCEDURES

A prehearing conference may be set up in which the parties agree on the list of witnesses and various procedural details.

At some point in the proceedings, the ABC Rating Bureau enters a motion to dismiss the action on the ground that Jones is not an aggrieved party and therefore does not have standing. This is usually overruled and the hearing proceeds, particularly if Jones can show that he or she has a homeowners policy and may be damaged. The prehearing conference should settle who has the burden of proof.

HEARING

At the hearing under general rules, Jones has the burden of proof, and it is up to Jones to present the testimony of actuaries and other expert witnesses to prove the points that (1) the underlying statistics were defective, (2) the trend factors and other adjustments were improper, and (3) in their expert opinion based on these facts the rates are excessive. Jones may also try to introduce newspaper clippings to indicate the large industry profits that insurers made. Counsel for the ABC Rating Bureau will object on the grounds that the clippings are hearsay. The commissioner admits them "for whatever they are worth."

As a practical matter, it usually falls on the Bureau to prove its case, which it will attempt to do with its own expert witnesses.

A court reporter records all of the proceedings. All documents will be marked for identification by consecutive letters or numbers, as the hearing officer prefers. After review of the documents, counsel moves for their acceptance into evidence. Opposing counsel may object for any relevant reason.

OPINION AND ORDER

Following the hearing, the commissioner reviews all of the evidence in the record. The commissioner may make a tentative order and submit it to the parties. However, generally the commissioner issues a final order that reads somewhat as follows:

In the Matter of
Homeowner Rate Filing   93-301
of April 1, 199X

Opinion and Order Disapproving Rate Filing

I. *Introduction*

On July 15, 1993, a hearing was commenced to consider the allegations of the complaint as set forth in the Notice of Hearing. The filing complained of was the Homeowners Rate Filing of April 1, 199X, made by the ABC Rating Bureau.

II. *Findings of Fact*

1. The applicants are aggrieved parties within the meaning of Section 1805(d) of the Insurance Law.

2. The actuarial methodology and data accumulation used in this filing were defective in that

   (a) The basic data contained several factual errors.

   (b) The trend factors overstated the effect of inflation on losses.

   (c) The actual loss ratio based on earned premiums and incurred losses for the past five years has never exceeded 50 percent, which is well within the permissible range.

3. A rate increase of 5 percent rather than 20 percent would be sufficient.

III. *Conclusions of Law*

1. The Commissioner has jurisdiction over the parties and the subject matters hereof.

2. The rates produced by the filing of April 1, 197X, are excessive and therefore in violation of Section 1803(a)(4).

Order

Therefore it is ORDERED that the Homeowner Rate Filing of April 1, 199X, be and is hereby disapproved.

The rates produced by such filing shall not be effective after midnight October 15, 199X.

A new filing containing a 5 percent increase and otherwise meeting the statutory standards will be entertained by the Commissioner if the ABC Rating Bureau so desires.

The Commissioner specifically retains jurisdiction of this matter and the authority to issue such further orders as may be necessary or appropriate.

H. Smith
Commissioner of Insurance

POST-DECISION PROCEDURE

At this point, it is up to the ABC Rating Bureau to decide whether the record is strong enough to appeal the commissioner's order to the courts. The rate law of the particular state outlines the procedure to follow.

Chapter Notes

1. 347 U.S. 483 (1954).
2. 384 U.S. 436 (1966).
3. 42 U.S.C. § 12101 (1990).
4. U.S. Const. art. VI, § 2.
5. U.S. Const. art. I, § 8.
6. U.S. Const. art. I, § 8, cl. 18.
7. National Labor Relations Board v. Jones & Laughlin Steel Corp., 301 U.S. 1 (1937).
8. U.S. Const. amend. V.
9. U.S. Const. amend. XIV.
10. U.S. Const. art. III, § 1.
11. Elder Witt, *Congressional Quarterly's Guide to the United States Supreme Court,* 2d ed., Congressional Quarterly, Inc., Washington, DC, 1990.
12. 5 U.S.C. § 552a.
13. 5 U.S.C. § 552.

CHAPTER 2

Elements of a Contract: Agreement and Capacity

Many of the daily activities that are routine in our lives involve contract obligations. People may not even think consciously of their activities as involving contracts. However, parties occasionally fail, or refuse, to perform as they promise. The question of whether a binding contract ever existed then becomes crucial.

Routine agreements are contractual arrangements for the purchase of food, clothing, or insurance, rental of housing, employment, enrollment in a course of study, and marriage. All of these agreements create contracts that courts may enforce. Promises to vacation with a friend, however, or to attend a social function, are not legally enforceable promises. Understanding the circumstances giving rise to binding contracts is at the heart of understanding contract law.

CONTRACT FORMATION

A *contract* is a legally enforceable promise. Another way to define a contract is "a promise or a set of promises for the breach of which the law gives a remedy, or the performance of which the law in some way recognizes as a duty."[1]

Promise

The law of contracts concerns the creation, transfer, and disposition of property and other rights through promises. A *promise* is an undertaking, however expressed, that something will or will not happen in the future.

When parties enter into a contract, they fix their own terms and set limits on their own liabilities. To create a valid contract, the terms must comply with the law. The form and subject matter of the contract, the age of the parties, and related matters are all considerations that determine the validity of the obligations the parties have agreed to undertake.

Parties

The parties to a contract mutually agree to create and undertake obligations that did not exist before. If a party does not fulfill these obligations, the other party may sue. The courts usually impose penalties consisting of money damages when they determine that a party has failed to perform contractual obligations.

Under some circumstances, as when a unique item, such as an antique, is the subject of the contract, the court may direct the parties to perform their obligations by transferring the property in question. The courts generally do not require such specific performance if the contract involves performance of personal services because it would be impossible for a court to supervise the performance. Nonetheless, a party who fails to perform a contract for personal services still may have to pay money damages.

Because a contract defines a legally enforceable promise, the party making the promise is referred to as the *promisor*. The party receiving the promise is the *promisee*. If there is a mutual exchange of promises, each party to the contract is both a promisor and a promisee with regard to the respective promises made and received. Legal language identifies the party who primarily performs a transaction with the "-or" suffix, as, "promisor." The party on the receiving end of a transaction is identified with the "-ee" suffix. Thus, the "promisee" of a contract is the person to whom a promise is made.

Contracts frequently involve the interests of third parties. For instance, the promisor and promisee may create a contract to benefit a third party, who is a *third-party beneficiary* (of the contract). If the contracting parties intend to benefit the third party by discharging a pre-existing obligation to that party, the third-party beneficiary has a legal right to enforce the contract if a breach occurs later. For example, Bill agrees with Joe that he will pay Mary the money Joe owes her. Mary is a third-party beneficiary of an agreement between Bill and Joe.

Privity

When two or more parties enter into a contract, there is usually privity of contract between these parties that imposes obligations on them with respect to their performance under the promises. *Privity of contract* is a legal term referring to the connection or relationship between parties to a contract. Ordinarily, one may not sue for breach of contract without being in privity of contract with the other party. A third party who is not a third-party beneficiary nor in privity of contract with the contracting parties usually has no right to sue under the contract if a breach occurs. A *breach* is a failure, without legal excuse, to perform all or part of a contract.

CLASSIFICATION OF CONTRACTS

Contracts fall into several classifications. The legal classifications include bilateral and unilateral contracts, executed and executory contracts, express and implied contracts, and void and voidable contracts. One contract may fall into more than one of these classifications.

Bilateral and Unilateral

In a *bilateral contract,* one party gives a promise in exchange for another party's promise. Most contracts are bilateral because they involve the exchange of mutual promises to be performed at a later time. Thus, Jay's promise to pay Tony $500 in exchange for Tony's promise to paint Jay's garage creates a bilateral contract in which Jay and Tony have exchanged mutual promises. Under this contract, each party makes and receives a promise. Thus, each party becomes both a promisor and a promisee. A *default* is a failure to perform a promise. If a default occurs, either party may enforce the other's promise in a legal action.

A *unilateral contract* involves the exchange of a promise for an act already performed. For example, if Jay promises to pay $500 when Tony has actually painted the garage, the performance of an act (painting) is required in exchange for the promise. No binding contract arises until Tony actually performs the act.

Executed and Executory

An *executed contract* is a contract that the parties have performed completely. Once a contract is executed, neither party has to do anything else. Thus, if one party buys and pays for clothes that another party delivers, the two parties have executed the contract. In contrast, the parties still have to do something in an *executory contract.*

If a tailor contracts to make a suit of clothes for a certain price, the contract is executory. In this case, the contract is executory because the tailor must make the suit and deliver it for the agreed-upon price. As long as something remains to be done, the contract is executory. An insurance contract is a good example of the executory contract. The insurer's promise to perform is an executory promise conditioned upon the happening of the event insured against.

Express and Implied

Express contracts are those in which the parties have made oral or written declarations of their intentions and of the terms of the transaction. These contracts exist in the majority of cases where the parties specifically have agreed by words or in writing to do certain things. For example, parties who agree either orally or in writing on the sale of an automobile for $5,000 create an express contract.

Implied contracts may be either implied in fact or implied in law. An *implied-in-fact contract* arises when the parties have expressed assent, but not by written or spoken words.

For example, one person performs services for another, who can reject those services but fails to do so. If a doctor finds a person injured and administers medical services, the injured person accepting the services without comment may be liable to pay the reasonable value of the services under an "implied-in-fact" contract. If Bill, who has a credit account at the local hardware store, picks up an item, shows it to his friend the store owner without comment, and then walks out of the store with it, an implied-in-fact contract to pay for the item exists. Implied-in-fact contracts often arise through and are governed by customs of trade, by prior relations between the parties involved, and by community customs of which all parties are aware.

Implied-in-law contracts, sometimes referred to as *quasi contracts,* arise when, even though the parties have not approved an agreement, the law imposes a contractual obligation because of the parties' special relationship or unusual circumstances of the case. A quasi contract is not an actual contract, but a promise the law implies to take care of situations that require a remedy. These obligations do not arise from the parties' apparent intentions but, rather, from courts' notions of justice and equitable principles within the contexts of particular cases.

A parent who does not provide a child with the necessities of life is liable to a third person who does provide those necessities under an implied-in-law contract for the reasonable value of those necessities. Similarly, if a doctor renders professional services to an unconscious person who cannot accept or refuse the services, then the law obligates the patient to pay the reasonable value of the medical services. A quasi contract is a duty the law imposes on someone who otherwise would be enriched unjustly.

Void and Voidable

Void agreements are those without legal effect. It is not logical to call them "void contracts" because they are not legally enforceable or binding in any way. No liability arises in these situations. An agreement to commit a crime, for example, is void and completely unenforceable. A contract between a sane person and an insane person is void because the insane person lacks the mental capacity to form a contract voluntarily.

A *voidable contract* is a contract that one of the parties can reject, or "avoid," based on some circumstance surrounding its execution. The right of avoidance is available only to an innocent or injured party.

A minor who has entered into a contract may avoid it any time during minority or within a reasonable time after reaching the age of majority. If both parties to a contract are minors, then either or both may avoid the obligations of the contract. This contract is only "voidable" and is not automatically void. Therefore, the contract continues in force, and the parties may execute it completely unless one of the parties first chooses to avoid it.

The behavior of one of the contracting parties also may make a contract voidable. Thus, a contract may be voidable because a party has committed fraud. An example of such fraud is a party's intentional misrepresentation of an important fact relating to a contract. Likewise, a party who has entered into a contract as the result of duress may avoid the contract within a reasonable period of time. For example, if a salesperson does not allow a potential buyer to leave a room until after signing a contract, the buyer later may avoid the contract.

An injured party may ratify, or affirm, a voidable contract later. Thus, if there is fraud or duress, the innocent party may later elect to abide by the agreement and may hold the other party to the contract.

ELEMENTS OF A CONTRACT

No matter what the type of contract, each of the following elements must be present for the contract to be legally binding and enforceable:

1. *Agreement.* An agreement consists of an offer by one party and an acceptance of that offer by another party. There must be real assent between the parties that is not negated by fraud, duress, concealment, or mistake.

2. *Competent parties.* Minority, insanity, or intoxication must not restrict the parties' legal capacity.

3. *Consideration. Consideration* is the price paid by each party to the other, or to what each party receives and gives up in the agreement. For the element of consideration to be present, there must be a legal benefit received by the promisor or a legal detriment suffered by the promisee.

4. *Legal purpose.* The contract must not be tainted by illegality. Instead, it must have a lawful purpose that is consistent with sound public policy.

The next section discusses the necessary parts of the first element of a contract, the agreement.

AGREEMENT

The first requirement of an enforceable contract is an *agreement* between the parties. An agreement consists of an offer and an acceptance of that offer. The parties to a contract at some time must mutually assent, or agree, to the same terms. Over the years, a considerable body of law has defined the circumstances under which a court will find that such an agreement exists. The basic defining circumstances are an offer and an acceptance of that offer.

Offer

An *offer* is a promise that requires an act or a return promise in exchange. The offer may have, as a condition, that the other party give a promise in return. This results in a bilateral contract if the other party makes a promise in return. If the offer is conditioned upon the performance of an act, a unilateral contract exists when the other party performs the conditional act. The person who makes the initial offer is the *offeror,* and the person to whom the offer is made is the *offeree.*

If the offeree can understand the communication as an offer to enter into an agreement on the terms as stated, an agreement becomes binding on both parties immediately upon the offeree's acceptance. The parties legally must fulfill the terms of the contract. No contract exists without both an offer and an acceptance.

Elements of Offer. The essential elements of an offer are the following:

1. Expression of present contractual intent
2. Definite terms
3. Communication to the offeree

The presence of all of these three elements gives the offeree the power of acceptance, which is, the ability to create a contract by accepting the offer.

Intent To Contract. The offeror must intend or appear to intend that the proposal will create a legal obligation if the offeree accepts it. Because the appearance of such an intent can be understood as an offer, the offeror's language is the most important factor in determining whether a communication is an offer. Because an offer is a promise, the language characterizing an intent to offer is language that includes words of promise. Without words of promise, the law will treat the communication only as a general statement of intention or an invitation for an offer.

Objective Test. The central question in each case involving contractual intent is whether, by words or conduct, the party showed an intent to be bound immediately. The intent of the party whose conduct is examined is usually of no importance. The manner in which an average, reasonable person would interpret that party's intent is the important factor here. The *objective theory of contracts* controls all rules of construction concerning communications between parties.

Reasonable Person Test. Many of the rules for formation of contracts require that the parties' actions be viewed from the standpoint of a *reasonable person*. This requirement provides an objective standard that may apply to people's conduct in general. A judge or jury must weigh all the circumstances of a case to make a determination of how a reasonable person acting under the same or similar circumstances would react in the same situation. The decision about what is reasonable in each case depends on the subjective judgment of the judge or jury.

General Statements of Intention. Statements that contain no inference of a promise are not offers. If Anne says to Bob, "I am going to sell my car for $5,000"; and Bob replies, "All right, I'll pay $5,000 for your car," they do not create a contract. The test is whether, under the circumstances, a reasonable person would conclude that Anne intended to promise to sell. A reasonable person would not draw that conclusion in this case. Instead, Anne's statement expressed only an intention to sell the car in the future and did not make an explicit offer to Bob.

If Anne says to Bob, "I will not sell my property for less than $20,000," and Bob replies, "I accept your offer," no contract results. Anne's mere statement of a minimum price does not allow Bob to conclude reasonably that Anne promises to sell at the figure mentioned. Anne again has given only a general statement of intention to sell at approximately the figure mentioned.

Invitations. People often communicate only to induce others to respond with offers. These communications are not in themselves offers because they express no present contractual intent. Instead, most advertisements, catalogues, and sales letters are *invitations* to negotiate or to make an offer. For example, a store that advertises a camera at $495 is inviting offers that it may accept later at that price. If the store runs out of these cameras, or if the cameras were mistakenly advertised for $4.95, a customer's acceptance does not bind the store. To the contrary, the usual advertisement or catalog does not define conditions so specifically that their acceptance would make a contract.

In some cases, however, an advertisement may constitute an offer that a reader may accept. If, for example, an advertisement indicates that the first person who enters the store can buy the goods at a specific price, the advertisement spells out the conditions of acceptance. When the first person who enters the store agrees to buy the goods, a unilateral contract arises. In other words, if an advertiser uses words of promise or specifies circumstances giving rise to a unilateral contract, a contractual intention may exist.

Bids. A party can call for offers that it may or may not accept. In construction, for example, a project owner asking for bids may elect to accept one bid or to reject all of them. Anyone bidding may withdraw the bid at any time prior to its acceptance. A party calling for bids may accept any bid, whether or not it is the lowest one unless a special law applicable to construction contracts applies.

Social Invitations. Courts recognize that it is difficult to enforce social invitations and that they do not involve contractual intent. Accordingly, social invitations do not create legal obligations because invitations to attend parties and weddings are not legally recognized offers under the law. If a person withdraws an invitation or cancels a party, there is no legal remedy for a person who received an invitation.

Opinion. A statement that is a prediction or an expression of opinion is not an offer or intent to contract. For example, one person mistakenly predicts that the weather will be good. Another person relies on that mistaken prediction, undertaking a course of action that results in a loss because of bad weather. The prediction did not create a contractual intention or binding offer. Similarly, if a doctor predicts that a patient will be in the hospital "only a few days," and the period of hospitalization turns out to be much longer, the doctor's prediction was not an enforceable promise or offer because there was no contractual intent.

Offers Made in Excitement or Jest. If a reasonable person were to recognize that a statement was made in jest or in the heat of anger and accept the statement regardless, that acceptance does not turn the statement into a contract. The person who made the statement did not intend to be bound by it. The person who heard the statement should have recognized that the person making the statement was joking or expressing emotions and should have known that an offer was not intended.

It is often difficult to distinguish cases in which statements are made in excitement or jest from those that can be reasonably interpreted as expressing an offer. In such situations, a contractual obligation may arise even though the person who made the statement may have been jesting or exclaiming. For example, Arthur in jest may offer to sell Bonnie a farm for $50,000 with an intent to embarrass Bonnie into admitting that she does not have $50,000. If Bonnie accepts the offer, and both parties sign a written agreement expressing Arthur's offer and Bonnie's acceptance, Arthur is bound if Bonnie reasonably could have believed that Arthur made a serious offer. In other words, Arthur's secret intention is not legally significant here. The objective manifestation of Arthur's intent, as viewed by a reasonable person, is the crucial test of contractual intent.

In another situation, Joe cries out in excitement, "Save my child from that burning building, and I'll give you $1,000!" In response, Bill runs into the building and saves Joe's child. If Bill reasonably could have understood Joe's statement as an offer, Bill's actions would create a binding unilateral contract.

If Joe's statement had been, "I'll give you a million dollars," then the statement would probably be viewed as the result of excitement. A reasonable person may not rely on or enforce the promise. In each case, however, the entire set of circumstances must be considered to determine whether the statement reasonably could be an offer to contract.

Auctions. Public auctions illustrate offer and acceptance. The seller at a public auction invites offers from those present and bidding. If nothing is stated to the contrary in a newspaper advertisement of the auction or at the auction itself, the auction is considered to be *with reserve,* which is usually the case. At an auction with reserve, the public is invited to make offers or bids for the items put up for sale. The auctioneer does not make offers, but merely solicits offers by holding up items for bidding.

Each new bid is a new offer that the auctioneer may either accept or reject. The auctioneer has reserved this right. The fall of the hammer, or some other sign the auctioneer gives, such as saying "sold," indicates final acceptance of the bid or offer and conclusion of the agreement. The auctioneer can withdraw the item prior to the time the hammer falls, even though the bidding has started. Likewise, until the hammer falls or some other signal of acceptance has been given, the bidder may retract a bid. The withdrawal of a bid does not revive previous bids. If the hammer is falling when a new bid is made, the auctioneer has discretion to accept the previous offer or to reopen the bidding.

In an auction announced to be *without reserve,* once the bids have been called for, the goods must go to the highest bidder. The seller has given up the right to withdraw an item up for sale, and the auctioneer has not reserved the right to accept or reject the highest bid but must accept it. Each item up for sale is offered to the public, and each new bid constitutes an offer at a higher level. An acceptance usually binds the parties immediately upon its making. In an auction without reserve, however, the bid or acceptance may still be withdrawn prior to the hammer's dropping. The bidder may withdraw a bid any time prior to the hammer's falling.

Unless otherwise announced before the auction, the seller has no right to bid at his or her own sale. For the seller to bid or to have an agent bid on the seller's behalf would be fraud. If the seller violates this rule, the buyer can avoid the sale upon learning of the improper bidding.[2]

Definite Terms.   An offer must be sufficiently definite, or certain, in its terms. Certainty makes an agreement enforceable and makes it possible to calculate damages. The terms of the agreement must be definite enough for a court to determine whether the parties have lived up to their promises.

Reasonable Certainty.   Before an offer created a possibility of acceptance, it must state its terms with at least a reasonable degree of certainty. Reasonable certainty means including essential terms that generally identify the contracting parties, the contract's subject matter, the price, and the time of performance. The absence of one or more of these terms, however, is not necessarily fatal to the offer.

To test an offer for sufficient certainty, courts often ask whether the offer's terms are clear enough to provide a reasonably certain basis for a remedy in the event of default. If possible, the courts will supply such missing terms as price or time of performance. For example, if there is no designated time for performance, courts usually find an implication that performance is to occur within a reasonable time, considering the subject matter involved.

However, inability to identify the parties to an agreement or the offer's subject matter creates sufficient uncertainty to make the offer indefinite and therefore not impossible to accept. If the offer is definite enough for a court to determine the parties' intent, then a court will enforce it even though it may be necessary to imply some terms. The requirement of reasonable certainty is relative and depends on the circumstances of each case.

Illusory Promises.   A statement can create the illusion of a promise when it really does not promise anything specific. Thus, Alice's promise to Bill to pay a "fair share of the profits" if Bill works for Alice is an *illusory promise* and too indefinite to be enforced. Similarly, a promise to "take care of" an employee who has been injured is too vague to afford a remedy.

Indefinite language creates the illusion of obligation but provides no means for determining the parties' true intentions. If, however, in the first case Bill actually goes to work for Alice, he is entitled to fair value of his services under the theory of implied-in-fact contract, even though the promise to pay a fair share of the profits is unenforceable.

Requirement Contracts.   Agreements to deal with one supplier, called *requirement contracts,* are usually enforceable even though the possibility exists that there may be no requirement for the goods. For example, Allen's promise to buy "all steel required" from Betsy is definite enough to enforce. Enforceable obligations arise on both sides because Allen promises to buy any steel required from Betsy, and Betsy promises to sell Allen the steel. In contrast, if the language of the agreement involved Betsy's promise to sell "all such coal as I wish to supply you," then the agreement is illusory and too indefinite to provide a remedy. The indefiniteness stems from the possibility that Betsy may not wish to supply any coal.

Certainty Under U.C.C.   The Uniform Commercial Code (U.C.C.) is a uniform law that most states have adopted to regulate the sale of goods and other commercial transactions. Although courts supply any important terms that are missing from a contract by ascertaining what the parties actually intended, the U.C.C. goes further by providing, for sales of goods contracts only, that the parties may agree in a binding contract to set terms in the future.[3] These *open terms* even may include the price of the goods. This U.C.C. approach differs from the general rule in contract law that it is ordinarily essential to ascertain the intended price at the time the contract was made unless the goods actually are delivered and accepted, in which case a "reasonable" price is implied. The U.C.C., however, rejects the usual rule that "an agreement to agree is unenforceable."

Communication.   An offer has no effect until the offeror or the offeror's agent communicates it to the offeree. Likewise, the offeree cannot accept a proposal before knowing about it. To illustrate, assume that Ruth offers to sell her library to Jackie for $3,000 in a letter to that effect. Before receiving the letter and without knowledge of Ruth's offer, Jackie sends a letter to Ruth stating that she will buy Ruth's library for $3,000. Jackie's letter is not an acceptance of Ruth's offer because Jackie did not know of Ruth's offer. The second letter was itself an offer, yet there is no contract because neither communication related to the other. The letters are mere *cross-offers,* which involve two offers "crossing" each other. No acceptance occurs until a reply responds to one of the two offers.

In another example, a newspaper advertisement offers "$100 to anyone who will enter the 100-yard dash on July 4 and beat David." Matt, having no knowledge of the advertisement or offer, enters the race and beats David. There is no contract, because Matt could not accept an offer of which he had no knowledge.

It is not necessary that an offeree completely fulfill the terms of the offer after learning of the offer. Indeed, the offeree may have already begun performance before learning of the offer. For example, an offeror makes an offer for information leading to the arrest and conviction of a person responsible for a certain crime. Paul already had investigated and had determined that Donna committed the crime. Then, upon learning of the reward, Paul turned Donna in to the authorities. If Donna is convicted, Paul may collect the reward even though part of his effort occurred before learning of the offer. The crucial fact is that Paul knew of the offer when he turned Donna in.

The law requires that the offeror communicate the offer to the offeree. Usually, this means that an offer is effective when delivered to the offeree or when the offeree learns of the offer. However, the law also holds that a person controls his or her own offer, and someone simply learning that an offer will be made may not seize upon that "offer" and insist that the item be sold to him or her. Thus, where Peter's friend learns of Angela's intent to offer a certain item for sale and advises Peter of the forthcoming offer, Peter may not accept the offer until Angela makes it to him or to the public at large.

Duration and Termination.   The length of time during which an offer is binding depends upon several considerations, including lapse of time, operation of law, the offeree's rejection, any counteroffers, and the offeror's revocation.

Lapse of Time.   Offers do not remain open indefinitely. Instead, an offer ceases to be binding upon the expiration of the time specified in the offer or, if no time is specified, after the lapse of a reasonable time. What is a "reasonable time" depends on such considerations as the contract's subject matter and the transaction's general commercial setting.

For example, in an offer for the sale of perishable goods, the length of time necessary for the goods to spoil is very important. Although the offer is still open, the offeree can accept it at any time. Once the offer is terminated, any attempted acceptance becomes a counteroffer, which the original offeror may either accept or reject.

Operation of Law. Any one of several events occurring before acceptance may automatically terminate an outstanding offer. If, for example, an offeror or the offeree dies or is adjudicated—or formally determined by a judge to be—insane, before the offer is made or accepted the law automatically terminates the offer. Once a contract has been created, death or insanity will not terminate the contract unless it involves the rendering of a personal or professional service by the deceased or insane party. In such a case, performance of the contract is excused. Otherwise, an agreement that does not call for personal or professional services is enforceable against the deceased party's estate.

If the subject matter of an offer is destroyed before acceptance of the offer, the offer is terminated at the point at which the destruction occurs—even if the offeree did not know that it had occurred, because operation of law automatically terminates the offer. "Operation of law" means that rules of law apply automatically to a situation without any act by the parties.

Similarly, if performance of a contract becomes illegal after the offer has been made, the offer ends. For example, if a statute makes it unlawful to deal in certain goods, then a preexisting offer to sell those goods before passage of the statute automatically terminates.

Offeree's Rejection. The offeree's rejection of the offer terminates that offer. A rejection occurs when the offeree notifies the offeror of an intention not to accept. An offeree may reject an offer either by an express refusal to accept or by making a counteroffer. As with the offer itself, the offeree's rejection is not effective until actually communicated to the offeror or to the offeror's agent. After the rejection, the offeree must not then change his or her mind and attempt to accept the offer. The attempted acceptance after a rejection is a new offer by the offeree.

Counteroffers. If the offeree makes a proposal to the offeror that varies in some material respect from the original offer, the proposal is a *counteroffer.* A counteroffer rejects the original offer and constitutes a new offer by the offeree. A counteroffer is not the same as a mere inquiry for further information because in the latter case, no rejection has occurred. For example, Gene offers to sell Pat a television set for $200. Pat replies, "I'll give you $150 for it." This reply is a counteroffer that automatically rejects Gene's original offer, and Pat cannot later accept the original $200 offer. Yet, if Pat had replied to Gene's offer by inquiring, "Will you accept $150?", the question is an inquiry and not a counteroffer or rejection. In that case, if Gene indicated that the lower figure was unsatisfactory, Pat could still accept the $200 offer.

The offer also remains open if the offeror makes an offer and adds, "This offer will remain open beyond any counteroffers." Based on the offeror's additional statement, the original offeree's counteroffer is not a rejection. Similarly, an offer also continues if the counteroffer makes it clear that it is not a rejection of the original offer.

Offeror's Revocation. A *revocation* is the offeror's withdrawal of the offer. Generally, an offeror may revoke an offer at any time before an offeree's acceptance. As in the case of the offer itself, the revocation is effective only when communicated, in this case to the offeree. Moreover, a letter or telegram revoking an offer is not effective until the offeree actually receives it. Up to that point, there has been no communication of the revocation to the offeree. Similarly, if the offeror mails a revocation but the offeree accepts it by telephone before receiving the mailed revocation, a contract exists.

Means of Communication. Offerors must revoke offers to the general public through the same means of communication used in making the original offers. For example, one who offers a reward in an advertisement may revoke it only in another advertisement. Once the revocation is advertised, the offer effectively is revoked—even if a party who tries to accept the original offer does not see the advertisement.

Option Contracts. The offeror's mere statement that the offer is irrevocable for a period of time is not usually sufficient to remove the right of revocation. Generally, the offeror may revoke an offer even after stating that the offer will remain open. However, there are some important qualifications to this rule.

An *option contract* is a contract to keep an offer open for a stated period of time. Consideration (payment of some kind) supports the promise to hold the offer open. Once an offeree has given consideration for the promise to hold the offer open, the offeror may not revoke the offer within the prescribed period. Option contracts frequently occur in real estate transactions, when a buyer provides consideration in the form of an amount of money, to secure a binding option to buy. "Binding" means that the option obligates the buyer to buy. The offeror then agrees to hold the offer open for a period of time and cannot revoke that offer within the option period. Moreover, the offeree may reject the offer but later accept it, as long as this occurs within the option period.

Firm Offers. Under the U.C.C., a merchant who makes a *firm offer* in writing to buy or sell goods and states that the offer is irrevocable for a stated period may not revoke that offer, even in the absence of consideration, up to a maximum period of three months.[4] The U.C.C. requires that the firm offer be in writing and signed by the merchant-offeror.

Unilateral Contract Offers. If the offeror has made a *unilateral contract offer,* and the offeree has partially performed the acts requested by the offer, most courts hold that the offer is then irrevocable after the performance. For example, Marie promises to pay John $2,000 if John excavates Marie's property. John has completed one-third of the excavation when Marie attempts to revoke the offer. The revocation is ineffective.

To render revocations ineffective, most courts require that a substantial start be made in the performance requested. The mere preparation for performance may not be a substantial start. Once a substantial start is made, the offeree has reasonable time to perform the entire acceptance. Whether substantial performance has begun is a question of fact.

Acceptance

No agreement exists unless an offeree accepts an offeror's offer. An *acceptance* occurs when an offeree agrees to a proposal or does what was proposed.

Elements of Acceptance. To create an enforceable agreement, an acceptance must include these elements:

1. The person to whom the offer was made must make the acceptance.
2. The acceptance must be unconditional and unequivocal.
3. The offeree must communicate the acceptance to the offeror by appropriate word or act.

An acceptance expresses the offeree's consent to be bound by the terms of the offer. While the offeree may state that the offer is "accepted," the term "accept" is not necessary. Instead, any language showing that the offeree agrees to the proposal suffices. Whatever the language, it must meet the above three conditions to form a binding agreement.

Person to Whom Offer Made. Only the person or persons to whom an offer is made may accept an offer because the offeror has the right to choose with whom to contract. Thus, if Alan makes an offer to Dan, who dies after receiving it, the executor of Dan's estate cannot accept the offer.

An offer may be made to one person, to a group or class of persons, or to the public at large. The language and circumstances of the offer determine the identity of the offerees. For example, if Janet promises to sell and deliver books to Lisa if Lisa's father will promise to pay $100 for the books, Lisa's father is the offeree. Only Lisa's father can accept the offer by making the return promise.

When an offer is made to a particular group, then any member of the group may accept it. Thus, when an offeror sends a form letter containing an offer to many persons, any recipient may accept the offer according to its terms. If an offer is made to the public at large, as in the case of a reward advertisement, any member of the public who knows of it may accept it. Once someone accepts the offer of reward, no one else may accept it.

Unconditional and Unequivocal. An acceptance must conform to the terms of the offer and be unconditional and unequivocal. If it deviates from those terms, the "acceptance" is actually a counteroffer. An offeree must comply strictly with provisions in an offer relating to time, place, or manner of acceptance. A conditional or equivocal response does not constitute an acceptance.

Conditional Responses. While an acceptance must not deviate from the basic terms of an offer, the law recognizes that, in customary business practices, a word-for-word response to the offer in the acceptance is unlikely to occur.

Some terms or words in an acceptance do not render the acceptance conditional if the law were to imply terms in any event. For example, an acceptance by a buyer in a real estate sale that states, "Good title must be passed," is an unconditional acceptance because the law implies good title in real estate transactions anyway. Good title would pass regardless of whether the parties say so. However, whether a purported acceptance that is subject to "details being worked out" is an unconditional acceptance depends on the extent of the "details." If the details are perfunctory clerical matters, then an unconditional acceptance results. If the details involve substantial matters, however, such as the boundaries of a piece of land, the acceptance is conditional. Likewise, a reply made subject to "details to be worked out between you and my attorney" is a valid acceptance if the "details" concern matters such as the agreement's form or a title search on property.

In contrast, a reply that leaves open essential terms that a court cannot imply according to legal rules cannot be an acceptance. For example, an offer to build a house and a reply that accepts the offer "subject to details to be worked out" does not create a binding agreement. Because the details of house building are not perfunctory, too many essential elements are missing. In this case, the response is not an unconditional acceptance.

Equivocal Responses. An equivocal response does not comprise a valid acceptance of an offer, but it also does not create a counteroffer or an outright rejection. An offeree's response that the offer "will receive our immediate attention" does not express a clear intent to contract and is too equivocal for an acceptance. Similarly, a mere expression of hope, such as "I hope to have the cash for you next Friday morning," is an equivocal acceptance. Therefore, no contract results from such a statement. Just as the vagueness of such equivocal responses precludes an acceptance, so does it fall short of expressing a counteroffer or rejection.

U.C.C. Provisions. If the contract offer concerns the sale of goods, the U.C.C. provides that a variance between the acceptance and the offer may not preclude contract formation. The U.C.C. provides as follows:

> A definite and reasonable expression of acceptance or a written confirmation which is sent within a reasonable time operates as an acceptance even though it states terms additional to or different from those offered or agreed upon, unless acceptance is expressly made conditional on assent to the additional or different terms. The additional terms are to be construed as proposals for addition to the contract. Between merchants such terms become part of the contract unless: (a) the offer expressly limits acceptance to the terms of the offer; (b) they materially alter it; or (c) notification of objection to them has already been given or is given within a reasonable time after notice of them is received.[5]

Under the U.C.C., unless the offeror and offeree are merchants, additional terms do not become part of the contract unless the offeror and offeree mutually agree to them. Thus, the proposal of additional terms in sales contracts involving goods is not a conditional acceptance and is not a rejection of the offer. Instead, the terms are additional proposals to the contract. If the offeror fails to object to the proposed additions within a reasonable time, the law agrees to their inclusion, and they become part of the contract. Thus, if the buyer's acceptance states "inspection of goods will be allowed prior to their acceptance," the addition becomes part of the contract unless the original offeror objects to it. The other terms of the contract remain unchanged.

However, if an intended acceptance of an offer for the sale of goods states terms that vary the agreement materially, the response is a counterproposal and a rejection of the original offer. In this case the offeror's notification to the offeree of objection to the added terms is unnecessary. To make the added terms a part of the contract, the offeror's express assent and acceptance of the counteroffer are required. For example, if the purported acceptance changes the quantity to be delivered or the unit price to be paid, the change is a counteroffer as well as a rejection of the original offer. The offeree can avoid the result that a material change constitutes a rejection only by (1) asking whether the offeror would consider new terms and (2) stating that the offeree's proposal to change the terms is not to be considered a rejection.

Appropriate Word or Act. An acceptance must involve more than the offeree's mere mental resolve to accept. The offeree must also communicate acceptance. What must be communicated depends on the contract offer. In a unilateral contract offer, acceptance occurs upon completion of the act the offeror requested. In a bilateral contract offer, two parties exchange promises, and acceptance occurs by the offeree's communication of the offeror's return promise.

Most offers are bilateral in the sense that they contemplate a return promise to perform. When it is unclear whether the parties intended a unilateral or a bilateral contract, courts usually find that they intended a bilateral contract, or the exchange of one promise for another. In any event, the law requires that the parties openly express mutual assent either by words or by conduct.

Manner. The acceptance must conform to the terms of the offer. If the offer specifies certain means of acceptance, those means are necessary to form a contract. If the offer does not require a particular method of acceptance, those means that are customary in similar transactions or reasonable under the circumstances are permissible. For an offer that prescribes that an acceptance be "in writing" or "by fax," an oral response is ineffective as an acceptance and does not create a contract. The offeror's definition of the method of acceptance is always the determining factor. Under the U.C.C., an offeree may accept in any commercially reasonable manner.[6]

If an offer requires acceptance "by return mail," an acceptance mailed the same business day of receipt of the offer generally is required. If the offeror does not set a time for acceptance, then acceptance must occur within a reasonable time under the U.C.C. The circumstances of each case determine what constitutes a reasonable time. Thus, if the offer involves the sale of highly perishable goods, such as strawberries, the reasonable time for acceptance obviously is much shorter than in the case of nonperishables, such as furniture.

Some situations do not require formal notice of acceptance. For example, if an offer to sell contains the words, "This proposal becomes a contract when an executive officer of the company accepts and approves it," the acceptance occurs when an executive officer indicates acceptance on the document by signing it. Thus, formal notice of acceptance is not necessary to form a contract. However, some courts still impose a duty on the offeree in this situation to inform the offeror of an acceptance within a reasonable time.

Complaining.   A complaint does not make an acceptance unnecessary. A contract still results even if an offeree replies to an offer by stating, "Your price is very unfair. If I didn't need the property so badly, I would never accept at this figure. Enclosed is my check for the unreasonable amount you demand." The acceptance is unequivocal, albeit grudging.

Silence.   An actual response or overt act is required to create an acceptance. Thus, an offeree's silence is not an acceptance. This rule cannot be circumvented by imposing a duty to respond on the offeree. If Jack offers an item for sale to Jerry by stating in a letter, "If I do not hear from you within ten days, I will assume the offer is accepted," no acceptance occurs if Jerry remains silent.

There is a qualification to this rule when the parties' *prior dealings* have imposed a duty to reject the current offer. For example, if the parties have been dealing for some time by sending goods and then later paying for them, the party who receives an unrequested additional shipment may have to reject it if he or she does not wish to accept the shipment.

In the absence of such a pattern of prior dealings, the person receiving unrequested goods has no duty to reply or to maintain the goods. For example, under the law of contracts a person receiving unordered merchandise has the right to use or dispose of it in any manner without returning or paying for it, and federal postal law explicitly confirms that right.

Unilateral Offers.   In the case of unilateral contracts, the offeror wants the offeree either to perform or not perform an act. The legal term for requested nonperformance of an act is *forbearance.* When the offeree, with knowledge of the offer, performs, or forbears, the offeree is accepting the offer. The offeree does not have to communicate performance because, presumably, the offeror will learn of the performance. The offer, however, may specify that the offeree must give notice of performance.

The most difficult problems arise when the offeree begins to perform the act, and the offeror then revokes the offer before completion of the performance. Most courts hold that an offeree's *substantial performance* suspends the offeror's right to revoke the offer. A unilateral contract offer includes the understanding that, if substantial performance occurs, the offeree can complete performance within the prescribed time.

No contract is formed until the offeree completes all the work, but the offeror's right to withdraw the offer is suspended temporarily. What constitutes substantial performance sufficient to suspend the offeror's right of revocation is a question of fact. Generally, mere preparations for performance are not substantial performance.

Bilateral Offers. In the case of a bilateral offer, the acceptance is not complete until the offeree assents by giving the offeror the appropriate return promise. The offeror may revoke the offer at any time until communication of the return promise. The communication may be to the offeror or to the offeror's agent authorized to accept such communications.

While the usual bargained-for response in a bilateral contract offer is a return promise, the offeree may choose simply to perform the act requested rather than to give a return promise. For example, Jill writes to Barry, "I'll pay you $500 if you'll promise to paint my garage by June 1." Barry does not reply to the letter but proceeds to paint Jill's garage, with her knowledge, and completes the work prior to June 1. A contract results. The reasonable interpretation of the parties' conduct is that, by commencing the work, Barry impliedly accepted Jill's offer and agreed to its terms. Jill impliedly agreed to this form of acceptance, and a bilateral contract resulted.

Time of Effect. An acceptance made in a manner invited by an offer is effective as soon as it leaves the offeree's possession, even if it never reaches the offeror, so long as the offeree intends the communication to be directly to the offeror. If the offeree simply tells a third person about acceptance of the offer, the purported acceptance is ineffective.

When acceptance by mail or telegraph is an approved mode of response to an offer, the acceptance is effective upon mailing the letter or handing the telegram to the telegraph clerk. Mailed and telegraphed acceptances create legally binding contracts when they leave the offeree's possession.

While this rule principally applies to mail and telegraph, the rule would apply equally to other communication services that the offeree does not control. Thus, delivery of the acceptance to a private messenger service creates a contract immediately upon the delivery to the messenger. This rule, unique to acceptances, furthers contract finality and formation. The offeree is not obliged to prove that the offeror actually received the acceptance.

Proper Dispatch. For an acceptance to be effective upon dispatch, the offeree must address it accurately to the offeror. The offeree may meet this requirement by using the return address indicated in the offer, whether on letterhead or otherwise. If, however, the acceptance is sent to the wrong address, it is effective only upon the offeror's receipt. For example, if an offeree receives an offer on stationery with a business address and the offeree mails the acceptance to the offeror's home, no contract results until the offeror actually receives the acceptance.

Loss or Delay.   If an offeree accepts in a manner the offeror has authorized, then the acceptance is effective when it leaves the offeree's control, directed to the offeror, even though the acceptance never reaches the offeror. If, however, the offer is conditional upon receipt of the acceptance, then the acceptance is effective only upon receipt and not when sent. For example, Amy mails an offer to lease land to Victor, stating, "Wire me a yes or no answer. If I do not hear from you by noon Wednesday, I will conclude that your answer is no." Victor telegraphs, "Yes," but Amy does not receive the telegram until after noon on Wednesday. Victor and Amy have not formed a contract because Amy did not receive the acceptance within the time period she prescribed.

Revocation.   An offeree cannot withdraw or revoke an acceptance once made. That the offeree conceivably can reclaim the acceptance from the post office or from the telegraph service does not prevent the acceptance from taking effect upon dispatch. The moment the letter or message is delivered to the postal department or telegraph company, the acceptance is effective. Attempts to revoke acceptances by retrieving them are legally ineffective.

Conflicting Communications.   While the majority of communications leading to the formation of contracts do not present complex legal questions, it sometimes becomes crucial to determine the exact time of a particular action. Unless the parties have provided otherwise, contract communications are not effective until actual delivery to the other party or to an agent authorized to accept delivery. The only qualification to this rule is in the case of the acceptance: if mailing the acceptance is the method the offeror expressly or impliedly authorizes, then the acceptance is effective upon mailing. To illustrate these rules, consider the following fact patterns:

Situation One.

May 3—Joel mails offer to construct a building to Carl and states that Carl should mail his response

May 4—Carl receives offer at 11:00 A.M.

May 4—Joel mails revocation at 3:00 P.M.

May 4—Carl mails acceptance at 6:00 P.M.

May 5—Carl receives revocation at noon

May 5—Joel receives acceptance at 2:00 P.M.

In Situation One, the contract was effective at the time of mailing of the acceptance on May 4 at 6 P.M. Joel's earlier revocation was not effective until Carl received it, although Carl's acceptance was effective when he mailed it. Therefore the acceptance is effective because

Carl mailed his acceptance at 6:00 P.M. on May 4, and he did not receive Joel's revocation until noon the following day.

   Situation Two.

   May 6—Joel mails offer to construct building to Carl May 7;
         Carl receives offer at 11:00 A.M.

   May 8—Carl mails letter of rejection at noon

   May 9—Carl telegraphs acceptance at 2:00 P.M.

   May 9—Joel receives rejection letter at 3:00 P.M.

   May 9—Joel receives acceptance telegram at 4:00 P.M.

In Situation Two, the parties do not have a contract because Joel received the rejection before receiving the acceptance. Thus, acceptance is usually effective immediately upon leaving the offeree's control. However, when the offeree takes the conflicting actions of first mailing a rejection and then following with an acceptance, the results depend on a race between the two communications. Technically, the first communication Joel receives—in this case the rejection letter—is binding.

In practice, if the rejection is the first communication received, most courts will favor the offeror and hold that no contract was formed, but may treat the succeeding attempted acceptance as a counteroffer.[7] In the same vein, if the offeree first mailed the acceptance and then telegraphed a rejection that the offeror received first, a contract technically would result because the acceptance was effective when mailed. However, if the offeror substantially relies on the rejection while unaware of the acceptance, the offeree may not enforce the contract.

COMPETENT PARTIES

The second essential element of an enforceable contract is the parties' legal *capacity to contract.* Capacity is competency or ability to understand the consequences of one's actions. People who have legal capacity to contract are *competent parties,* and the contracts they make are enforceable against them. A party who lacks legal capacity to contract is described as *incompetent.* An incompetent person can challenge the validity of any contract he or she makes. Successfully challenging a contract is called *avoiding* it.

Incompetency to contract, or legal incapacity, may result if a party is one of the following:

- A minor
- Insane
- Under the influence of alcohol or drugs

- An artificial entity (such as a corporation lacking capacity to enter certain contracts)

The law protects incompetents, who often cannot protect themselves from exploitation. They have the opportunity to disaffirm contracts entered into while incompetent. At the same time, the law enforces the justifiable expectations of parties to contracts and promotes the validity of transactions generally.

Minors' Contracts

Under early common law, any person under the age of twenty-one was a minor, or "infant." That the minor may have become *emancipated*—or no longer in need of parental support and entitled to keep earnings—by leaving home, marrying, or being orphaned did not affect the minor's capacity to contract because no contractual capacity existed until the minor reached the age of majority.

Minors' contracts were not void, but were voidable at the minor's option. Void agreements have no legal effect, but a voidable agreement is a legal contract that a party may reject, or "avoid," based on a circumstance surrounding its execution, such as the party's being underage at the time. An adult dealt with the minor at his or her peril because the minor could enforce the agreement against the adult, and the right of avoidance rested only with the minor.

Today it is necessary to consult each state's statutory law to determine the age of majority for contracts. Historically, some state statutes provided for a lower age of majority for women, but charges of sex discrimination have eliminated the differences in the age of majority for males and females. The most common age of majority today is eighteen for males and females.

Avoidance. The law protecting minors from disposing of their property while they are underage reflects public policy. Generally, a minor always may assert minority as a defense against liability in contracts not involving the purchase of necessaries.

Although earlier common law considered whether the contract was beneficial to the minor, that is no longer true. The minor still has the right to avoid a contract for nonnecessaries at any time during minority or within a reasonable time after reaching majority. This means that claim settlement files involving minors' claims should be retained until the age of majority, plus the "statute of limitations period," in the event the minor later repudiates settlement. A statute of limitations limits the time period within which a person may sue.

A minor may avoid a contract by any expression of an intention to renounce the agreement. Accordingly, any act inconsistent with the contract constitutes avoidance. Thus, if a minor contracts to sell property to one person but sells it to another immediately after reaching the age of majority, the sale renounces and thereby avoids the minor's original agreement. A minor who elects to avoid a contract must repudiate the entire contract and may not affirm some parts while seeking to avoid others.

If a parent or adult also is a party to a minor's contract, the adult must perform the contract even if the minor avoids it. An adult may not claim that a minor's incapacity negates a contract unless the adult acts on a deceased minor's behalf as administrator of the minor's estate or in a similar capacity.

Time. A minor may avoid a contract at any time during minority or within a reasonable time after reaching the age of majority. A court must, in each case, determine what constitutes a "reasonable time." If a minor has not avoided a contract within a reasonable time after coming of age, most courts hold that the minor has ratified the contract by failure to avoid it. Although a minor may avoid a contract during minority, a minor may not confirm a contract during minority.

Courts limit minors' rights to avoid contracts for the sale of real estate. To protect a minor's interests, some courts give the minor the right to repossess any real estate sold during minority. This right is valid until the minor reaches the age of majority, but the minor may not challenge such a contract until that event occurs. If an adult purchaser possesses the real estate, the minor who challenges the validity of the contract at majority can receive rents and profits for the period the adult was in possession of the real estate.

Courts may consider whether the contract is executory (not fully performed by the parties) or executed (fully performed by the parties) in determining the right of avoidance at majority. They may hold that executed contracts are binding on the minor unless actually disaffirmed after reaching majority. Executory contracts are not binding unless actually ratified by conduct of the minor after reaching majority. Executed contracts are valid until rescinded, and executory contracts are invalid unless ratified. Courts attempt to prevent exploitation of minors in all cases.

Restitution. *Restitution* is making an injured party whole again. For example, most courts require a minor to return any goods obtained before avoiding a contract. A minor may not challenge a contract and at the same time retain benefits from the contract. A minor who has received consideration, or something of value, must return it upon rejecting the contract. For example, if a minor has purchased a car and later trades the car for something else, the minor must return whatever comparable consideration is available upon rejecting the contract.

The minor must make only that restitution which is possible. In those cases in which the minor has spent or damaged the consideration received under the contract, most states permit the minor to avoid the contract, despite the impossibility of full restitution. Thus, if the minor purchases an automobile and demolishes it, most courts permit the minor to reject the contract by returning the wreckage to its original owner. Moreover, the minor can obtain a full refund of the purchase price upon rejection of the contract. Courts in some jurisdictions consider this rule too harsh and allow for the depreciated value of the property before permitting the minor to reject the contract. In the case of the demolished car, for instance, these courts would order the return only of its salvage value. A majority of courts continue, however, to assert that people take great risks in dealing with minors, and they permit minors to avoid contracts and return whatever remains of money or other consideration received. The other party cannot collect damages under the contract because permitting recovery would be permitting indirect enforcement of the contract against the minor.

Misrepresentation of Age. A minor's misrepresentation of age to induce another party to enter into a contract does not prevent the minor from avoiding the contract. The other party to the contract, however, can avoid it, too, on the grounds of misrepresentation.

Contracts for Necessaries. The law recognizes that certain transactions clearly benefit a minor and that the minor, therefore, has a duty to meet obligations assumed under such contracts. The term *necessaries* describes the subject matter of contracts benefiting minors and includes anything related to a minor's health, education, and comfort. A minor must pay the reasonable value of necessaries.

This special rule of law assures that minors are not deprived of the necessities of life because others refuse to deal with them. In this way public policy protects minors. If courts strictly applied the rules of law relating to dealing with minors, then they would have difficulty obtaining necessaries.

Necessaries include anything befitting a minor's mind and body and appropriate to that minor's standard of living. The law is not egalitarian here. What constitutes necessaries for a wealthy child might not be necessaries for a poor child. If a minor lives with parents who supply the necessities of life, the minor is not personally liable for necessaries. If, however, the parents have refused or cannot supply necessaries, and the minor must contract for them, the minor is liable for the reasonable value of any necessaries supplied. For example, if a minor's parents do not provide clothing, and the minor purchases clothing to wear, he or she must pay for them. If, however, a wealthier minor buys clothes on credit, and then sells them for profit, the creditor cannot collect from the minor because the items are not necessaries.

The majority view is that an automobile is not one of life's necessaries. However, the increasing use of the automobile and the fact that in many areas public transportation is not available to get to school or to work have led several courts to permit determination of the question on a case-by-case basis.

The concept of necessaries usually does not apply to items used for business purposes. Minors have been held not liable under contracts of fire and life insurance because insurance contracts are not for necessaries. Mandatory automobile insurance, however, when an automobile is one of a minor's necessaries, could arguably be necessary for that minor.

A minor is liable only for the reasonable value of necessaries actually received. If a minor bought and received a suit of clothes, the minor must pay the reasonable value of the clothing if the minor's parents were unwilling or could not provide the suit. If, however, the contract was executory and the seller agreed to make a suit for the minor, then the executory agreement would not be enforceable against the minor or the minor's estate. A minor may avoid a contract to deliver or to make necessaries. Only when the minor receives the necessaries does an obligation to pay arise.

If a minor borrows money to purchase necessaries, most courts would require the minor to repay the loan, even though the minor elected to squander the money on something else. The purpose is to encourage people to make available to minors the necessities of life or the means to purchase necessities without fear that they will not receive compensation. If a loan to a minor is not for the purchase of necessaries, even though it may be used in that manner, the minor may avoid the loan contract just as any other contract not involving necessaries.

Other Contracts. There are several other situations in which minors may not avoid contractual obligations. For example, if a minor has married, has enlisted in the armed services, has assumed the obligation of a bail bond, or has the duty of child support, overriding public policy considerations require the minor to be bound by those commitments. Similarly, if a court has approved a contract for the performance of services by a child, such as a child actor, that a contract may then be enforced against the minor.

In some jurisdictions, minors actively engaged in business pursuits are liable on contracts involving the conduct of those pursuits. For example, some states impose liability on minors in matters involving transferring stock, handling bank accounts, and obtaining loans for higher education. In the absence of a more important public policy or the existence of special statutes, however, the rule is that a minor may avoid any contract not involving necessaries.

Parents' Liability. A parent is generally not liable for a minor child's contracts. For a court to hold otherwise would permit indirect enforcement of a minor's agreement. For example, if a minor contracts to purchase a boat, and a parent does not become a party to the agreement by signing or otherwise promising to assume the obligation, then the parent is not liable if the minor defaults.

In some situations, however, the law does impose liability on a parent for a minor child's contracts. For example, if the child acted as an agent for the parent in the transaction, then liability is imposed on the parent as a principal under the normal rules of agency, discussed in Chapter 11. If a parent directs a child to sign a contract for the parent's benefit, the child would be the parent's agent. Similarly, if a parent has neglected or refused to pay for necessaries for a child, most jurisdictions enforce a contract against the neglectful parent for necessaries actually supplied. The party dealing with the minor can take legal action to obtain the reasonable value of the necessaries against the minor or against the parent.

Finally, in those cases in which the parent has acted as a cosigner for the minor's contract, the parent is personally liable if the child fails to perform obligations, usually payment, under the contract. This liability is the same as that imposed on any other cosigner who assumes liability for the default of another, regardless of minority or majority status.

Third-Party Rights. An adult dealing with a minor obtains only a voidable title to goods. "Title" means legal ownership. If the minor refuses to honor the contract by claiming rightful ownership of the goods, the adult must surrender the goods to the minor. Special problems arise when the adult has sold the goods to a third party, who purchased the goods in good faith without any knowledge of the minor's prior ownership or interest. At common law, the minor's rights would prevail, even against an innocent third party, and a minor could repossess goods in a third party's possession.

Under the U.C.C., which applies to the sale of goods, a person with a voidable title, such as a party dealing with a minor, has the power to transfer a good title to a person who purchases in good faith for value.[8] Thus, a person who purchases items in good faith that were, in turn, purchased from a minor is immune from a minor's later decision to reclaim title to those goods.

The U.C.C., however, applies only to personal property, and the common law rule still applies to real property. The minor may reclaim real property upon refusing to honor a contract even though the property has been transferred to a third person.

Insane Persons' Contracts

With regard to contractual liability, the law recognizes two classes of insane persons:

1. Those "adjudged insane"
2. Those who claim actual insanity or mental incompetence

Some people have been adjudged insane by a court of law, which means that they have been formally declared insane. An agreement entered into by any one of these two classes of insane persons is completely void; and, thus, the act of a person who has been adjudged insane is without any legal effect. A court's adjudication is conclusive that the person is insane. This adjudication makes any contract that person has entered into void, whether or not anyone challenges it.

The more troublesome problems involve persons who have not been adjudged insane, but who attempt to avoid liability under their contracts on the ground that they were actually insane or otherwise mentally incompetent at the time they entered into the contracts. Contracts of people who claim insanity, but whom courts have not adjudicated insane, are voidable, although they do remain in full force and effect until the parties claiming insanity avoid them. Other parties to these agreements have no right of avoidance.

For a person who has not been adjudged insane to avoid a contract, that person must be so mentally deranged that one of the following is true:

1. The person did not know a contract was being made.
2. The person did not understand the legal consequences of what was being done.

Mental incapacity can result from insanity, idiocy, senility, or any other mental defect. Merely having a mental weakness is not sufficient to avoid the contract unless one of the two tests above is met. That a party suffers from delusions, has insane intervals, or is eccentric does not affect a contract in the absence of one of the two conditions listed above. It is not necessary to show that a person is permanently insane. It is sufficient that the individual was insane at the time the contract was created. Contracts made by mentally ill persons during lucid intervals are binding.

A person confined to or being treated in a mental institution may be competent to contract. If a court either does not adjudge a person as insane or does not find that the person meets one of the two tests above, that person's contract will be enforceable even if he or she has been confined for mental illness. A party asserting incompetency must prove whether the person is or is not insane.

Avoidance.   As in the case of minors' contracts, only the incompetent or insane party has the power of avoidance or ratification. If the insane person has a guardian, then the guardian may avoid the agreement. An insane party who regains competency may then affirm a contract. An insane party who avoids a contract must make full restitution if the other party acted in good faith and was unaware of the insanity. The insane party must prove the fact of his or her insanity, as well as the other party's knowledge of the insanity.

Contracts for Necessaries.   Insane persons' contracts for necessaries result in the same kind of liability for them that minors have. The insane person must pay the reasonable value of necessaries received.

Necessary goods and services for insane persons are the same as those for minors. The individual's station in life is considered, and the need for nursing and medical attention are considered necessities for insane persons. If the insane person is, for example, institutionalized, legal services to obtain release from custody are also necessary, as is money to obtain necessaries.

The public policy protecting insane persons also protects their families and personal estates. The insane person is obligated for necessaries provided to his or her spouse and family and for items needed for preservation of his or her estate, which are not limited to things related to the personal maintenance of the individual, as in the case of minors. Thus, repairs to the insane person's home are necessaries.

Beneficial Contracts.   If an agreement is beneficial to an insane person, and the other party was ignorant of the infirmity, the insane person who has benefited by the other party's performance cannot disaffirm the contract. The sane party to a contract with an insane person can enforce the contract by proving the following:

1.   His or her lack of knowledge of the insanity
2.   The contract benefits the insane person

For example, an insane person contracts to have her house painted. The other party, who does not know about the insanity, paints the house. The painter has a right to compensation for those services, and the insane person cannot disaffirm the contract.

If, however, one knows, or should know, of a person's insanity at the time the parties create the contract, the insane person is not liable if the contract is executory, or still has not been performed. In that case, the insane person may disaffirm without paying back consideration upon offering to return what is left from an executed contract, if anything.

Intoxicated Persons' Contracts

As a general rule, a person's intoxication when entering a contract does not permit avoidance of that contract. The law usually does not protect persons from their own follies. If an individual becomes drunk enough to impair his or her judgment, that person must suffer the legal consequences. Case law has tempered the general rule, however, and exceptions in the law have developed.

Test. If a person was so under the influence of intoxicants (or narcotics) as not to understand the consequences of what was being done or that a contract was being made, then that person may avoid the contract. Thus, the same tests applied to the determination of insanity are applied here. That is, the person (1) must not have known a contract was being made and (2) did not understand the legal consequences of what was being done. Unless the degree of disability required to prove insanity also can be shown by the person alleging intoxication, the contract will be enforced even though the person may have acted under the influence of alcohol or narcotics.

Other Qualifications. If one party to a contract purposely caused the other party to become drunk to obtain an unfair advantage, the innocent party can avoid the contract. Likewise, in most states, persons may be adjudged habitual drunkards, just as they may be adjudged insane. If this adjudication is made, it is a matter of public record that contracts that these people subsequently make are completely void. In any other case, the other party to the transaction must know, or have reason to know, that the person is intoxicated or under the influence of drugs.

For example, Donna, who is extremely intoxicated, signs and mails a written offer to sell a business to John. John, who has no reason to know of the intoxication, accepts the offer. Under these circumstances, Donna cannot avoid the transaction.

Avoidance. A person who was intoxicated or under the influence of drugs when the contract was entered into, and whose mental impairment was sufficient to meet the tests just discussed, may either avoid or ratify the contract upon becoming sober. The intoxicated party is the only one with the right of avoidance. The party who avoids a contract cannot later retract avoidance or ratification and must return any consideration received. If, however, the consideration was wasted, or spent, before the party's sobriety, its return would probably not be required. A drunken person is liable for necessaries, as are minors and insane people.

Corporations' Contracts

Corporations, as artificial creations of the state, are persons in the eyes of the law. They can hold property, sue and be sued, commit crimes and torts, and enter into contracts. The extent of a corporation's competency to enter into contracts depends upon the scope of the power granted by its charter.

At one time, all corporate charters contained some limitation on the powers of corporations. With the rise of modern diversified business, that rule was no longer practical. Consequently, most states permit a business to incorporate without restriction on its activities, enabling it to engage in any lawful business. Therefore, corporations usually are not restricted in the types of contracts they may make. This is not true, however, of specially licensed and controlled businesses such as insurance, banking, and transportation.

Under an older rule, an attempted contract that is not within corporate powers was called *ultra vires,* which means, literally, "beyond its power." Under that doctrine, a corporate contract beyond the scope of the corporation's charter authority is voidable by either the corporation or the other party while it is fully executory (still unperformed).

If either party has performed its part of the bargain, however, the other party must perform. If the contract is fully executed, neither party can avoid the agreement even though an *ultra vires* act was involved. At least half the states have abolished the defense of *ultra vires.*

Capacity and Insurance Contracts

Capacity issues with regard to insurance contracts arise with regard to insurers, insurance agents, and insureds.

Insurer Capacity. At common law, a corporation, an association, or a natural person could be an insurer. In modern times, because of statutory requirements, corporations are the principal conductors of the insurance business. As a legal entity, the life of a corporation extends beyond that of its owners or management. This continuous existence is necessary to protect the long-range security interests involved in insurance.

Insurance companies obtain their legal capacity to do business from the state in which they are incorporated, but they also must be licensed to conduct business in each state in which they operate. Each state's regulatory authorities and statutes establish the financial requirements for incorporation in that state to engage in the insurance business, as well as the requirements to become licensed to write insurance in the states if the insurer is incorporated outside the state.

The states stipulate conditions on the right to conduct the insurance business, the types of contracts that may be entered into, and the language in the contracts. A state may refuse to grant a license or may withdraw it if a company does not meet all of the legal requirements stipulated by the state.

State statutes and insurance department regulatory requirements must be consulted to determine the qualifications necessary to engage in the business of insurance. These laws and regulations affect the nature and scope of insurance contracts. Regulatory authorities usually must approve insurance language before insurance companies can sell policies in the states. If a state requires actual approval of the language, it is a *prior-approval state*. If it requires only review and filing of the language, it is called a *file-and-use state*.

An insurance contract that exceeds or is different from the authority granted the insurer nevertheless may bind the insurer. Regulatory authorities may revoke the insurer's license, but the insured may enforce the contract as written. The insurer may not assert its own wrongdoing as a defense to an action on the contract.

The contracts of insurers not licensed to do business in a state are enforceable against them. For example, if Insurance Company X is licensed to write health insurance in State A and also solicits applications by mail from residents of State B, the contracts entered into may be enforced in either state. These contracts also must conform to the law of the state in which they are issued.

While courts may offer relief, regulatory authorities have some difficulty in states in which the nonadmitted insurer does business. These regulatory agencies attempt to enforce the agreements and communicate with regulatory authorities in the insurer's *state of domicile* (state in which the insurance company was incorporated) to achieve compliance with state law.

Insurance Agent Capacity. State statutes and regulations control individuals' capacity to act as insurance agents. Each state administers tests to prospective insurance agents before issuing licenses to assure a certain degree of competency. A license grants the privilege of writing a certain type of insurance for a designated company. One agent may be licensed to write business for more than one company.

As a result of the licensing requirements for insurance agents, few cases have arisen concerning agents' legal competency. As will be seen in greater detail in Chapters 11 and 12, the principal's legal capacity to contract is more important than the agent's. The agent merely acts on the principal's behalf. Since the agent's act is considered the principal's act, the agent need not have contractual capacity.

Thus, a principal cannot avoid at a later date a contract completed by an agent who is a minor or an incompetent because of mental disability as long as the incompetent can carry out instructions. It is the principal's responsibility to appoint a competent representative to carry out the principal's business.

Capacity of Insureds. While insureds' capacity to enter into insurance contracts seldom has become a legal issue, insureds are subject to the same general rules of law that apply to others. Unless the insured was incompetent by reason of insanity, minority, or intoxication, he or she may not avoid insurance contracts.

Thus, if an insured was insane at the time of making the agreement, and did not know a contract was being made, the insured could avoid the contract. There are few such cases, because the insured can always avoid an insurance policy by ceasing to pay premiums. The insurer then cancels the contract, making an adjustment, in the case of life insurance, for payment of any existing cash values due under the policy. The insured can terminate any insurance agreement by ceasing to pay the premium or by cancellation.

In a number of jurisdictions, people as young as fifteen years of age may obtain life insurance policies on themselves. A minor's right to avoid a life insurance contract and to obtain a refund of all premiums paid during minority is precluded in those states after the minor reaches fifteen years of age. In the few cases that have arisen concerning insureds' capacity, those who were incompetent for any reason could obtain return of the full amount of the paid premiums after avoiding the insurance contract because of incompetency.

SUMMARY

A contract is a legally enforceable promise. Every day people perform contract commitments voluntarily, and they seldom think of many of these commitments as contracts. Occasionally, however, parties fail or refuse to perform, necessitating queries as to whether contractual obligations existed in the first place. This chapter described contract formation, including promises, parties, and privity of contract. The classifications of contracts include the following:

1. Bilateral and unilateral
2. Executed and executory

3. Express and implied
4. Void and voidable

The elements of a contract are as follows:

1. Agreement
2. Competent parties
3. Consideration
4. Legal purpose

This chapter examines the first two elements, the agreement and competent parties. The agreement includes an offer and an acceptance. The elements of an offer are as follows:

1. Intent to contract
2. Definite terms
3. Communication of the offer

Issues concerning offers are general statements of intention, invitations, bids, social invitations, expressions of opinion, offers made in jest, and auctions. The law applies objective tests, including the "reasonable person" test. Definite terms must convey reasonable certainty about the offer, and terms cannot consist of illusory promises.

An acceptance must include the following elements:

1. Offeree's acceptance
2. Unconditional and unequivocal acceptance
3. Communication to offeror by appropriate word or act

Issues concerning acceptances include conditional and equivocal responses, as well as the manner of acceptance, such as complaining and silent acceptances.

After examining the first element of a contract, the agreement, the chapter discusses the second element, that only competent parties, or those with capacity to contract, can contract. Questions arise with regard to minors, insane persons, intoxicated persons, and corporations. Finally, the chapter discusses capacity issues in insurance, which focus on insurers, insurance agents, and insureds.

Chapter 3 will examine the final two elements of contracts, consideration and lawful purpose.

Chapter Notes

1. Restatement (Second) of Contracts § 1 (American Law Institute, 1973). Restatements of the law are a series of books from the American Law Institute (ALI) that generally describe American law in specific areas, such as contracts, torts, and agency. They also tell how the law is changing and explain changes in the law. Because the books are written by ALI, which is not a government entity, the restatements are not themselves the law. They are, however, regarded very highly by lawyers, judges, and legal educators and commentators.

2. The Uniform Commercial Code (U.C.C.), a statute that most states have adopted, sets forth these rules in some detail. The U.C.C. embodies the common law rules relating to auctions.

3. U.C.C. §§ 2-204(3), 2-305.

4. U.C.C. § 2-205.

5. U.C.C. § 2-207(1).

6. U.C.C. § 2-206(1)(a).

7. Restatement (Second) of Contracts § 39 (1973).

8. U.C.C. § 2-403.

CHAPTER 3

Elements of a Contract: Consideration and Lawful Purpose

Chapter 2 discussed the first two necessary elements of a contract, the agreement and the capacity of parties to contract. This chapter discusses the final two elements necessary for a valid contract, consideration and lawful purpose. Even if an apparently valid contract contains all four necessary elements, it still may be unenforceable because one of the parties may not have given genuine assent. Therefore, this chapter also examines fraud, mistake, duress, and undue influence, all of which can negate a party's genuine assent and therefore void a contract.

CONSIDERATION

The third element of an enforceable contract, in addition to an agreement (offer and acceptance) and competent parties, is *consideration*. Most contracts involve agreements in which one party says to another, in effect, "If you will do this for me, I will do that for you." What one person asks another to do in return for the promise is that person's consideration. The consideration necessary to make a promise enforceable may consist of one of the following:

1. A return promise
2. An act performed
3. A forbearance to act

A promisor demands and receives consideration in return for the promise. It is the "bargained-for exchange." To constitute consideration, a performance, forbearance, or return promise is bargained for if the promisor seeks it in exchange for the initial promise. The promisee gives it in exchange for that promise.[1] A promise is binding on a person only upon receipt of consideration in return for the promise.

Consideration is needed only to make a promise legally enforceable. Lack of consideration is not a basis for avoiding promises already performed. That a promise was made does not mean that a contract was made. A promise to make a gift or a promise to do something without receiving consideration is not enforceable. The statement, "I'm going to give you this ring," involves a promise to make a gift and does not bind the promisor. Once a gift has been made of the ring, however, the executed gift or completed performance cannot be rescinded for lack of consideration.

Types of Consideration

Types of consideration include valuable consideration, forbearance, present and past consideration, binding promises, promises to perform existing obligations, and compromise and release of claims.

Valuable Consideration. The consideration needed to support a valid contract is a *valuable consideration.* The law distinguishes between "good" and "valuable" consideration. *Good consideration* is not sufficient to support a contract. Valuable consideration has inherent value. For example, a parent signs a writing stating that, "For and in consideration of the love and affection I have for my daughter, I will convey my property Whiteacre to her on November 1, 2001." This expression of love and affection is "good" consideration, but not valuable consideration that can create an enforceable promise.

Good consideration is a reason for making a promise, and the other party cannot respond to a promisor's request because the promisor did not make a request. If the father actually conveyed the property to the daughter, then the transaction would be executed completely and would not be subject to attack for lack of consideration. The transaction is unenforceable for lack of consideration, however, if it has not been performed.

Gratuitous promises, regardless of the motivation for them, are not binding. While love and affection form the basis for many such promises, the promisor may wish merely to obtain the promisee's friendship or good will. Whatever the motivation for a promise, unless the promisor receives valuable consideration, there is no binding contract.

Forbearance. *Forbearance,* which may constitute consideration, is giving up or promising to give up a right to do what one is legally entitled to do. Forbearance is commonly the consideration in cases of compromise. For example, a person injured in an automobile accident may have a right to sue for damages. A promise to refrain from suit in return for the other party's promise to pay a sum of money constitutes valuable consideration for the promise to pay. If, however, the claim had no basis either in fact or in law, then a promise to forbear to sue does not involve valid consideration. Under such circumstances, a suit is solely to vex and harass; and, therefore, forbearance to sue is ineffective as consideration. One has no right to bring a baseless suit, and a promise not to bring a baseless suit is not surrendering a right.

Forbearance may constitute valuable consideration even though the act requested may be for the good of the party asked to make the promise. The consideration is valid as long as that party has given up some right of action.

In an early case, an uncle promised $5,000 to a sixteen-year-old nephew to refrain from smoking, drinking, or gambling until age twenty-one. The court held that this forbearance was sufficient to enforce payment of the money.[2] Similarly, an agreement by the seller of a business not to compete with the buyer involves forbearance. Mutual promises to forbear are sufficient consideration to support each other.

Present and Past Consideration. To constitute valuable consideration, the act or promise must involve a present or future commitment. Past consideration is not valid consideration. Thus, if a person cuts another's lawn without the property owner's knowledge, the owner's subsequent promise to pay for the work is not enforceable. The owner did not demand cutting the lawn in return for a promise. There was no demand for the performance, and the performance cannot later become the bargained-for exchange. Similarly, if one finds a wallet and returns it to the rightful owner, who then promises to pay a reward, the consideration for the owner's promise (the return of the lost wallet) represents a past consideration and is not sufficient to support the promise to pay a reward. The finder cannot enforce the promise of a reward made after the return.

In many states, courts and legislatures have created exceptions to the rule concerning past consideration. If a person promises anew to pay a debt that has previously been unenforceable because (1) one of the parties is a minor, (2) the promisor is bankrupt, or (3) the time period for payment has run out, most jurisdictions hold the new promise to pay binding. No consideration supports the new promise to pay the obligation. Still, no new consideration is necessary, and the new promise is a waiver of the previous inability to enforce the debt. Some courts state that the new promise couples itself to the preexisting debt and that valuable consideration does support it. Other courts find renewal promises enforceable because there is a preexisting moral obligation sufficient to support the new promise.

To illustrate, Francine, a seventeen-year-old, promises to pay Joy $200 for Joy's car. Because a minor made the promise, it was not enforceable. Upon reaching eighteen, the age of majority, and having paid none of the purchase price, Francine promises to pay $100 for the vehicle. Although Joy could have disaffirmed the contract entirely and owed no duty of performance, the renewal promise to pay $100 is enforceable. However, Joy cannot legally collect the price agreed upon initially.

A promise to pay a debt barred by the statute of limitations or by bankruptcy is also enforceable without any additional consideration. The promisor must express clearly the promise to pay, and in some states renewal promises must even be written. A mere acknowledgment of the debt or partial payment of it, without an actual promise to pay all or part of the preexisting obligation, is not sufficient to create a binding renewal promise to pay.

Binding Promise. To be valid consideration, a promise must create a binding obligation. Thus, the promise of one party to "make certain payments to you for such work as I request you to do" is the illusion of a promise when no binding obligation has arisen. These "illusory promises" do not create obligations. The promisor may not request any work at all, and no obligation arises. A promisor who requests work may be bound to pay for it, but the promisee cannot claim that the promisor is legally obligated to provide any such work. The promisor is free to hire anyone to do the work.

Similarly, a promise "to stay in business as long as it is profitable" is an illusory promise that is not valid consideration. A promise "to buy all the coal we may order" is also illusory because the party making the promise does not promise to buy any coal. No binding obligation arises.

Courts generally have taken a different position if the promise involved *requirements* or *output contracts*. Thus, if the promisor agrees to buy requirements, or all the coal she needs or will require during a given period, from the promisee, a binding obligation usually arises.

Similarly, a promise to sell all of the coal produced, or outputs, to a particular promisee creates a binding obligation. In each case, however, it is necessary to inquire whether any requirements or output are involved. If some level of previous or expectant need, or output, is present, then the obligation to continue meeting those needs, or providing the output, for just one party creates a sufficient consideration to support the agreement. If the promisor actually did not anticipate any need for coal, then the promise would be illusory and does not constitute consideration.

Promise To Perform Existing Obligation. A promise to perform a duty that the promisor is already obligated legally to perform is insufficient consideration. The promisee receives nothing in return for his or her promise because the performance promised is required by another obligation and does not constitute promising to do something that one has no legal duty to do. For example, a police officer's promise to the public to arrest a law violator is not enforceable because the arrest is something to which the public promisee already had a right. However, if a public officer renders service beyond the call of duty, the consideration supports a promise. If someone offers a firefighter a reward to run into a burning building to retrieve property at great risk to the firefighter's life, such service supports a claim for the reward.

A contractor may refuse to complete the construction of a building according to an original agreement without an additional payment. If the other party promises to pay an additional amount if the contractor will complete the project as originally promised, the promise to pay a greater consideration is not enforceable. Promises to abide by one-sided modifications of existing contracts are purely gratuitous, and additional consideration does not support them. If, however, the contractor promises to do some additional work, a promise to pay more is enforceable.

There are two qualifications to the rule that the parties do not have to abide by one-sided modifications of existing contracts. First, if extraordinary circumstances cause entirely unforeseen difficulties in construction, then a promise of additional compensation may be enforceable because of *changed conditions*. For example, if the contractor had no reason to expect the presence of a large body of quicksand under the construction site, or an earthquake changed the conditions expected in performing the agreement, then a promise to pay additional compensation may be valid even though the contractor is agreeing simply to complete the building as agreed. The law implies a condition in the contract that the facts will be as the parties think they are.

The second qualification to the rule regarding one-sided modifications is that, under the provisions of the U.C.C., agreements between parties modifying a contract for the sale of goods need no consideration. The purpose is to facilitate agreements for the sale of goods. For example, Jean agrees to manufacture and sell goods to Frank for $1,000. Subsequently, market conditions make it impossible for Jean to sell the goods without suffering a loss. Frank agrees to pay an additional $500 for the goods. Later Frank refuses to pay more than $1,000. At common law, Frank's promise to pay the $500 was not enforceable because there was no consideration. There was a preexisting duty to deliver the goods. The U.C.C., however, changes the situation and requires no new consideration.[3]

Compromise and Release of Claims. As a general rule, partial payment of money a debtor owes is insufficient consideration to discharge the original obligation. When a debtor owes $100 and promises to pay $50 if the creditor will accept that amount as full payment, the creditor's promise to pay $50 is not binding. Partial payment of what is owed does not support an agreement to take less, and the one-sided modification is not binding. There are situations, however—such as bona fide dispute, payment before debt is due, and payment of part of debt—in which a promise to take less than the original amount of the debt may be binding.

Bona Fide Dispute.   Many claims between parties involve genuine disputes—also called *bona fide,* or good faith, disputes—about the amounts of money owed. In these situations the parties have sincere beliefs that their claims are just. Such debts are *unliquidated,* or not certain. Claims involving damage to property or injury to persons often involve unliquidated amounts. The promise of each party to surrender a claim that the amount is more or less than the originally claimed amount is sufficient consideration for the return promise. A similar finding would result if the parties to a construction contract disagreed in good faith concerning price. In the latter case, a compromise agreement concerning the extent of the debt is binding on both parties.

Payment Before Debt Due.   An obligation may not be due until a certain date. Before that date the debtor pays an amount less than that agreed upon because the creditor led the debtor to assume that the payment would discharge the entire obligation. The promise to accept the lesser amount is binding on the creditor. In this situation, the debtor has changed the performance of the obligation by paying before the due date. The debtor's modification of performance is sufficient consideration to support the creditor's promise to accept a lesser amount in that the debtor pays earlier than he or she otherwise would have to pay. Both parties have agreed to a different performance involving legal detriment to each because the debtor pays earlier and the creditor receives less money. The changed consideration by each makes the promises mutually binding. Similarly, an offer to pay the debt at a different place from that specified in the original agreement is binding on the parties if the creditor agrees. Both parties here also experience changes.

Payment of Part of Debt.   If the debtor makes part payment and also offers additional consideration in some form other than money, the creditor's agreement to accept is binding. For example, where the original debt involves a $100 obligation, and the debtor promises to repay $50 plus a book, the creditor's assent to such agreement is binding, notwithstanding the value of the book.

Accord and satisfaction is the term referring to agreements to take part payment and something else of value, however slight that value may be. In the example, the accord and satisfaction involves an agreement to substitute a different performance for the one in the contract (that is, accord), and the performance of that substitute agreement (that is, satisfaction). These agreements are binding on the parties.

Composition of Creditors. A *composition of creditors* forms when a number of creditors combine and each agrees to take a certain percentage of the original obligation owed. The combining of creditors is a composition of creditors, and they form a *composition agreement*. These agreements are binding on the assenting creditors. Each creditor's assent to take a percentage of the full debt is sufficient consideration for the same promise of the other creditors and makes their assent to receive a lesser amount binding upon each of them.

A composition agreement extinguishes the original debt altogether because the creditors have agreed to forfeit the original amounts and to accept new amounts as payment in full. If, following such an agreement, a debtor promises to pay one of the creditors 100 percent of the obligation owed, the renewal promise would not be binding on the debtor. This result differs from the bankruptcy situation, mentioned previously, in which a promise of a debtor to make good on the debt discharged by bankruptcy is binding on the debtor without need for additional consideration. The reason for the distinction is that composition agreements extinguish debts, but bankruptcy bars only the right to sue. A bankrupt party's renewal promise to pay may revive the right to sue. This promise waives the bankrupt person's right to defend a lawsuit on the basis of bankruptcy.

Adequacy of Consideration

Courts generally do not inquire into the adequacy of consideration. Attempts to weigh the fairness of the numerous bargains in business would result in excessive litigation. That a person was willing to pay $50 for a book worth only $5 is a matter beyond the province of the courts, which do not attempt to unravel or remake agreements by inquiring into the adequacy of the legally valuable consideration passing between the parties.

For example, Mike writes a novel and gives it to Bridget to read. Bridget concludes that it is publishable and offers Mike $5,000 for the manuscript, which Mike accepts. Before paying the $5,000 to Mike, Bridget attempts unsuccessfully to find a publisher and concludes that the manuscript is completely worthless. Mike sues for the $5,000, and Bridget attempts to defend on the basis that she received no consideration because the manuscript was without value. In this case, such a defense is not valid. The mere giving of the manuscript was sufficient consideration. That it proved valueless is immaterial. Bridget must pay the $5,000, and the court will not rule on the adequacy of the consideration.

There are some situations, however, in which a court may review the value of consideration. For example, a court may find an unconscionable agreement in a situation where a very large supplier has charged an excessively high price to a small buyer who had no alternative but to deal with the seller, or where the price of goods sold on credit is exorbitantly higher than the cash price.

Exceptions to Consideration Requirement

Certain exceptions to the rule that a contract requires consideration have developed. Situations involving promissory estoppel, charitable subscriptions, the U.C.C., and other state statutes can present outcomes different from those in other cases.

Promissory Estoppel. Promises to make gifts, *gratuitous promises,* which are promises that do not involve payments of any kind and which are mere gifts, are generally unenforceable. Because no payment of any kind is given in exchange for these promises, no consideration is present. In many cases, however, the application of this rule has led to inequities. The doctrine of *promissory estoppel* is sometimes applicable when there is no consideration. This doctrine permits the enforcement of a promise even in the absence of consideration when the following three elements of promissory estoppel exist:

1. A party makes a promise, and he or she should expect that another party will act or forbear to act in reliance on that promise.
2. The other party justifiably relies on the promise by acting or forbearing to act.
3. Only enforcement of the promise will achieve justice.

For example, Nancy promises to employ Barry, who is unemployed, for no definite term of employment. Barry lives a thousand miles away and incurs considerable expense to move closer to Nancy's company in reliance on her promise. When Barry shows up at Nancy's office to accept the job, Nancy reneges on her promise. Barry can sue Nancy for damages although there is no valuable consideration from Barry to support Nancy's promise to hire him.

In another example, Ben says to his granddaughter, Gail, "None of my other grandchildren has to work in a factory like you do. I'm going to give you my promissory note for $50,000 so that you will not have to do factory work if you do not wish to." Gail later quits her job, acting in reliance on her grandfather's offer. Because Ben made a promise that reasonably induced Gail to quit her job, and because it is likely that the only way to avoid injustice is to enforce the promise, Ben must keep his promise under the doctrine of promissory estoppel. If Ben had made the offer to Gail "if she were to quit her job" or "in consideration of Gail's quitting her job," then Gail's act of quitting would have involved real consideration in the form of a detriment to her. In this example, however, Ben's gratuitous promise, requiring nothing in return, was not a bargain in exchange for Gail's quitting her job. It was an unconditional promise made "in the event" that she left her job. A party's reliance on such a promise resulting in his or her detriment results in the application of promissory estoppel. The party making the promise (Ben) cannot deny (will be estopped from denying) making the promise or Gail's reliance on that promise to her detriment.

Each of the elements of promissory estoppel gives rise to a question of fact that the trier of fact will determine, whether it is a judge or a jury. Generally, evidence of substantial economic loss is necessary before a court will determine that justice can be achieved only through enforcement of the promise. Under the doctrine of promissory estoppel, a court grants whatever remedy it thinks is necessary to avoid injustice.

Charitable Subscriptions. Whenever a person makes a subscription or otherwise pledges money to a charitable organization that depends on voluntary contributions, the obligation involves more than a gratuitous promise to make a gift. The commitment is as fully binding on the party pledging as if consideration had supported it. In this situation, some courts refer to the doctrine of promissory estoppel, finding that the organization relied on the pledge to its detriment by undertaking projects the pledge would support and that injustice would result if the court did not enforce the promise. In practice, many pledge solicitations state that the pledge is not legally binding.

U.C.C. The U.C.C. provides that consideration is not necessary to make a contract enforceable in contracts that involve the sale of goods where one of the following is true:

1. A party has given a written waiver or discharge of a claim involving an alleged breach of a commercial contract.[4]
2. There is an agreement to modify a contract for the sale of goods.[5]
3. A merchant has made a firm written offer for goods, and the writing made the offer irrevocable for a fixed time, not to exceed three months.[6]

The U.C.C. thereby reinforces the commercial need to provide additional certainty of result in contracts involving the sale of goods.

A party may raise the lack of consideration given for commercial paper, such as a check or promissory note, as a defense against someone who possesses such paper. The result is that in some situations commercial paper may be enforceable even without consideration.

State Statutes. Many states have adopted the *Model Written Obligations Act* or similar statutes. In those states, if a person signs a writing indicating an intention to be legally bound by a promise, that person cannot assert the defense of lack of consideration later.

Consideration in Insurance Contracts

The insurance contract, like any other contract, requires valuable consideration. The consideration an insurer gives is its promise to indemnify an insured upon the occurrence of a situation insured against. The value the insured gives is the payment of a premium or the promise to pay a premium. Some differences exist with respect to the insured's obligation to pay the premium for property and liability insurance, as distinguished from payment of the premium in life insurance.

Property and Liability Insurance. In property and liability insurance, prepayment of the premium is not strictly required as a condition to the validity of the contract. Courts readily find an implied promise to pay a premium. Therefore, an insured's failure to pay a premium at the outset of a policy period will not result in an insurer's successful defense based on failure of consideration.

The contract of property and liability insurance usually applies to the entire period of the contract coverage, whether for six months or for one, two, or three years. The whole premium becomes an obligation as soon as the coverage begins. It is possible for parties to agree to payment on a three-year policy made on a year-to-year basis. Whatever the premium payment arrangements, the consideration is generally due and payable at the beginning of that period. The premium owed then becomes the insured's debt and the insured must pay it to the extent that policy coverage for a period was actually granted. Cancellation of the policy during the period of coverage necessitates an appropriate adjustment for a premium refund, or unearned premium, depending on whether the insurer or insured instituted the cancellation.

With most property and liability coverages, coverage begins immediately. With direct writers, represented by their own agency forces, payment of the premium is usually on a cash basis, though direct writers may extend credit.

Under the general agency system, when independent agents write business for a number of companies, insurers often do not require that agents pay the premium to the company for a period of thirty to sixty days. The agent in turn may extend credit for the premium to the insured for lesser periods. An agent who extends credit to an insured must settle with the company within the fixed thirty- or sixty-day period. When coverage has begun, the insured must pay the premium for the policy. The implied obligation to pay the premium arises out of the acceptance of the policy, even in the absence of an express agreement.

Life Insurance. In life insurance the life application or life policy almost always provides that the insurance shall not take effect until payment of the first full premium. Life insurance is essentially a cash transaction. The insured usually assumes no duty to pay any premiums after the first one.

Nonpayment of premiums may result in forfeiture of rights under the policy, but no duty to pay premiums exists. If the insured has paid premiums for a number of years, certain cash values may have accumulated under the policy. The insurer may be obligated to return those values to the insured upon termination of the policy. Refusal to pay a premium usually results in the insurer's right to avoid the life policy.

LAWFUL PURPOSE

The final element of an enforceable contract is that it must have a lawful purpose. A contract is illegal when either the formation or performance of the agreement constitutes a crime or a tort. Ordinarily, an illegal contract is void, and neither party can sue the other under the contract. Courts will not aid parties to illegal agreements.

The result of this rule is that the parties to an illegal contract cannot recover damages for breach of contract, nor can they recover damages recovered for the value of any partial performance they have made. Although this rule may result in a wrongdoer's unjust enrichment, a court will impose this harsh result to deter parties from entering illegal contracts.

Types of Illegal Contracts

Contracts may be illegal either because they are contrary to constitutional or statutory law or because they are against public policy as the courts define it. A contract that is illegal at the outset does not become enforceable by a subsequent change in the law that makes similar contracts legal. Conversely, if a contract is legal at the outset but subsequently becomes illegal as the result of a statute or court decision, the parties need not perform further. In this situation, called *supervening illegality,* the parties may recover the value of performance while the contract was still lawful. A party may not continue to perform, however, because there can be no recovery for acts performed after the declaration of illegality.

Contracts To Commit Crimes or Torts. Any agreement between parties by which one is to commit an act that would constitute a crime or other wrongful act (tort) is illegal and void. Thus, contracts to obtain another's injury or death, to slander or libel someone, to induce a breach of contract, or to accomplish the infringement of a patent are illegal and unenforceable agreements. In these cases, a breach of the agreement by one of the parties, such as failure to pay the agreed fee for the illegal acts, does not give rise to any remedy enforceable in a court of law.

Contracts Harmful to the Public Interest. Courts have found a number of agreements illegal because they are injurious to the public interest. Among them are contracts involving injury to public service, such as offers to buy or sell public offices. Similarly, agreements for illegal procurement of government contracts, agreements to contribute more than legal amounts to political campaigns, and illegal lobbying agreements are contrary to public policy and are therefore void.

Agreements to interfere with or obstruct legal processes are also illegal. Thus, agreements to bribe a witness, to drop a criminal charge, or to suppress lawful evidence are harmful to the administration of justice and against the public interest. Likewise, agreements that stir up unnecessary litigation, such as lawyers finding people to sue a particular party and then splitting the legal fees, are illegal and unenforceable.

Usury Contracts. The law of each state limits the interest for the loan of money. Any contract allowing a lender more than the maximum legal interest is a *usury contract* and is therefore illegal. In most states a lender who has agreed upon an illegal rate cannot collect interest on the principal sum. The lender still may obtain the principal amount loaned. Many states permit the recovery of the legal rate of interest only, construing the agreement to permit recovery up to the maximum legal rate.

Loans fall into three general classifications, each of which the usury statutes treat differently:

- The first classification is loans to corporations and to individuals who borrow large sums of money for business purposes or on the security of very large mortgages. These loans are not subject to usury statutes. Presumably these borrowers are financially sophisticated enough to bargain effectively.

- The second classification is loans by lending institutions, such as banks and insurance companies, but loans also by private persons for lesser amounts on personal credit or on security. These loans are subject to state-imposed maximum interest rates, which vary with time and place.

- The third classification is small consumer loans and retail credit transactions. These loans emanate from a wide variety of institutions, including licensed small loan companies, credit unions, banks, and pawnshops, to name a few. The retailer who extends retail credit also fits in this category. Because of abuses in the third class of loans, legislation to protect the consumer has multiplied in recent years.

Wagering Contracts. Most states have statutes making wagering, or gambling, contracts illegal. Courts cannot, therefore, enforce betting or gambling transactions. In most cases it is not difficult to determine whether an agreement is a wager. Clearly, a bet placed on the outcome of a sporting event constitutes a wager. It is the essence of a wager that neither party has any interest in the event that is the subject of the wager except the interest created by the agreement. The wagering agreement thus creates or increases a risk that the parties otherwise would not face.

It is important to distinguish contracts of insurance from wagering agreements. In the insurance contract, the involved risk shifts or decreases by a person's obtaining insurance to protect against possible loss. The hazard, such as fire, is already there. The insured, who has an interest in a property, tries to protect against the hazard.

In the gambling contract, on the other hand, the gambler creates a risk that did not otherwise exist. For this reason, the law does not permit a person to obtain insurance coverage on property or on another's life when that person has no insurable interest in the property or life. Unless the insured stands to suffer some financial loss as the result of destruction of property or loss of the other's life, no insurable interest exists. The insurance contract in such a case would be essentially a gambling transaction and would not be enforceable.

Other types of contracts present more difficult questions in determining whether the transaction involves gambling. Futures agreements in the commodity markets are an example. Under these contracts, a seller promises to sell goods, usually an agricultural product, that the seller does not presently own. These futures contracts generally involve what are called "hedging transactions," which involve making simultaneous contracts to purchase and sell a particular commodity at a future date. The intention is that a gain on one transaction will offset a loss on another transaction. These agreements protect against the fluctuation in market prices and are not gambling transactions because they protect legitimate business profits.

Unlicensed Practitioners. Numerous state statutes require licenses for persons to engage in particular trades or occupations. These statutes are intended to protect the public against unqualified and incompetent individuals performing specialized callings. Statutes require licenses for lawyers, doctors, dentists, and other professionals.

Many careers involve special state licensing or certification before a person can pursue the occupation legally. Typical state statutes require licensing of barbers, pharmacists, insurance agents and brokers, real estate brokers, surveyors, architects, stockbrokers, and others. If a person engages in any of these occupations without the necessary license, the people receiving the benefit of such services may refuse to pay for the services later, on the ground that the contract was illegal, because an unlicensed practitioner performed it. Thus, an unlicensed surveyor who performs work under contract may not sue for a fee. This is true even if the person was licensed in another state as a surveyor and did the work correctly. Compliance with the law in the state in which the services are performed is necessary.

Legal Advice. Many difficult problems arise in the area of violating licensing requirements, such as the practice of law by unauthorized persons. People who practice law without a license are not entitled to a fee for their services and are subject to criminal prosecution. Because legal practice involves giving advice, problems arise when specialists such as insurance brokers, real estate salespersons, bankers, and accountants give legal advice.

Distinguishing between advice given by lawyers and by the professionals in other fields presents difficult ethical questions. Rules about what constitutes the practice of law differ among the states. One state may permit a real estate broker to draft a deed or lease in a transaction negotiated by that broker. Another state may require that a lawyer draft a deed or lease. Still another state may permit the broker to fill in blanks on a printed form that a lawyer has drafted.

An accountant can file an income tax form, but not a refund claim based on an intricate question of law. People specializing in various business areas must be aware that giving legal advice and preparing legal documents may result not only in lost compensation, but also in criminal sanctions.

Commerce Regulation. In addition to licensing requirements for particular occupations, most states regulate dealings in certain articles of commerce. Such statutes also protect the public against fraud or the sale of improper articles. Licenses are often required for the sale of intoxicating liquors, firearms, poisons, and other potentially harmful goods. People selling goods in violation of these licensing requirements engage in illegal transactions and may not resort to the courts to enforce such agreements.

Revenue Purpose. Some statutes requiring licenses raise revenue rather than protect the public against practice by unauthorized persons. If the licensing requirement protects the public, then agreements by unlicensed persons are illegal and void. If, on the other hand, the purpose of the statute is to raise revenue, the protection of the public interest is not the primary motive; and the contract may be enforceable.

A builder failing to obtain a building permit under an ordinance designed primarily to provide revenue may collect damages for breach of a construction contract. Similarly, a business failing to pay a license tax for sale of a product may collect damages for breach of contract. In these cases the licenses have revenue purposes, rather than protection of the public against unskilled workers.

Sunday Laws. During the nineteenth century, most states enacted legislation prohibiting certain kinds of business on Sunday. Many of these laws, sometimes called "blue laws," have been repealed. However, where they are still in effect, some types of contracts entered into on Sunday or contracts that require performance of work on Sunday are illegal and void. Courts will not enforce these contracts and will not allow recovery for work performed under these agreements. When parties negotiate a contract on Sunday, but actual acceptance does not occur until a secular day, a court will consider the contract to have been made on the day of acceptance and therefore will enforce it.

Nearly all the Sunday laws contain an exception for works of necessity and charity. Thus, acts necessary to preserve life, health, or property still may give rise to an enforceable contract even though performed on Sunday. If a property is in great danger, work done to protect or save it may form the basis of a contract. However, when the work on Sunday is merely a matter of convenience to avoid having to close the business on a weekday, the work is not a necessity, and a court will not permit recovery for the work done on a Sunday. State courts differ as to what constitutes works of necessity and charity.

Restraint of Marriage. Agreements restraining the freedom to marry are contrary to public policy and therefore illegal. Agreements between two persons to obtain or prevent the marriage of a third person are illegal and void, as are marriage brokerage contracts restraining the freedom of choice in entering into marriage. A promise to pay money for a parent's permission for a child to marry is also illegal.

Some limited restraints on marriage that are incidental to some other legitimate purpose may not prevent recovery. For example, the promise of a housekeeper or teacher not to marry while employed may be a legitimate basis for discharge from employment if the person marries during the employment period. So, too, young people who promise not to marry until age twenty-one can enforce such contracts against parties who promised to pay them to delay marriage. Refraining from marriage for a limited period of time is valuable and sufficient consideration to support a contract. Agreements not to marry that are not limited as to time are unenforceable.

Just as agreements restraining the freedom to marry are discouraged on social and public policy grounds, so are agreements that seek to dissolve marriage. A promise to pay a woman or man money to divorce a spouse is illegal.

Liability for Negligence. A contractual provision purporting to relieve, or "excuse," a party of liability for negligence is an *exculpatory clause*. Courts generally do not favor these disclaimers of liability. Courts interpret them narrowly against the party attempting to limit its liability, and they often declare them illegal as contrary to public policy, especially when the other party is at a bargaining disadvantage. An example of such a clause is a term in a residential lease excusing the owner from liability if the building burns down as a result of the owner's negligence. In most situations courts would not enforce such clauses.

When the owner of personal property temporarily gives its control to another, as by entrusting car keys or a coat to an attendant, the transaction is a *bailment*. Bailments commonly take place when attempts to limit liability occur. The receiver, or bailee, of the goods generally has a duty to exercise reasonable care under all the circumstances. Receivers frequently attempt to limit their liability for negligence in such places as parking lots or coat checkrooms by placing on the receipts for the goods a notice that disclaims liability for lost or damaged property. Some courts hold these clauses to be illegal because these limitations, if upheld, would result in all bailees attempting to restrict liability, which is contrary to public policy.

Common carriers, such as trains, airplanes, and buses, attempt to restrict their liability for negligence, as do certain public utilities and other monopolies. These entities may not limit liability for negligence except as permitted by statute, administrative agency ruling, or international agreement. An important consideration here is the lack of equality of bargaining power between a large and powerful entity on the one hand and the relatively powerless consumer on the other.

Restraint of Trade. The rule of both common and statutory law in the United States is that contracts unreasonably restraining trade or stifling competition are illegal and void. Agreements involving potential restraint of trade arise very frequently in contracts for the sale of business and in employment contracts. Some of these agreements are legal. If restrictions are reasonable and do not impose undue hardship on the party restricted, courts will uphold them. The limitations must be necessary to protect the parties and must be reasonable as to time and distance.

Business Noncompetition. A common provision in a contract involving the sale of a business is that the seller not open a new business to compete with the buyer within a certain distance and for a certain period of time. Thus, a person buying an insurance agency would have a legitimate interest in wanting protection against the seller's setting up a new agency nearby and retaining the customers of the agency sold.

Whether a restriction is legal depends on the extent of the limitation. Clearly, if the provision stipulates that the seller may never again compete in the line of business or in a particular city, the limitation is unreasonable and invalid. If the restriction is that the seller may not compete with the buyer of the business for one year and for a distance of two miles from the place of the business sold, the restriction is more reasonable and probably enforceable. The tests are whether the restriction was necessary to protect the buyer's interests and whether the restriction was reasonable as to time and distance.

Employment Noncompetition. An employer may impose on an employee the obligation not to compete in the same business for a reasonable period following termination of employment. Again, if the restriction is necessary to protect the employer and is reasonable as to the time and distance constraints placed on the employee, courts will enforce it.

An agreement by a prospective insurance agent that, upon later termination of the employment contract, the agent will not compete for a period of one year and within a radius of ten miles probably is reasonable and enforceable. Attempts to violate the agreement could result in a court action to restrain the agent from competing and also constitute a breach of the employment agreement, justifying forfeiture of rights to commissions and other benefits under the employment contract.

If an agreement not to compete constitutes an unreasonable restraint of trade, a court will strike out the entire provision and will not attempt to reform the contract to apply only to a reasonable restriction. A few courts find these agreements valid for a reasonable time and distance. Courts generally look more favorably upon agreements not to compete that are connected with the sale of business interests than those that apply to employment contracts. Businesses generally have greater equality of bargaining power in contracts than do individuals in employment situations.

Unconscionable Bargains. At common law, courts of equity would not enforce contracts containing provisions so harsh and unfair that the party resisting performance would be oppressed unduly. The U.C.C. contains a provision relating to sales contracts that incorporate this common law viewpoint. The U.C.C. also provides that a court that finds a contract or clause was unconscionable at the time it was made may refuse to enforce the contract or unconscionable clause or may limit the application of the clause to avoid an unfair result.[7] The U.C.C. intends to prevent oppression and unfair surprise. The court, if it so desires, can revise sales agreements to more reasonable standards.

Illegality in Insurance Contracts

Insurance contracts must involve legal subject matter. Courts refuse to enforce any insurance contract that injures the public welfare. It is against public policy to issue such contracts. Thus, an insurance policy purporting to pay for traffic violations is invalid because it encourages insureds to disregard the law. Contracts that increase crime or violations of the law are invalid. Several states prohibit insurance coverage for punitive damages.

Contraband. Insurance coverage on illegally owned or possessed goods is invalid. Property such as illegal drugs and illegal weapons may not be legally possessed, and insurance on these items is void and unenforceable.

If it appears that the insurance is incidental to an illegal purpose, then the contract is enforceable. For example, a fire insurance policy on a building in which illegal gambling or prostitution is carried on is still enforceable, notwithstanding the illegal activity in the building. The coverage is considered only incidental to the illegal purpose. The primary purpose of the fire policy is to protect the building and not the activity carried on there. The illegal business in the building does not taint the fire insurance contract so as to render it void. However, business interruption insurance on an illegal gambling activity or house of prostitution is void and unenforceable.

Insurable Interest. Public policy requires that a person have an insurable interest in another's property or life to insure that property or life. If an insurable interest does not exist, the policy is illegal and void.

In property insurance, an insurable interest exists if a person has any right or interest in property so that its destruction will cause the insured direct monetary loss. In life insurance, everyone may obtain insurance on his or her own life. An insurable interest in another's life exists if one can expect monetary gain from the other person's continued life. Relationship by blood or marriage is generally sufficient.

The insurable interest in a life must exist at the time the insurance coverage is obtained. In property insurance, the insurable interest must exist at the time the loss occurs. Absent these conditions, the policies are illegal and void because they essentially involve gambling on the lives or property of others and thereby increase the moral hazard of intentional harm or destruction.

No Profit From Wrong. The insurance contract may have been legal when obtained, but the insured's wrongful conduct may render the policy unenforceable against the insurer.

In the case of a fire insurance policy, for example, when the insured either burns or obtains the destruction of insured property, no recovery will occur under the policy. The insured's illegal activity precludes any right to payment of benefits. The insured need not be convicted of arson for the policy to be unenforceable. The insurer, to avoid payment, need only establish by a preponderance of the evidence that the insured committed arson. An insured may have been acquitted of criminal arson, for which a case must be established beyond a reasonable doubt. The acquittal on the criminal charges, however, would not preclude a suit based on intentional burning in a civil action for proceeds under an insurance policy. In a civil case, a mere preponderance of the evidence can prove intentional burning, and proving intentional burning may be sufficient to establish the insurer's lack of responsibility to pay. An innocent insured spouse of the person who burned the property, however, may be able to obtain a fair share of the insurance proceeds in a majority of states.

Similar questions arise regarding a beneficiary's illegal conduct of a life insurance policy. When the beneficiary causes the insured's death, courts in many states limit the conditions under which the beneficiary may recover the benefits of a life policy. Generally, if the killing was in any way willful on the beneficiary's part, there is no recovery. The beneficiary is passed over as if he or she had predeceased the insured. As a result, benefits go to the deceased insured's estate or to a secondary beneficiary.

Under the law of most states, when the killing of the insured by the beneficiary is clearly accidental, the unintentional killing does not result in a forfeiture of life insurance benefits. This is true if the beneficiary kills the insured in self-defense, or if the beneficiary was insane at the time of the killing.

If a beneficiary obtained a life insurance policy with the intent to kill the insured to obtain the proceeds, the insurer may avoid payment of the proceeds. Both the beneficiary's illegal intent and fraudulent conceal-ment are bases for avoidance of the contract. When this happens, the policy is entirely void, and no benefits are payable to anyone.

Qualifications to Rules

A contract that might be illegal may still be totally or partially enforceable under a number of conditions. Each situation involves over-riding considerations of equity or public policy.

Protective Laws. In some cases, a contract is illegal because of a legislative enactment that protects a specific group of persons. Courts interpret these contracts so as to protect the group's rights. For example, when a statute or charter prohibits a corporation from issuing a certain type of stock, and the corporation contracts to sell this stock, the pur-chaser of the stock nevertheless may sue to collect money paid under the illegal transaction. The restriction against the sale protects potential stockholders and will not prevent them from suing because of wrongs.

Similarly, an insurance company that issues an illegal policy can-not use its own wrongdoing to defend itself in an insured's lawsuit to collect benefits under the policy. Restrictions on policy issuance protect the public, and the illegal nature of a policy will not prevent a member of the public from asserting the right to protection under the policy.

In Pari Delicto. The concept of *in pari delicto,* or "in equal fault," concerns whether the parties to a transaction were equally at fault in producing an illegal contract. If one of the parties was induced by fraud or duress to enter an illegal agreement, the courts may still permit that innocent party to sue on the basis of an otherwise illegal agreement. Thus, a weak father who was persuaded by his son to transfer property to that son to defraud creditors may sue the son under the illegal agree-ment to recover the property transferred.

Courts apply the concept of *in pari delicto* only when there is a clear disparity of guilt between the contracting parties. The general rule is that the parties to an illegal agreement cannot sue on the basis of the agreement.

Illegality Incidental. When an agreement is merely incidental to an illegal transaction, courts do not consider the incidental agree-ment so tainted as to preclude its enforcement. If a fire insurance policy covers a house in which an illegal activity is conducted, the illegality does not preclude insurance coverage. The insurance provides protec-tion against damage to the house by fire and does not further the illegal activity. If, on the other hand, the insurance protects against the pos-sibility of destruction of illegal goods, the contract is directly related to an illegal transaction and is void. Insurance protection for contraband whiskey or weapons, for example, is illegal and void, and no recovery will occur under the policy.

Severable Contracts. Many contracts involve a number of promises and stipulations. When contracts contain some provisions that are legal and others that are illegal, courts may enforce the legal parts. Enforcement is at the court's discretion and occurs only in cases in which the legal and illegal parts are readily separable. If the illegal provisions have tainted the entire transaction, the courts will void the agreement entirely and will not give legal relief to either party.

For example, a contract to deliver goods to a sporting goods store, including separate provisions for sale of camping equipment, bows and arrows, and high-powered weapons, does not become illegal and void if the weapons subsequently are declared illegal for sale. The court will enforce the sale of camping equipment and bows and arrows but will not enforce the sale of the weapons.

Repentance. The law discourages the performance of illegal acts. In keeping with this policy, courts in some jurisdictions permit a party to repent for having entered an illegal agreement prior to its completion and to obtain return of whatever consideration the party has paid.

Thus, in the case of a wager on a race, with two parties placing $100 each in the hands of a stakeholder, either of the parties may repudiate the agreement before the race and get the $100 back. A person electing to repent an illegal act before it is consummated may recover any money or goods transferred under the agreement. Once an agreement has been performed completely, courts will not assist a repentant party.

GENUINE ASSENT

A contract may contain all four necessary elements and appear to be valid but still may be unenforceable if either party did not give genuine assent. *Genuine assent* means that the parties actually intended to enter into a contract or that their external actions and words indicate intention to contract. An innocent party whose genuine assent was lacking may avoid the contract. Absence of genuine assent may be found in the following situations:

1. Fraud
2. Mistake
3. Duress
4. Undue influence
5. Innocent misrepresentation

In such cases, courts do not uphold the contracts and, under some circumstances, award money damages to aggrieved parties. In contracts, as in all other fields, the law does not permit one party to take wrongful advantage of another.

Fraud

Fraud involves an intentional misrepresentation resulting in harm to someone. When one party to a contract has committed fraud, the contract is voidable if the innocent party chooses to repudiate the contract. Although the law protects against fraud, it does not protect against carelessness. The law therefore attempts to distinguish between fraud, folly, and mere carelessness.

The infinite variety of ways to deceive makes it difficult to define fraud precisely. Instead, the courts apply well established elements of fraud to the case.

If all the elements of fraud are present, the defrauded party may choose one of two remedies. First, the party may bring suit to negate the contract. If the court does not uphold the contract, the defrauded party has no further duties under the contract and is entitled to repayment of all that the party paid or gave to the other party. The party also must return what he or she received. A court attempts to put the parties back where they were before they entered the contract. *Rescission,* the usual remedy, is the complete unmaking of a contract. ("Rescind" is the verb form of rescission.) Alternatively, the defrauded party may choose to sue for damages. This is a tort action, usually called an *action in deceit.* In an action in deceit, the plaintiff must prove that he or she incurred damages, in addition to the elements of fraud necessary for rescission.

A principal is responsible for an agent's fraud committed within the scope of the agent's authority, as well as for that principal's own fraud. Although a principal does not authorize an agent to make a fraudulent statement, if the agent does so in connection with the principal's business, both the principal and the agent are responsible for it in an action in deceit. The defrauded party may bring an action for rescission of the resulting contract.

Elements. Fraud is a false representation of a material fact, knowingly made, with an intent to influence or deceive, resulting in the receiving party's reasonable reliance to his or her detriment. Courts generally require the presence of the first five of the six elements to rescind a contract on the basis of fraud. The sixth element is necessary for a plaintiff to obtain damages. The following repeats and explains the six elements:

1. *False representation*—of a past or existing fact
2. *Knowingly made*—party must know a fact to be false or must have made the representation in reckless indifference toward the truth or falsity of the statement made
3. *Intent to influence or deceive*—party must have intended to influence or deceive
4. *Material fact*—the misrepresented fact influenced or induced the other party to enter the contract
5. *Reasonable reliance*—it must appear that the innocent party was justified in relying on the statement
6. *Detriment*—in a suit for damages, the plaintiff must show injury or loss

False Representations.   A false representation relating to a past or existing fact is the first element of fraud. False representations regarding the profit a business made last year, or the identity of the artist who created a painting, are statements of fact.

Opinion.   False statements of opinion, however, do not constitute fraud. If one knows that another is stating an opinion, one relies on that opinion to one's peril.

To express a false opinion that one does not really hold, however, lays the basis for a possible fraud action. Courts have held false opinions to be fraudulent in cases in which the utterer knew the truth to be different. For instance, a statement by a seller of real estate that a tenant is "very desirable" when the seller knows that the tenant's rent has been in arrears can be a sufficient basis for rescission.

Statements regarding one's opinion concerning the value of a property are not statements of fact, but are expressions of personal judgment or feelings. However, misstatements by one who is or claims to be an expert with superior experience and knowledge of the subject matter are fraudulent if the other elements of fraud are present. Thus, a layperson's statement concerning the value of a painting could not form the basis of fraud because it is not an expert opinion. A similar statement by an expert, falsely made and reasonably relied upon, could constitute fraud.

Law.   People often make statements about the law. A layperson's statement concerning the law is a statement of opinion. An attorney's legal opinion, however, is an assertion upon which the hearer reasonably can rely. If the statement was false and the other elements, such as intent to deceive, were present, fraud may exist.

Whether a statement is fact or opinion is a matter for the trier of fact to resolve. The representation may be oral or written, may consist of conduct such as merely shaking one's head, or may in some instances consist of silence. A misleading partial truth may be as fraudulent as one that was entirely false.

Silence. Silence in the absence of a duty to speak does not constitute fraud. The law does not impose a duty to speak on parties who deal at arm's length, in the marketplace, and in a purely businesslike manner. However, the law recognizes at least four situations in which there is a duty to speak the truth and in which failure to do so is fraud. In each of these cases it is unfair to permit one of the parties to remain silent.

The first exception exists when the parties stand in a *fiduciary relationship,* which imposes special duties of trust and confidence on the parties. In a fiduciary relationship, the relationship between agent and principal, guardian and ward, director and corporation, or among partners is so close that the parties must disclose all facts relating to the transactions between themselves. The partner who sells property to the partnership and fails to reveal material facts relating to the condition of that property may, because of the close nature of the relationship, be as culpable for fraud as if he or she had stated the facts falsely.

A second exception is for property that contains *latent defects* that a reasonable inspection cannot reveal. For reasons of equity and fairness, a person who sells a house knowing that it is infested with termites must reveal that information to a prospective buyer. In such a case the seller must have known of the defect, and it must appear that the defect was one that the buyer would not uncover by making a reasonable inspection. Mere reason to know, rather than actual knowledge, of the defect is not sufficient in itself to hold the seller liable.

When the parties had previous negotiations during which certain representations were made, but the facts changed before the contract was actually made, there is a duty to disclose the change. The representation was true, but conditions later changed to make that representation false. Under these circumstances, the party who makes the representation and subsequently learns of the changed condition has a duty to inform the other party. Failure to do so constitutes fraud.

A fourth situation in which the law imposes a duty to speak is in contracts that require the *utmost good faith* between the parties. The parties must each be able to rely upon information received from the other. This exception most frequently applies to insurance contracts. The parties to the insurance agreement owe a duty to reveal all material facts relating to the contract. Failure to do so affords a basis for avoiding the agreement on the grounds of fraud.

The saying that people are usually not their brothers' keepers prevails in most contract negotiations. Other than the exceptions discussed above, parties do not owe a duty to one another to reveal all facts known to them regarding a transaction.

Knowingly Made. The party alleged to have perpetrated a fraud must have made the false representation knowingly. An innocent misrepresentation does not amount to fraud. Further, the party charged with fraud must have been competent to commit fraud.

Intent To Deceive. For a court to find fraud, the party making a false representation must either (1) intend to deceive or (2) be recklessly indifferent to the truth or falsity of the representation. The deceiver must also intend that the injured party rely on the statement. Fraud includes any representations calculated to mislead or deceive. Surrounding circumstances in each case may establish intent. That a person made a false statement or made a statement without caring whether the statement was true or false is evidence of an intent to deceive.

If the seller of an automobile has no idea of its mileage, but represents that it is 20,000 miles without even attempting to verify the figure, the statement constitutes fraud if the true mileage significantly exceeded that figure. The wrongdoer has been recklessly indifferent to the truth and has committed fraud only as to persons he or she intended to receive the information. A person who happened to overhear the false representation and relied upon it to his or her detriment may not charge the seller with an intent to deceive that person.

If, however, the wrongdoer makes a false public announcement concerning the subject matter offered for sale, then any member of the public who reasonably relies on that announcement can sue for fraud. Thus, an advertisement that falsely describes the goods for sale may form the basis for avoidance of the contract because of fraud.

Material Fact and Reasonable Reliance. A *material fact* is one that influenced or caused a party to enter a contract. For example, a material fact in an automobile sale would be that a car has only 10,000 miles on it. However, reliance would not be reasonable if the buyer could have looked at the odometer, which had a much higher mileage displayed.

A misrepresentation is not fraud if the party to whom it is made knows the truth to be different or investigates and learns the true facts. The question is whether the false representation induced the party to enter into the contract. If, in a court's judgment, the misrepresented fact induced the formation of the contract, the fact was material.

For example, Sam offers to sell a horse to Barbara and tells Barbara, falsely, that Charles bred the horse. Charles is not a renowned horse breeder, and Charles's horses do not bring premium prices. The misrepresented fact is not material because it would not have induced a reasonable person to enter into the contract.

Suppose, however, that, in the example given, Sam had told Barbara that Charles was a renowned horse breeder, knowing that he was not, knowing that Barbara was not knowledgeable, and intending to deceive her. Should Barbara be required to investigate? Should Sam be able to defend himself in a suit for fraud on the ground that his victim should have investigated Charles's reputation?

The older view was that an investigation should be made if the injured party had a ready means of investigation and failed to do so. Judgments of that nature are so difficult to make, however, that modern courts and legal commentators have adopted the view that actual reliance rather than reasonable reliance is sufficient.[8] Of course, the less reasonable the reliance, the less the misrepresentation is likely to have induced formation of the contract.

The question of reliance often arises when one of the parties fails to read the contract. Of course, if a party is induced to sign a document different from the one that was negotiated, as by some sleight of hand, a clear case of fraud exists. Suppose, however, that one party induces the other not to read a contract and misrepresents its contents. If the parties are in a relationship of trust and confidence, failure to read the contract is probably reasonable. Some courts hold that there is no excuse for failing to read a contract. Other courts hold that fraud is no less fraud even if the plaintiff was careless, because the very purpose of the misrepresentation was to induce carelessness.

Detriment.   As a practical matter, *detriment,* which is damage or injury, occurs in most cases involving fraud. For example, the value of property received is less than the property was supposed to be worth. Injury results when a party is not in as good a position as he or she would have been if the statements had been true. The injured party may request rescission of the contract or may request monetary damages.

If a party requests rescission of the contract, courts have not insisted on a showing of actual monetary damage because rescission is cancellation of the contract regardless of whether the plaintiff proved damages. The presence of the other elements of fraud is generally sufficient to justify cancellation of the contract and restoration of the parties to their original positions.

Compensatory damages compensate an injured plaintiff for actual, quantifiable harm, and *punitive damages* punish a defendant. Beyond recovery for compensatory damages, a plaintiff may also obtain punitive damages. Because fraud is intentional, juries sometimes award damages in excess of the actual loss to punish the defendant and deter future fraudulent actions.

Fraud in Insurance Contracts. A victim may avoid an insurance contract induced by fraud. A person fraudulently induced to make or sign an application for a policy may sue to cancel or rescind that policy. If an insurance agent fraudulently misrepresents the nature of the document the applicant is signing, or the protection that is being purchased, the victim of the fraud may rescind and recover any premium paid.

As far as the insurer's right to cancel an insurance policy for fraud is concerned, any material fraudulent conduct in the procurement of the policy permits the insurer to avoid the contract. For example, when an insured who applies for a health policy misrepresents the material fact that he or she was receiving X-ray treatments for a tumorous condition, this fraud permits avoidance of the policy.

Impersonation of Applicant. The substitution of one person to take a medical examination for another in connection with life, accident, and health policies is one of the more blatant types of fraud in insurance transactions. Because the fraud is usually not discovered until after the insured's death, proof largely depends upon the recollection of the medical examiner, who must recall the deceased's identity through photographs. If a substitution can be shown, courts uniformly hold the contracts void rather than merely voidable. The contract, thus, is treated as though it never existed.

When fraudulent impersonation of an applicant is involved, it is not necessary for the insurer to prove that the misrepresentation was material, such as that the named applicant was uninsurable. The substitution itself justifies an inference of materiality. Neither is it necessary to prove that the named applicant was a participant in the fraud. A finding that the applicant's signature was forged, or that the applicant was induced to sign by a fraudulent misrepresentation as to the nature of the instrument signed so taints the transaction as to render the policy void from the beginning.

Collusion. *Collusion* is an agreement by two or more people to defraud another. A person who knowingly colludes with an agent to defraud the agent's principal cannot hold the principal to the contract, and the knowledge of the agent in this circumstance is not imputed to the principal. Thus, if the applicant for health insurance and the insurance agent cooperate to withhold the adverse information concerning the applicant's medical history from the insurer, the fraudulent collusion provides grounds for the insurer's later avoidance of the policy. If, however, the applicant informs the agent of negative information that the agent fails to record, or assures the applicant that a report is unnecessary, there is no collusion. The insured may recover damages under the policy. Once the applicant steps over the ill-defined line separating ignorant innocence from fraudulent collusion with the agent, the insurer may win the case.

Concealment in Insurance. In insurance, misrepresentation by silence is technically called *concealment.* The insurance contract is a personal contract requiring the utmost good faith between the parties. The insured in each case has superior knowledge concerning the loss exposure involved and owes a duty to the insurer to reveal this information. The insurer must rely upon the applicant's full disclosure regarding that loss exposure to make a reasonably correct estimate of the characteristics of the loss exposures to be undertaken. Thus, the parties to an insurance contract do not deal at arm's length, but on the basis of mutual confidence and good faith.

Another reason for the importance of full disclosure in insurance contracts is the nature of these contracts. For the promise of a relatively large sum of money to be paid upon the happening of some uncertain event, the insured pays a much smaller sum, the premium. It is not good faith for one who knows that a covered event has occurred or will occur to obtain insurance without disclosing all material information. For example, a homeowner who finds his or her home on fire at 2 P.M. and immediately calls an insurance agent to obtain fire coverage effective at noon on that date has concealed a material fact and cannot obtain recovery from the insurer.

The defense of concealment is of great importance in both property and life insurance. The concealment rule for property and life insurance contracts is that intentional concealment of a material fact by an applicant for insurance is a good defense for the insurer if an insured sues. The requirements of the rule are as follows:

1. The insured knew that the fact concealed was material.
2. The insured concealed the fact with intent to defraud.

If the insurer does not ask questions upon suspicion of an insured's concealment, the insured's silence concerning a material fact is not a ground for avoidance of an insurance contract absent intent to defraud. The insured may assume that the insurer is satisfied as to the characteristics of the loss exposure.

Requisites. To constitute the defense of concealment, the fact concealed must have been material to the transaction. The test for materiality in insurance contracts is whether the disclosure of the fact would have influenced the insurer's decision to accept the application. If it did influence that decision, the fact was material. Materiality is primarily a question of fact. Whether the insured thinks a fact is or is not material is not the determining factor, for only a judge or jury can make that decision.

Courts agree that any fact that is the subject of a specific inquiry is material. Thus, standard applications for life insurance ask questions regarding drug use, scuba diving, auto racing, parachute jumping, aviation, speed contests, body-contact sports, and other risky activities. Because the questions are specific, facts relating to these activities are material. Failure to disclose them is strong evidence of concealment that may give the insurer adequate grounds for defending against claims made under the policy.

A question may concern a loss exposure that a policy does not cover. A life insurance application form, for example, may ask questions concerning participation in aviation, but the written policy contains a specific exclusion for death that results from aviation. If the policy does not cover the peril or hazard, may the insurer assert that the fact was material?

Most courts would find that the facts that do not relate to the policy coverages provided are not material. Thus, if an applicant for life insurance either fails to answer or incorrectly answers a question regarding participation in aviation, and the policy specifically excludes death from aviation activities, the concealment is not material under the policy. A court will permit recovery.

If, however, the falsely answered question relates to drug use, the relationship between the question and the event insured against (death) clearly is material. If the applicant dishonestly answered the drug usage question in the negative, the insurer later can avoid the contract even though the applicant died of a nondrug-related accident.

When the application asks no question, but the insured is aware of an unusual hazard, the test of materiality is the same. Would the fact influence the insurer's decision to enter into the contract? In an application for a life or accident policy, the applicant's plan to embark on a dangerous trip probably is material. Even though the application contains no question about expected travel plans, a trier of fact will probably conclude that knowledge of the trip would have influenced the insurer's decision to accept the application. The loss potential clearly is affected. Still, it is necessary that the concealment relate to the intention of the party concealing the fact.

The test to determine whether there is an intent to defraud is whether the fact was clearly and obviously material, and whether the insured knowingly and in bad faith failed to disclose it. If so, an intent to defraud exists.

A court finds intent to defraud only when the facts are clearly and obviously material. Some courts require that the facts be obviously material if life or accident insurance is involved. Obviously material facts would be that an applicant's hobby was skydiving or that an applicant was about to embark on a hazardous venture. If one's hobby is making explosives in a home basement laboratory, this fact is material to many types of coverage and must be disclosed.

When a fact is the subject of a specific inquiry—when the insurer raises the question on the application, for example—the fact is conclusively deemed material. The insured must answer fully and accurately. However, an applicant need not disclose facts of general knowledge, such as that a war is going on, or facts relating to well-known trade usages applicable to the loss exposure. An insurer is charged with knowledge of general facts but not with information peculiarly within the applicant's knowledge.

When the insurer asks no specific question regarding a particular transaction or activity that may affect the loss exposure, the question of intention is, again, for the trier of fact. Would the fact that the applicant is about to undertake a long hunting trip be a clearly and obviously material fact that the applicant must reveal to the insurer? The trier of fact must attempt to determine in each case whether the insured honestly believed a fact was not material and therefore innocently failed to disclose it. The test is subjective because the insured's belief is the crucial consideration. The trier of fact weighs the insured's past experience and knowledge in deciding whether the insured knew the fact was material.

In a case involving concealment in the purchase of credit life insurance, which is protection of a creditor when a debtor dies, the court found that the defendant's wife had died of cancer sixty-eight days after he purchased a car in their joint names, financing $5,000 of the price with a bank in a transaction secured by a credit life policy on the wife. The court recognized the conflicting interests involved. If the court did not permit the defense of concealment, spouses of terminally ill persons might make purchases that would shift the costs to policyholders generally. Permitting the insurer to avoid these claims, however, ignores the fact that credit life policies are written without requiring medical examinations, or inquiries into health, on an aggregate loss exposure basis. The court held that there was a duty to disclose under the circumstances. The purchase of a credit life policy that any reasonable person knows an insurer would not write if the facts were disclosed constitutes concealment of a material fact and provides a basis for avoiding the obligations of the policy.[9]

Prior Losses.   Courts generally have not imposed a duty to reveal prior losses or claims in the absence of a specific question on an application regarding loss history.[10]

In one case, a woman lost her jewels on a West Indies cruise. She had a habit of losing things, particularly those things she had insured. The insurer rejected the claim on the ground that, in applying for the policy, she should have disclosed her history of similar losses as well as her history of financial difficulties. The insured "had a right to assume that the fact concealed was not material unless she knew, even though no inquiry was made, that the fact was material and with that knowledge she willfully concealed it with intent to cheat and defraud" the insurer.

The jury held for the insured. The jury had the discretion to find that no fraudulent intent to conceal information was involved. In the absence of the insurer's inquiry prior to issuing the policy, the insured properly assumed that concealment of prior losses of similar articles was not material. Under the rule in nonmarine insurance, the insured must know the fact was material and must conceal the fact with intent to defraud.[11]

Embarrassing Facts. Many cases have dealt with the question of whether applicants for insurance must reveal intimate and embarrassing facts. In the absence of a specific question, should a person have to reveal a past venereal disease to an insurance agent when making application for a life or health policy? If a highly embarrassing fact is material, fraudulent nondisclosure will void the policy.

Courts have found no fraud and affirmed policies although insureds failed (1) to disclose excessive use of intoxicants in making an application for a life policy, (2) to reveal a previous insanity commitment, (3) to reveal pregnancy in making a life application, or (4) to reveal that the insured was about to lose his job. In each of these cases, the application made no specific reference to the fact in question, and no fraud was involved in failing to volunteer the information.

An applicant's failure to reveal a previous history of syphilis on a life insurance application has been found to be fraudulent. Another case found concealment where the applicant concealed a prior conviction for conspiring with others to submit a false proof of claim under an insurance policy. Fraudulent concealment is generally a question of fact that is determined by a jury.

In one unusual case, a court found that the insured concealed a material fact even though he told the absolute truth. Joseph DeBellis applied for life insurance in the amount of $5,000. DeBellis was his correct name. Five months after the policy was issued, the insured's body was found, stabbed to death, under a railroad bridge. The death certificate named the deceased as Joseph DeLuca. This was the first notice to the insurer that the insured had an alias. The insurance company denied the claim on the ground that the insured had concealed a material fact from the company by not revealing his correct identity. The insurer introduced evidence showing that "Joseph DeLuca" had an extensive criminal record.

The court found in favor of the insurer and stated that the insured should have told the insurer of the alias, whether or not the insurer asked about it specifically. The insured should have told the whole truth even though the insurer had not inquired about aliases. The insurance contract requires good faith, and the insured's concealment of his alias breached the obligation of good faith.[12]

In a similar case, an applicant for life insurance indicated his occupation as "plasterer" and employment as such for fourteen years. In fact, for almost half that period, he had been in a penitentiary serving a sentence for robbery. A policy was issued to the insured, and he later died in a gun battle. The court held that the policy was voidable by the insurer because of the insured's intentional concealment of his past and denied recovery.[13]

Termination of Duty To Disclose. Most courts agree that an applicant for insurance must be reasonably diligent in notifying an insurer of material facts that come to the applicant's knowledge after making the application and up to the time the contract becomes effective. The insured, however, owes no duty to disclose facts learned after entering into the insurance contract even though actual delivery of the insurance policy may not occur until after the insured learned of pertinent facts. The effective date of inception of the policy thus becomes crucial. An insured must reveal any material fact coming to his or her attention prior to the time the policy actually goes into effect. Once a binding contract has been concluded and coverage is in force, however, the duty to disclose material facts ceases.

To illustrate, suppose Bert applies for health insurance, and the policy is not effective until Insurance Company's home office approves it. After submitting the application, but before the home office has approved the correctly completed forms, Bert discovers that he suffers from an ulcer. Under these conditions, Bert would owe a duty to disclose the new condition. Nondisclosure would constitute concealment of a material fact.

A case in Illinois illustrates further the possible effect of non-disclosure of information during the application process. On June 22, at 5:00 P.M., Mimms completed an application to Adams Mutual Insurance Company for automobile liability insurance at the Iberra Insurance Agency, applying for coverage commencing at 12:01 A.M. on June 22. The agency mailed the application to Adams that day, and Van Gundy, vice president and underwriting manager of Adams, reviewed it on June 25. Mimms had stated on the application that he had no prior accidents. Iberra had no authority from Adams to issue a binder for auto liability insurance to Mimms. On June 25, Adams processed and approved the application and on June 26 mailed Iberra the policy, bearing an effective date of June 22 at 12:01 A.M. Mimms was in an accident on June 22 at 10:00 P.M. Later, Adams recovered the policy from Iberra, and it never appeared on the insurer's books. Mimms never paid a premium on the policy.[14]

The company's acceptance had not been conditional on either delivery of the policy or prepayment of the premium. The issue arose as to whether the applicant's uninsured motorist coverage was in force. The court held that the company was not liable under the policy, stating that the applicant had a duty during pendency of the application to notify the insurer of any changed condition, such as an accident, materially affecting the risk. Not having done so, the applicant did not satisfy the good faith requirement, and the insurer had relied on his previous statement that he had experienced no accidents. Hence, the uninsured motorist coverage was not in force.

Silence.   Most courts impose a duty on the insured to reveal material facts to the insurer. The insured's silence or failure to advise the insurer of material facts may constitute concealment. Words or actions constituting concealment are not required. An applicant who knows that the property is subject to some unusual hazard must reveal that information to the insurer. Failure to do so may constitute concealment and permit avoidance of the policy. The law imposes a duty to speak when a fact is clearly material.

Mistake

A *mistake* is a perception that does not agree with the actual facts. Many different kinds of mistake are possible, and the law does not treat each one the same way. Mistakes may be made regarding the facts of the transaction or the law affecting the agreement. Mistakes may involve errors in typing, in arithmetic, or in the value of property in question. While some mistakes do not affect the rights of the parties, others make the agreement voidable or unenforceable.

A common way of classifying mistakes is to determine whether one or both parties were mistaken. If only one party was mistaken, there was a unilateral mistake. If both parties were mistaken, there was a bilateral mistake.

Unilateral Mistake.   A mistake or error on the part of only one party, or a *unilateral mistake,* does not affect a contract. For example, an offeree may accept an offer mistakenly transmitted when the offeree receives it.

An important qualification to this rule occurs when the offeree knew or had reason to know that the offer was made mistakenly. Thus, when a contract bid is so low that it is obvious that a clerical or mathematical mistake has occurred, the offeree may not take advantage of the error by accepting the offer. Courts do not permit one party knowingly to exploit another's mistake. The law does not lend its support, however, if the carelessness or lack of diligence of one of the parties results in a mistake the other party does not know about.

Some courts recognize in construction bids another exception to the rule that a contract may not be avoided because of a unilateral mistake of fact. By way of illustration, a contractor bids on a public works project and makes an error in the bidding process. The contractor may retract the bid if (1) the contractor makes the retraction promptly after discovery, and (2) the governmental agency involved did nothing more in reliance on the bid than accept it.

In these cases, it must appear that the contractor's error was material in terms of costs. Thus, if a contractor overlooks certain substantial items in the bidding process, the contractor may make a timely withdrawal of the bid immediately upon discovery of the mistake. As a matter of policy, it is not in the best public interest to enforce bids mistakenly made against contractors for public works projects.

Ordinarily, however, one party's mistake of fact does not affect the rights of the parties. To illustrate, Lee contracts with Jenny to buy an expensive ring from Jenny on credit. Jenny believes Lee to be a wealthy man who has the same name as Lee's, and her belief is one reason she wishes to purchase the ring. Lee does not know of Jenny's belief and acts in good faith. Jenny's unilateral mistake is immaterial, and the contract is enforceable against her.

Bilateral Mistake. *Bilateral mistakes,* or mutual mistakes, occur when both parties to an agreement make the same mistake of fact. Agreements under such conditions are generally voidable. Because both parties have acted upon factual assumptions that were false, no genuine assent to an agreement exists and no contract is created. The mutual mistake must relate to a material fact about one of the matters that form the basis of the agreement. Mistakes regarding collateral considerations, which the parties did not perceive as crucial to their agreement, do not provide grounds for avoidance.

Value.   In many cases the parties are mistaken as to the value of the subject matter. Courts should not remake bad bargains, and there is a distinction between mistakes merely pertaining to value and mistakes made about the identity of the subject matter. Mutual mistakes as to the value of the subject matter are not a basis for avoiding a contract. Thus, where the parties contract for the sale of a particular stone, with neither of them knowing the stone's true value or making value a condition of their agreement, they may not avoid the contract if the stone has a different value than either or both parties anticipated. However, if the mistake relates to the identity of the subject matter, then the parties may rescind the agreement.

In the illustration about the stone, the parties knew the identity of the subject matter. If later it appears that both parties incorrectly estimated the value of the subject matter, the courts do not remake the bargain. A mutual mistake regarding the true identity of the subject matter would, in such case, permit avoidance of the contract for lack of genuine assent. As in the case of mistakes of value, mistakes of opinion or mistakes in judgment do not render a contract voidable. Only mutual mistakes of material fact afford such a remedy.

Responsibility for Mistake. Parties make many contracts with full knowledge that they do not know all the facts. When an insurance company issues a "lost or not lost" policy on a ship, it takes the chance that the ship may already be lost, even though both parties think the ship is safe. In agreements to settle disputes, both parties give up their rights to sue even though facts later may be discovered that provide a basis for suit. Neither the buyer nor the seller of a used car can know the extent of wear on each and every part of that car. These assumptions and lack of knowledge do not constitute mistakes.

Mistakes in Insurance Contracts. Of the many thousands of insurance policies issued each year, a considerable number contain mistakes. The correction of mistakes over one party's protest can create difficult legal problems. The law does not correct mistakes in judgment or relieve a party of the consequences of an act simply because that party did not foresee or desire those consequences. While courts do not relieve parties from the consequences of their folly or misjudgments, under some circumstances they do correct errors in expression. Court interpretation and reformation are two remedies for mistakenly worded insurance policies.

Court Interpretation. An ambiguity or incorrect description in an insurance policy may require that a court interpret the policy to conform with the parties' true intent. The court's ability to interpret the policy is limited to some extent by the restrictions of the *parol evidence rule,* which requires that the court refuse to hear any parol (oral) evidence to show that the terms of the contract were different from those in the written policy. However, there are several well established exceptions to the parol evidence rule. Thus, if an insurance policy contains a unilateral mistake that indicates the wrong address for an insured property, if a loss occurs, a court will reject the incorrect street number and interpret the policy to cover the building the parties intended. Similarly, if the beneficiary of a life insurance policy is designated "my brother-in-law, Charles Jones" and there are two brothers-in-law with that name, the court will permit the introduction of parol evidence to clarify the ambiguity.

Reformation. A court will grant the remedy of *reformation* only upon proof of mutual mistake or of unilateral mistake of which one side was aware. Reformation means to "reform," or rewrite, a contract to reflect the parties' intentions. A court will not grant reformation for a unilateral mistake, or one party's error, unknown to the other party.

Although courts will not add to the coverage of a policy through interpretation, if clear and convincing evidence of the parties' true intent is produced, a court of equity may reform the policy to conform with the parties' intent. Thus, if both the applicant for insurance and the insurance agent understand clearly that particular coverage is to apply, but that coverage is not available, the court may reform the policy in keeping with the agreement.

Mistake of Law. Mistakes of law, whether unilateral or bilateral, do not affect the binding nature of a contract. This statement is true to the extent that the law is not clear, and court decisions may change the law after the contract has been made.

The doctrine that mistakes of law do not entitle either party to a remedy originated in nineteenth-century England, where several cases held that parties could not regain money they paid because of mistakes of law. However, the distinction between a mistake of law and a mistake of fact is often difficult to make. Consequently, courts have engrafted so many exceptions to the rule that many modern legal authorities no longer recognize the distinction.[15]

For example, both parties to an insurance contract erroneously believe that property insurance obtained in an individual partner's name will protect the partnership's interest in the property. Upon the occurrence of a loss, the court may correct the policy to cover the firm's interest, even though it is a mistake of law.

Duress

A party may seek to avoid or rescind a contract on the ground that the other party used wrongful force, or *duress,* to obtain assent to the agreement. To establish sufficient duress to escape liability under a contract, the plaintiff must show that the threat of violence or other harm actually restrained the victim's free choice. In weighing this decision, a court considers the victim's physical health, mentality, experience, education, and intelligence. The question for a fact-finder is whether this person was deprived of free will in entering the agreement. If so, the court may void the contract.

Circumstances. Threats to do bodily harm to the victim or to the victim's close relatives clearly involve sufficient duress to justify avoidance of a contract. Similarly, a threat to burn down the victim's home or to destroy the victim's other valuable property constitutes duress.

A threat to prosecute a person for a crime also constitutes duress. Thus, for example, David confronts a businessman with the fact that the man's son, who is also his employee, had embezzled funds from the man's business. The businessman threatens to prosecute the son unless the father agrees to assign stock to David in an amount equal to the amount of the missing funds. If the father agrees to meet David's demands, he later may avoid the assignment on the ground of duress.

Generally, the threat of economic loss is not sufficient to constitute duress. Even in the situation involving the man's son, however, a court may find duress if the victim were to suffer irreparable loss. A contract entered into under threat of eviction or threat of action to affect the individual's credit standing adversely may be sufficient to constitute duress. Again, the combined circumstances of each case govern the outcome. The crucial question is whether the wrongdoer's action caused sufficient fear to deprive the victim of free will, or volition, with respect to the transaction.

Insufficient Facts. Some cases involve insufficient facts for a court to find duress. The threat of economic loss or the threat to bring a civil action is not enough to deprive a reasonable person of free will. Thus, the threat to cease business with a person does not constitute sufficient duress to permit avoidance of a contract. Likewise, a threat not to pay for work already done unless additional work is performed free of charge does not justify a finding of duress. A threat to bring a civil action on a promissory note that was due but not paid before the maker died does not constitute duress against an executor, even though the action may delay settlement of the estate. In such cases, the fear of force imposed on the victim is not considered sufficient to permit avoidance of contract obligations.

Undue Influence

Undue influence, like duress, includes the essential element that a person did not exercise free will in making a contract. In the case of undue influence, a confidential relationship must exist between the parties. One party must exercise some control and influence over the other. Thus, the relationships of parent and child, nurse and invalid, attorney and client, doctor and patient, guardian and ward, or agent and principal give one party a position of dominance over the other.

An element of helplessness or dependence must be involved. In contracts between such individuals, the law will assist a person who is a victim of undue influence. The law assumes undue influence whenever the dominated person receives inadequate benefit from a contract made with the person who is dominating.

Proof. The dominating party must prove that a contract entered into between parties to a confidential relationship from which the dominated party obtains inadequate benefits is free of undue influence. Although it is difficult to prove such a negative point, the rule protects the integrity of such relationships as well as the weaker party's interests. If the dominating party does not disprove undue influence, the court will void the contract.

Mere persuasion and argument are not of themselves undue influence. The nagging insistence of a spouse or friend usually is not undue influence. A confidential relationship involving clear elements of dependence must be involved. Undue influence is sometimes a catchall defense for matters not embraced in other elements affecting genuineness of assent, such as fraud or duress.

Mental Infirmity. A mental infirmity may form the basis for a claim of undue influence. Even in absence of a fiduciary relationship, where a person has a mental infirmity that seriously impairs judgment, even though insufficient to constitute lack of legal capacity, a court may find undue influence. The mentally infirm person may have known the nature or subject matter of the contract, but the motive for entering into the contract may have been the product of seriously impaired judgment.

Thus, courts look carefully at contracts entered into by bereaved widows, widowers, and others who suffer from mental infirmity even though temporarily. Undue influence thus may involve a party taking advantage of the fiduciary relationship or mental infirmity. Most cases that involve undue influence concern gifts and wills made by people whom others dominated.

Innocent Misrepresentation

In general the person making a misrepresentation honestly and reasonably believes the statement to be true. The materiality and reasonable reliance requirements of fraud, however, also apply to misrepresentation. If a party innocently misrepresents a material fact, and that fact is material and the other party reasonably relies upon it, the injured person who relied on the misrepresentation later may avoid the transaction. If wrongful intent is involved, the transaction involves fraud rather than misrepresentation. Misrepresentation, however, is easier to prove because intention to deceive need not be shown.

The victim of an innocent misrepresentation can always obtain rescission of the contract. However, a court will not award money damages for an innocent misrepresentation because in many instances, an innocent misrepresentation is difficult to distinguish from a mutual mistake of fact.

For instance, relying on an expert's mistaken identification of a painting, Diana represents to Ed, a potential buyer, that a famous artist painted the work. Ed purchases the painting. There is a mutual mistake, but there is also an innocent misrepresentation by Diana to Ed. However, many cases of innocent misrepresentation cannot be treated alternatively as cases of mutual mistake. The reason for the dominant rule is probably the long-standing rule of case law that a court will grant damages only for fraud.

SUMMARY

The final two elements necessary for a contract are consideration and lawful purpose. Consideration must be valuable and can take the following forms: forbearance, present and past consideration, a binding promise, a promise to perform an existing obligation, and compromise and release of claims. The adequacy of consideration can be an issue, and other issues arise when fraud may have occurred, when there was an exchange of identical units, and when the parties made an unconscionable agreement.

Exceptions to the consideration requirement include situations involving promissory estoppel, charitable subscriptions, certain transactions subject to Uniform Commercial Code provisions, and transactions that state statutes govern. Property and liability and life insurance contracts also require consideration.

To be binding, a contract must have a lawful purpose. Types of contracts that do not have lawful purposes include contracts to commit crimes or torts, contracts otherwise harmful to the public interest, usury and wagering contracts, contracts with unlicensed practitioners, contracts in violation of Sunday laws or in restraint of marriage, contracts affecting liability for negligence, contracts in restraint of trade, and unconscionable bargains.

Qualifications to the rule requiring lawful purpose in contracts include contracts covered by protective laws, contracts where the parties are not *in pari delicto,* contracts in which illegality is only incidental, severable contracts, and contracts involving repentance by one party. Illegality in insurance contracts includes contracts involving contraband, policies where the insured has no insurable interest, and situations in which an insured may gain no profit from his or her wrong.

Even if a contract contains all the elements necessary to be binding, a court still may not enforce it if there was no genuine assent in the making of the contract. Fraud, mistake, duress, undue influence, and innocent misrepresentation all can negate a contract that is otherwise valid.

To constitute fraud, a situation must involve a false representation made with the intent to deceive, concerning a material fact, and resulting in the other party's detrimental reliance. Fraud in insurance contracts usually involves impersonation of an applicant, collusion, or concealment. A mistake can be either unilateral or bilateral. Mistakes in insurance contracts often require court interpretation, and a common remedy is reformation of the contract.

Duress involves wrongful force to obtain assent to an agreement, and undue influence involves duress by a party in a position of power or dominance over another party. An innocent misrepresentation of a material fact requires detrimental reliance by the other party. However, the person giving wrong information, unlike fraud, innocently believes that information to be true. A victim of innocent misrepresentation can obtain rescission of a contract.

Chapter Notes

1. Restatement (Second) Contracts, § 75.
2. Hamer v. Sidway, 124 N.Y. 538 (1891).
3. U.C.C. § 2-209-1. Example drawn from *Uniform Commercial Code in a Nutshell,* Stone, West Publishing Co., 1989, pp. 26-27.
4. U.C.C. § 1-107.
5. U.C.C. § 2-209(1).
6. U.C.C. § 2-205.
7. U.C.C. § 2-302.
8. Restatement (Second) Contracts, § 471, Comment (i).
9. National Life Ins. Co. v. Harriott, 268 So. 2d 397 (Fla. App. 1972).
10. Hartford Protection Ins. Co. v. Harmer, 2 Ohio St. 452 (1853).
11. Blair v. National Security Ins. Co., 126 F.2d 955 (3rd Cir. 1942).
12. DeBellis v. United Benefit Life Ins. Co., 93 A.2d 429 (Pa. 1953).
13. DePee v. National Life & Accident Ins. Co. 62 P.2d 923 (Kan. 1936).
14. Carroll v. Preferred Risk, 215 N.E.2d.801 (Ill. 1966).
15. Restatement (Second) Contracts § 502, Illustration 4.

CHAPTER 4

Contract Formality, Interpretation, and Discharge

Chapter 3 concluded the discussion of the elements of a contract and discussed mutual assent of parties to a contract. This chapter examines the formality in wording or form, if any, necessary for certain contracts and explains court rules for contract interpretation, as well as discharge and breach of contracts.

The Uniform Commercial Code (U.C.C.) applies to sales of goods, and most states have adopted it. This chapter discusses applications of the U.C.C. to contracts, when appropriate, and compares U.C.C. provisions with the common law when the U.C.C. restates, enhances, or differs from the common law.

Statutes of frauds require writing in certain situations, but oral contracts are usually valid in all other situations. Courts usually look only at a contract writing to interpret meaning, unless parol (oral) evidence is necessary to clarify a writing. Courts apply several rules in interpreting contracts and can imply terms or resolve contradictory or otherwise ambiguous terms.

Third-party rights are those belonging to parties other than the parties to a contract and include those belonging to parties who have contractual rights by means of assignment or who are third-party beneficiaries. Third-party beneficiaries include creditor, donee, and incidental beneficiaries. This chapter, in discussing third-party beneficiaries, examines the differences between these categories and their relative rights under contracts.

Parties complete their contractual obligations by performance or agreement, but events sometimes can make contract performance impossible. Conditions in contracts affect fulfillment of contractual obligations, or *discharge,* and they can be either precedent, concurrent, or subsequent conditions, or a combination of the three. Breach, or failure to adhere to contracts, includes breach by repudiation, and anticipatory breach. A breach can be either important or minor. The remedies for breach of contract include various kinds of damages and specific performance, injunction, or reformation.

Following this final chapter of basic contract law analysis, Chapter 5 focuses on contract law applied to insurance policies.

STATUTE OF FRAUDS

Most contracts are oral. Although many people believe that a valid contract must be in writing, most oral agreements are readily provable and enforceable in courts of law. The law, however, requires that contracts be in writing in some situations to be enforceable. Statutes called *statutes of frauds* now create the requirements for many written contracts, but at early common law contracts did not have to be in writing. All contracts were valid and enforceable so long as the parties could establish their terms in a court of law.

It became increasingly apparent in the seventeenth century that some modification of the common law was necessary to establish the existence of certain agreements. The rules of evidence in English courts prevented a party from testifying in his or her own behalf, and many persons were defrauded of their property as the result of perjured testimony concerning the existence of oral contracts. In other words, witnesses could testify falsely that a person had agreed orally to sell a property, and the alleged seller then had to prove that there was no agreement. Producing other witnesses to prove that an oral agreement had not been made was very difficult.

To deal with this problem of fraud and perjury in connection with certain types of contracts, in 1677 Parliament passed the most famous act in English commercial law, the "Act for the Prevention of Frauds and Perjuries." This act, commonly known as the "Statute of Frauds," provided that contracts susceptible to perjury had to be in writing to be enforceable in a court of law.

All states of the United States subsequently have enacted statutes of frauds using essentially the same format as the early English statute. The purpose of each of these statutes is to provide certainty with respect to an obligation undertaken by requiring written proof of intentions and to reduce the possibility of fraud.

Contracts Requiring Writing

While state statutes sometimes include additional provisions, most statutes, as well as the original English Statute of Frauds, set forth six situations in which a contract must be written to be enforceable:

1. Contracts involving the sale of land or any interest in land
2. Agreements that cannot be performed within one year
3. Promises to answer for the debt of another
4. Promises in consideration of marriage
5. Promises by executors of decedents' estates to pay debts of estates from executors' own funds
6. Contracts involving sale of personal property for a price of $500 or more

Sale of Land. An important statute of frauds provision relates to the sale of real estate or legal interests in real estate, which is land and such things as buildings attached to the land. Legal interests can include many things, from actual ownership to a tenant's interest. Oral contracts for the sale of these interests are unenforceable.

The requirement extends to all interests in land, including mortgages, easements, and leases. A transfer of an interest in land for a transferee's life creates a life estate, and the transfer must be in writing. For example, John's Aunt Sarah gives him a life estate in her farm. This means he can use and enjoy the farm during his life, as if he owns it. However, he cannot sell the farm, and his interest terminates completely upon his death.

While it is not difficult in most cases to determine whether a transfer of an interest in land is involved, problems of interpretation sometimes arise in sales of minerals, timber, and growing crops. Do contracts involving the sale of these items involve the sale of real estate or of personal property? Generally, if title to the property passes along with the real estate itself, there is little dispute. The property is part of the realty. When a seller harvests a growing crop and sells it to a buyer, the contract involves personal property and need not be in writing unless the value reaches or exceeds $500. The U.C.C. provides that a contract for the sale of such items as timber and minerals is a contract for the sale of goods if the seller is to sever them from the property.[1] If the buyer severs them, the contract involves land and is subject to the land provisions of the statute of frauds.

Part Performance of Oral Real Estate Contracts. When the purchaser of real estate has taken possession of the property and made substantial improvements to it in reliance upon an oral agreement to sell, most courts consider it unfair to permit the seller to avoid the agreement. Under these conditions, the case is "outside the statute of frauds," and the contract may be enforceable, notwithstanding the absence of a writing. The trier of fact must decide what constitutes substantial performance. A buyer's simply taking possession of real property without making substantial improvements is not sufficient performance to avoid application of the statute of frauds. Neither does payment of the purchase price alone satisfy the statute if the contract is not in writing.

Executed Agreements. The statute of frauds does not apply to executed agreements (those already carried out). A party who has purchased or sold land under an oral contract cannot obtain a refund of money or a return of the deed to land. The statute of frauds does not allow rescission but only serves as a defense to a suit for breach of an executory, or incomplete, contract.

The usual statute of frauds provision states that "no action shall be brought unless the agreement, or some memorandum or note thereof, shall be in writing, and signed by the party to be charged therewith...." Lack of compliance with the statute may be a procedural defense between the parties but, when neither party raises the statute as a defense in a lawsuit, the agreement may be carried through to completion. Oral contracts not complying with the statute of frauds are not void, but are merely voidable. Third parties who are not participants in an agreement may not raise the defense of lack of compliance with the statute of frauds.

Performance Within a Year. Disputes over the terms of long-term oral contracts are frequent. For this reason, statutes of frauds frequently include provisions that make unenforceable those contracts that the parties cannot perform within one year from the date of their making.

Strict Construction. Courts have not favored the one-year requirement of the statute of frauds. They generally hold the provision inapplicable if it was possible to perform the agreement within one year. For example, a promise to perform an act "upon John's death" does not have to be in writing, even though John may not die for many years. Because John may die within a year, and it is therefore possible that performance will occur within one year, the one-year provision is not applicable. Similarly, a fire insurance contract covering a three-year period need not be in writing to be enforceable because the contract could be performed upon the occurrence of fire within a one-year period. The possibility of performance controls the applicability of the one-year provision.

Personal Services.   If a contract for personal services calls for a period of services longer than one year, the agreement must be in writing to be enforceable. An oral contract under which Annie agreed to work for Bob for a period of two years would not be enforceable because it violates this provision of the statute. Similarly, an oral contract involving the sale of a business and an agreement by the seller not to compete for three years would not be enforced because the period of the agreement exceeds one year.

Complete Performance on One Side.   Another situation in which most courts have restricted the application of the one-year provision involves unilateral contracts in which one party has fully performed. For example, if Jim sells and delivers a car to Karen for a price of $400, and Karen orally promises to pay for the car eighteen months after delivery of the car, the agreement is enforceable. Here, Jim has completely performed his side of the agreement, and his performance made Karen's promise unilateral. Hence, Jim can recover the $400 from Karen based on the oral promise. The one-year provision of the statute of frauds is applicable only when mutual promises to perform, or bilateral contracts, are involved.

Cancellation Provision.   Courts disagree about the question of enforceability of an oral contract that extends for a period of more than a year but that also contains provisions that permit cancellation by one or both parties within a year. Some courts hold that such an oral contract is not enforceable because it may not continue beyond a year. The majority hold that such an oral contract is enforceable because there is a possibility of discharge within one year.

Another's Debt.   If Annie promises Carol to pay Bob's debt to Carol if Bob does not do so, Annie's promise must be in writing to be enforceable. Annie's obligation is secondary to Bob's. Annie is promising to pay Carol only if Bob defaults upon the obligation to Carol. Annie makes her promise to the creditor, Carol, and not to the debtor, Bob. The promise must involve the discharge of an obligation owed by someone other than the promisor, Annie. If the debt is either directly or indirectly that of the promisor, Annie, then the statute is not applicable and no writing is necessary.

When the promisor's main purpose in making the promise is not to answer for the debt or default of another but to secure some personal business purpose, then the case does not fall under the statute of frauds and no writing is necessary. In each case, two obligations must exist for the statute to be applicable. A primary obligation must have been assumed whereby a new promisor has agreed to pay the debt in the event that the primary obligation is in default. The primary agreement need not be in writing, but the secondary agreement must be written if it is to be enforceable. In a case in which Annie promises to pay Carol for such clothing as Bob may obtain from Carol, the promise need not be in writing. Annie is promising to pay for the clothing and is not promising to answer for Bob's debt or default, because in this situation there is none. Only one obligation exists in this case, Annie's obligation to pay for clothes that Bob obtains from Carol. Annie has assumed primary liability and cannot assert the lack of a writing as a defense.

Similarly, when a prime contractor orally promises a subcontractor's supplier that the prime contractor will pay the supplier if the subcontractor does not pay, the oral promise is enforceable. In this case, the promise to pay the subcontractor's debt is primarily for the benefit of the prime contractor, who wishes to keep the work progressing. Because the prime contractor's objective is to accomplish his or her own business purpose, the case is not within the statute of frauds and no writing is necessary.

Consideration of Marriage. Another area subject to fraud and abuse at common law involved promises made in consideration of marriage. The statute of frauds requires that promises to pay money or property if someone marries or promises to marry another must be in writing in order to be enforceable.

While the statute of frauds is not applicable to mutual promises to marry, it does apply to the situation in which one party promises to give a certain sum of money to another if the other will marry either the promisor or a third party. For example, if Will orally promises $5,000 to Bea if Bea will marry Carl, and Bea accepts the offer by marrying Carl, there is no recovery unless the contract is in writing. Marriage is not sufficient substantial performance to take the case outside the requirements of the statute of frauds under this provision.

In another example, two provisions of the statute of frauds apply. If Carl promises to marry Bea on the condition that Bea transfer a house to Carl, and the marriage takes place in reliance on Bea's promise to transfer the house, the oral promise is not enforceable. The provision of the statute of frauds relating to transfer of real property, as well as the provision relating to promises in consideration of marriage, would each prevent enforcement of the oral agreement.

Estate Debts. An *executor* manages an estate left in a will. An *administrator* manages an estate left without a will, which occurs by inheritance under the rules governing inheritance. Most contracts made by an executor or administrator in settling an estate do not require writings. When, however, the executor promises to pay a debt of the estate from the executor's personal funds, the promise must be in writing to be enforceable. The rule applies only to promises to pay debts against the decedent's estate that arose during the decedent's life. Generally, an executor or administrator would have no legal obligation to pay the decedent's debts out of personal funds. Therefore, a writing is the only way the executor or administrator can make such a binding commitment.

For example, if a decedent had owed Peter $2,000, and the executor of decedent's estate orally promises to pay Peter the money from personal funds, no one can collect later from the executor on the basis of the oral promise. Such promises must be in writing to be collectible.

In another illustration, David dies and Eve is executor of David's estate. Eve then makes an oral promise personally to pay Paul the general legacy of $1,000 provided under the will if David's estate runs out of money. This legacy is usually payable only if funds remain in the estate after all obligations are met. Assume that, after David's estate expenses are met, no money remains to pay the legacy to Paul. Paul then sues Eve under the oral promise to pay. A legacy is not a debt that David owed while he lived, and this provision of the statute of frauds is applicable only to debts incurred during the decedent's lifetime. Thus, Eve's promise may be oral, and its enforceability depends on ordinary rules of contract law. In this case consideration is lacking.

Sale of Personal Property. The original English Statute of Frauds contained a provision requiring a written document as evidence of a contract for the sale of goods. Today the U.C.C. provides that a contract for the sale of goods for the price of $500 or more is not enforceable unless it is in writing.[2] The written document must be signed by the party against whom enforcement is sought or by that party's authorized agent.

The limitation of enforceable oral contracts to those under $500 applies only to the sale of goods. Whether the $500 limit has been reached depends upon the total price of all the goods sold under the contract. Thus, if several items, each with a value under $500 but totaling over $500, are the subject of one contract, then the contract must be in writing to be enforceable. If the parties intended several contracts, no writing is necessary as long as the price or value of the goods did not exceed $500 in any one of the contracts.

Writing Requirement. Today in most states the U.C.C., which supersedes the common law, provides that the contract writing required need not set forth all the material terms of the contract to be binding. It can omit some terms and incorrectly state others. The only term required is that relating to the quantity of goods to be sold, and even that term need not be stated accurately. The contract is not enforceable, however, beyond the quantity written in the contract. The plaintiff or party bringing the action need not have signed the contract. Only the person against whom the contract is enforced need sign.

Merchants. The U.C.C. treats merchants who deal in goods of a particular kind specially. In the interests of furthering trade and of providing certainty of obligation between merchants, the U.C.C. provides that one merchant can satisfy the requirement of a writing by sending a written confirmation of a transaction to another merchant within a reasonable time following the oral agreement. Unless the merchant receiving the communication responds within ten days with a written notice of objection, the confirmation satisfies the requirements for a writing. To be valid, the confirmation also must be sufficient to bind the merchant sender.[3]

Part Performance. Other situations in which the U.C.C. provides that oral contracts for the sale of goods are enforceable involve (1) the buyer's acceptance and receipt of part of the goods or (2) the buyer's part or full payment of the price of the goods. Each of these conditions reflects an admission by the parties that a contract does exist. There is no need, therefore, to produce something in writing to establish the existence of the agreement manifested by the parties' conduct. Part performance, either by acceptance of goods or payment of a portion of the price, is effective to bind the parties only to the extent to which the buyer actually accepted or paid for the goods.[4]

Specially Manufactured Goods. Still another situation in which an oral contract for the sale of goods may be enforceable involves goods manufactured specifically for the buyer. Under the U.C.C. (1) if the goods are not suitable for resale to others in the ordinary course of business, and (2) the seller either has made a substantial beginning in their manufacture or has made commitments for their procurement, the contract is enforceable even though there was no written agreement.[5] Thus, where the manufacturing process has begun in accordance with the buyer's specifications and the goods are not of the type that can be resold readily in the seller's business, a writing is not necessary. It is necessary, of course, for the seller to establish the terms of the agreement as part of the proof of the claim.

There are two types of personal property, which is all property other than real property. The first type, goods, has been discussed. Goods are tangible, and their existence does not depend upon law. The second type of personal property is an intangible claim or right that the law creates, such as a claim arising out of a contract or out of ownership of a bond, or a right to intangible property such as a patent or copyright. Goods can be possessed physically and in law are called *choses in possession*. *Choses* is the French word for "things." Because legal claims or rights cannot be possessed physically, but can be enforced only by a legal action, they are called *choses in action.* A promissory note, for instance, is not the debt, but merely evidence of the debt and is, therefore, a *chose* in action. The destruction of the note does not destroy the debt, but the existence of the debt must be proved by other legally acceptable means.

The U.C.C. requires a writing for the enforceability of all sales of investment securities, such as stocks and bonds.[6] A writing also is required in credit sales or secured loans that provide special protection for the seller or lender.[7] Oral contracts in both cases are not enforceable regardless of amount. Thus, an agreement to sell a share of stock for $10 must be in a writing to be enforceable under the U.C.C.

A special section of the U.C.C. covers all other types of *choses* in action. Sales of contract or royalty rights, notes, insurance policies, and similar intangibles are not enforceable "beyond five thousand dollars ...unless there is some writing that indicates that a contract for sale has been made between the parties...."[8] Although oral assignments of these contracts are enforceable if the amount is below $5,000, the difficulties of proof are such that a written agreement, signed by the party against whom enforcement is sought, is very desirable.

Form Required

The writing required as evidence of a contract under the statute of frauds may be a simple note or memorandum. No formal written contract is required. The agreement may be in any form and may consist of several communications, so long as it provides evidence of the existence of a contract.

A written memorandum made sometime after the original negotiations may be sufficient to satisfy the requirement. This is true even if what is in writing appears to avoid the original agreement. For example, if Millie has agreed orally to sell Blackacre to Tina but later writes a letter to Tina stating, "I don't want to go through with our contract to sell Blackacre to you for $5,000," signed "Millie," the letter makes the original oral contract enforceable against Millie. Communication reflects the essential elements of the agreement, including the parties, subject matter, and price. This writing would be sufficient to satisfy the requirements of the statute of frauds.

The statute of frauds requires that the writing be signed by the party against whom the agreement is to be enforced. The signing can consist of a signature, initials, typewritten name, telegraph signature, or any mark that appropriately identifies the party acknowledging the memorandum or communication as his or her writing. Similarly, the signature, in any of the forms listed above, of an agent who is authorized to execute such contracts on a principal's behalf will satisfy the statute's requirement of a signed writing.

Insurance Contracts

Oral insurance contracts are valid and enforceable. The customary statute of frauds provisions are not applicable to insurance agreements. While it is desirable that insurance contracts be in writing, the hardship of enforcing this requirement would fall upon insureds, and courts therefore do not require written agreements.

While a few states have specific legislative requirements that contracts of fire or life insurance must be in writing, most jurisdictions hold oral contracts of insurance valid and enforceable. In fire and casualty insurance, oral contracts are common. For example, Joe calls his insurance agent and asks for homeowners insurance for his new home, and the agent says, "Fine. You're covered." Joe has coverage immediately, even without a written policy. In life and health insurance, oral contracts are not common, but temporary written receipts provide evidence of interim coverage. For example, an agent cannot initiate life insurance coverage orally. In virtually all insurance contracts, the contract is reduced eventually to writing as a policy. Generally, the policy stands by itself as the best evidence of the agreement between the parties.

Once created, insurance policies are *choses* in action. To the extent the law permits, therefore, any assignment to another person of an insurance policy or of rights under the policy for an amount over $5,000 must be in writing and signed by the party against whom enforcement is sought.

Of the six basic statute of frauds provisions, only two may apply to insurance contracts. Courts have dealt with the questions of whether the requirements for a writing in contracts that cannot be performed within one year and of promises to answer for the debt of another should also be applied to insurance agreements.

Performance Within a Year. The statute of frauds provision requiring a writing for contracts that cannot be performed within a year is never applicable to contracts of insurance. As previously noted, an oral contract of fire insurance for a three-year term would be enforceable because the agreement might be performed at any time a loss occurs. This provision of the statute of frauds is interpreted strictly, and the possibility of performance within one year takes such policies outside the statute of frauds.

When an insurance broker enters into an agreement with a property owner to procure yearly renewals of insurance upon property for a definite future period beyond one year, a contract to procure insurance exists. Such an agreement would not be enforceable unless it was in writing. Because the agreement cannot be performed within a year and because it involves an agreement to procure insurance rather than an agreement to insure, the usual statute of frauds requirement for a writing is applicable. Some courts hold in this situation that, if the insured has reserved the right to terminate the agreement with the broker, then an oral agreement also would be enforceable. The insured's option to terminate would, in the view of some courts, take the agreement outside the one-year provision.

Another's Debt.   The statute of frauds provision requiring a written memorandum of contracts of guaranty, involving agreements to answer for the debt, default, or miscarriage of another, has no application to insurance contracts. The agreement of guaranty is a three-party relationship in which one party guarantees payment of another's debt to a third party. For example, Joe promises Lois to pay for Dan's debt if Dan does not pay his own debt. The reason a writing is required is to protect Joe from being defrauded by someone falsely asserting Joe's obligation to pay and from being made to pay an obligation he did not assume.

When surety and guaranty companies replaced private sureties, the legal assumption was that the statute of frauds might apply to such contracts. Today, however, courts do not see these agreements as contracts to perform an original debtor's obligation, but contracts to indemnify the creditor against loss or damage as the result of the debtor's default or nonperformance. Thus, oral guaranty contracts are not subject to the requirements of the statute of frauds.

PAROL EVIDENCE RULE

The *parol evidence rule* limits the terms of a contract to those expressed in writing. The parol evidence rule assumes that all prior negotiations, conversations, and agreements were merged into the final, written contract and that the final contract is the complete statement of the agreement. Once the parties have reduced any agreement to writing, no oral evidence may contradict its terms.

The parol evidence rule therefore prevents the introduction of any oral or written evidence of an agreement to contradict or vary the terms of the final written contract. Words that parties may have spoken before or at the time of contracting, and letters that parties may have written or memoranda they may have prepared before the drafting of the final contract, may not alter the written words of the contract. The written contract is the only admissible evidence of the agreement.

For example, Roy sells a car to Steve and orally warrants during their dealings that the car will develop no mechanical defects within six months of the date of sale. The parties then sign a written agreement of sale, but the writing contains no warranty. Steve may not introduce evidence later concerning the oral warranty. A court would assume that the parties have merged all negotiations in the written contract, and it would exclude evidence of the oral warranty under the parol evidence rule.

In another example, Roy sells a power boat to Steve. The bill of sale indicates the make, model, and year of the boat and the make and model of its compass. Steve later claims that Roy had promised to include other equipment, such as a marine radio-telephone, and wants to support his claim in court with a letter Roy wrote and signed prior to the date of the final bill of sale, promising to include the claimed items. If the court finds the bill of sale to be the final contract, it will not, under the parol evidence rule, admit the letter into evidence because its terms were not part of the final contract.

A contract may consist of a series of letters or other documents. In such a case, a group of documents may, together, constitute the final contract. The possibility that several documents may constitute a contract instead of just one can give rise to uncertainty concerning the contract's terms. Therefore, parties to a contract should include the entire agreement in the final contract and not rely on other documents or conversations.

The parol evidence rule applies only to prior or contemporaneous statements and is not applicable to oral or written agreements made subsequent to the written contract. This subsequent evidence is admissible in a court to show that, after entering into the written agreement, the parties agreed to modify, or even cancel, their written contract.

Scope of Rule

The parol evidence rule applies to all written documents. In addition to ordinary contracts, it applies to such writings as deeds, wills, leases, insurance policies, releases, and similar legal instruments. The purposes of the rule, which applies equally to all written agreements, are as follows:

1. To carry out the presumed intention of the parties
2. To achieve certainty and finality as to the rights and duties of the parties
3. To exclude fraudulent and perjured claims

There are exceptions to the parol evidence rule that have lessened the harshness of the doctrine. The rule has been liberalized to produce a better understanding of what the parties actually meant by their written contract. Oral evidence is always admissible to interpret or explain a written agreement, but not to alter its terms.

Exceptions to Rule

A number of exceptions to the parol evidence rule are well established in the law. Justice dictates that oral evidence of prior or contemporaneous agreements be admissible in the following situations.

Incomplete Contracts. When some essential term of an agreement is missing, parol evidence is admissible to prove that term. For example, Sharon orally agrees to sell Blackacre and Whiteacre to Tom for $50,000 each, and they agree that they will execute a written agreement to that effect. Sharon prepares the agreement of sale for $100,000, which she and Tom both sign, but which makes no reference to Whiteacre. In an action to reform the contract, Tom may show that the contract was incomplete by introducing evidence of their oral agreement regarding both Blackacre and Whiteacre.

Ambiguity. If the written contract contains ambiguous language, oral evidence is admissible to clarify the parties' intent. For example, when provision is made for payment of money "to my nephew, Bill," and the party in question has two nephews named Bill, parol evidence may determine which nephew the maker of the will intended. The testimony does not change the wording or intent of the agreement, but establishes the parties' true intent.

When ambiguity exists in an insurance policy, such as when the policy purports to cover "property of the Smith sisters," evidence may establish whether the parties' intention was to provide coverage for property the Smith partnership owned, property the sisters owned individually, or both.

Fraud, Accident, Illegality, Mistake. When fraud or illegality taints a transaction, oral evidence may support an allegation of wrongdoing. If one of the parties substituted the wrong document while obtaining the other party's signature, oral testimony may prove fraudulent conduct. Similarly, if a sale of guns occurs under illegal circumstances, oral testimony may prove the illegality even though the writing itself does not reflect the wrongful nature of the transaction. If, by accident or mistake, a copy of a contract is not a true copy of the agreement, the parties may show the mistake using oral evidence. The parties' oral testimony also may show errors made through reducing the contract to writing.

Condition Precedent. Parol evidence is admissible to show that a written document that appears to be a contract never became a contract because of failure of some condition precedent to the agreement. A *condition precedent* is an event that must occur before a duty of performance arises. Nondelivery or conditional delivery of the contract reflects conditions that a party may show orally. When one party delivered the contract to the other with the understanding that it was not to take effect until certain conditions had been met, parol evidence can prove the conditions did not occur. As with other exceptions to the parol evidence rule, the oral evidence does not vary the parties' written agreement. The objective is to permit a showing of the parties' true intent.

To illustrate further, a writing provides for completion of a building by December 1, 1990. The written agreement does not include the time at which work was to begin. Oral evidence can show that work was not to begin until official recording of the new owner's mortgage in the appropriate local governmental office. It is not evidence as to time of performance but speaks to the question of whether the parties complied with a condition precedent to performance. The evidence does not vary or contradict the terms of the writing and does not violate the parol evidence rule. A written promise may be affected by oral evidence when pertinent facts are not set forth in the writing and oral evidence is admissible to prove the condition.

U.C.C. The U.C.C. specifically recognizes the parol evidence rule. It provides that "Terms...set forth in a writing intended by the parties as a final expression of their agreement...may not be contradicted by evidence of any prior agreement or of a contemporaneous oral agreement...."[9] It also states that (1) a prior course of dealings between the parties, (2) usage of the trade, or (3) the course of performance may explain or supplement a written contract.[10] It allows introduction of oral evidence of consistent additional terms unless the court finds that the parties intended the writing as a complete and exclusive statement of the terms of the agreement.[11] Again, these provisions help in ascertaining the parties' true intent. The assumption is that the parties took prior dealings and usages of the trade for granted when they formed the contract.

CONTRACT INTERPRETATION

Courts apply many principles and maxims to determine the meaning of contract language. Just as they interpret legislative enactments and constitutions, courts also interpret contracts. Their purpose in interpreting a contract is to determine the intention of the parties who drafted it. If the language is clear and unambiguous and construction or interpretation is easy, the intent expressed in the contract applies.

When the language of a contract is ambiguous or obscure, courts apply established *maxims of construction* to ascertain the parties' supposed intent. Maxims of construction are not hard-and-fast legal rules but are well accepted guidelines for interpretation. These maxims do not make a new contract for the parties or rewrite an old one. Courts apply them only to resolve doubts and ambiguities in a contract.

Application of the maxims of construction is more an art than a science. The maxims do not point with unerring accuracy to particular interpretations and are not "rules" of construction. They are instead the customary way of attempting to interpret contracts, and they sharpen analysis and bring out possible alternative interpretations of contractual terms.

The general standard of interpretation is to use language that would have meaning to a reasonably intelligent person familiar with the circumstances in which the language is used. Thus, courts judge language objectively rather than subjectively. What one party thinks a contract means is immaterial because words mean what a reasonable person would think they mean under the circumstances. In determining the parties' intention, what parties express is the decisive factor, and this expression is decisive unless it conflicts with a rule of law or public policy.

Plain Meaning

A fundamental maxim of contract interpretation is that words are to be understood in their plain and normal meaning, or by the *plain meaning standard*. This maxim applies even though the parties who agreed to the wording may not have anticipated the consequences. A court looks at contract language within the context of the contract's subject matter, nature, objectives, and purposes.

Although courts interpret everyday language using its ordinary meaning, they also interpret technical words with technical meanings. Courts give words with established legal meaning their legal meanings. In interpreting the words and conduct of the parties to a contract, a court seeks to put itself in the position the parties occupied at the time they made the contract. The law of the place where the parties made the contract controls the formation of the contract. For example, if the parties made a contract in New Mexico, New Mexico law applies.

In every case, the circumstances under which the parties entered into the contract are relevant, whether the contract was oral or written. The circumstances of the agreement, the subject matter, the relationship of the parties, and the subject of the agreement are all relevant in determining the meaning of the agreement and in giving effect to the parties' intent.

Although the plain meaning standard may help ascertain the intention of both parties to a contract, it might not apply when only one party's intention is unclear. For example, an applicant for life insurance may name as his beneficiary "my wife." At the time the insured obtained the policy, he was living with a woman who was not his legal wife because he had gone through a ceremony of marriage with her without divorcing his first wife. The plain meaning of the term "my wife" clearly conflicts with the insured's actual intention, and a court may ignore the plain meaning and apply the insured's intention.

Effectuation of Intent

A fundamental principle of contract construction is that courts apply an interpretation that best carries out the parties' intentions. To ascertain that intention, a court reads the contract as a whole. If several writings relate to the transaction, a court considers all of them together.

A court interprets individual clauses and specific words in relation to the main purpose of the contract. The intention expressed in the contract applies, not the subjective intention of one of the parties. If the intention appears clear from the words used, there is no need for the courts to go further, and the words apply.

Courts do not attempt, under the pretext of interpretation, to make new contracts for the parties. Neither do they change written contracts to make them express intentions different from those expressed by the parties in the contractual language. Courts generally take people to mean what they say. Courts do not make agreements for the parties but ascertain what their agreements were.

Entire and Divisible Contracts

In an *entire contract,* the party who must perform first must render full performance to be entitled to the other party's performance. For instance, unless a contract provides otherwise, delivery of goods is necessary before payment. In a *divisible contract,* however, the performance of a portion of the contract entitles the performing party to immediate payment. A contract providing for the delivery of goods in installments usually states the price for each installment upon delivery, and each installment is due upon delivery. Similarly, in most employment contracts the courts permit an employee to sue for compensation for the number of weeks or months of service rendered on the theory that these contracts are divisible. Therefore, employees who sign contracts are entitled to be paid before the end of the contract.

A contract is divisible if each party's performance is divisible into two or more parts, and if it appears that the parties agreeing to the contract contemplated separate compensation for each installment of the performance. Failure to perform one installment is not failure to perform the entire agreement.

Court Interpretation. Parties seldom say in a contract that it is divisible or entire. If the parties intended that each would accept the other's part performance in return for his or her own full performance regardless of subsequent events, the contract is divisible. If, however, the division of the contract into parts was only to provide periodic payments applicable toward the amount due upon contract completion, it is an entire contract.

Courts prefer to interpret contracts as divisible whenever they can, and to avoid hardships that can result from interpreting them as entire. If a court interprets a contract as requiring an entire performance, no duty to pay arises under the contract until completion of full performance.

U.C.C. The U.C.C. provides that a sales contract is entire unless the parties have agreed otherwise. Thus, all of the goods a contract calls for must arrive in a single delivery, and payment in full is due upon that delivery.[12] If the contract permits installment deliveries, the seller can demand a proportionate share of the price as each delivery occurs, provided the price can be apportioned, as when goods cost a certain price per item. If there is a substantial default on an installment, as when goods do not conform to a contract, a buyer may reject the installment.[13]

When an installment breach cannot be cured, or if the seller will not give adequate assurance that the breach will be cured, the buyer can rescind the entire contract. If the buyer accepts a nonconforming installment without giving notice of cancellation or without demanding that the seller deliver goods that conform, the breach may not be a basis for rescission, and the contract stands.[14]

Clerical Errors and Omissions

Courts correct obvious clerical errors or mistakes in writing and grammar. Thus, courts may transpose, reject, or supply words, if necessary, to make the language clear. In every case a court attempts to read the contract as the parties intended, unless the error or omission makes it impossible to determine the parties' intent.

Implied Terms. Courts read certain terms into contracts even though the parties did not express them, unless the parties expressed a contrary intention. The law presumes that the parties intended some provisions. For example, courts generally presume that payment under a contract is to be in legal tender, and not in foreign currency or some substitute for money. In service contracts, courts imply that the parties will render the service with reasonable care and skill.

If the parties have not specified the time of performance, performance must take place within a reasonable time. If it is customary in the trade to extend credit, a court will read that trade practice into the contract. Thus, the parties need not have set forth every provision of a contract.

Court Interpretation. Courts imply some terms in a contract if needed to carry out the parties' intent. The unexpressed or implied obligations in these instances are those the court believes to be inherent in the transaction. The parties must abide not only by what they expressly intended, but also by intentions the court presumes the parties would have had if they had given more thought to the matter. For a court to read an intention into a contract, however, that intention must concern a necessary legal implication.

U.C.C. The U.C.C. restates and expands the rule that parties need not set forth every provision in contracts for the sale of goods for those contracts to be binding on the parties. The U.C.C. provides that, "even though one or more terms are left open a contract for sale does not fail for indefiniteness if the parties have intended to make a contract and there is a reasonably certain basis for giving an appropriate remedy."[15] Thus, in contracts for the sale of goods, if the parties fail to state a price for the goods, a reasonable price is implied.[16] If the parties do not mention a time for performance, performance is to be within a reasonable time.[17] In both of these cases, a reasonably certain basis for affording a remedy exists.

If the parties have failed to specify the quantity of goods, the courts are reluctant to speak for the parties concerning the amount the parties intended. If the parties have not mentioned a quantity, a court probably will find that the contract is invalid because of indefiniteness, and the court will not imply the amount of goods. If one of the parties has agreed to purchase all the goods that party requires from the other party in a requirements contract, or to sell all output to the other party in an output contract, the U.C.C. implies that these provisions mean "such actual output or requirements as may occur in good faith...."[18] In those types of contracts, therefore, a court determines whether the output tendered or requirements demanded were in good faith or whether they were "unreasonably disproportionate to any stated estimate or...to any normal or...comparable prior output or require-ments...."[19] Strictly speaking, output and requirements contracts are not indefinite. They are indefinite only as to quantity at the time the parties agree, but actual events make the quantities definite as output or requirements become known.

Contradictory Terms

If clauses in a contract conflict, but an interpretation made by the court is possible to make them effective, a court will adopt that inter-pretation. When the parties have made typewritten or handwritten changes in a printed contract form, the courts apply a system of priori-ties:

1. Handwriting prevails over typewriting.
2. Typewriting prevails over printing.
3. Words prevail over figures.

This is a common-sense approach, because parties usually make handwritten changes last. If a writing is printed, it is safe to assume that any typing on the document occurred later. Words on a check, for example, prevail over figures.

In interpreting conflicting language, the courts give preference to acts that require greater attention to detail and effort. The result pre-sumably reflects the party's true intent most accurately.

Ambiguity

The term *ambiguity* has two legal meanings:

1. It may mean that a provision of the contract can be interpreted reasonably in more than one way.
2. It may mean that, after using all the tools of interpretation, the court cannot determine the meaning of the language.

If a provision reasonably can mean more than one thing, the courts adopt the interpretation least favorable to the party who put the provi-sion into the contract and most favorable to the party who merely as-sented to it. For example, a court interprets an insurance policy against the insurer who designed it. Similarly, courts interpret words in offers against the proposers, and words in acceptances against the acceptors. They interpret words in promissory notes against the makers and words in transfers of property against the grantors. The principle for this rule is that people are responsible for ambiguities in their own expressions. If they initiate expressions and have the power to phrase them as they please, they cannot expect courts to interpret ambiguities in their favor.

If a provision is so ambiguous that a court cannot determine what it means with the usual tools of interpretation, the court may admit evidence from outside the contract. For example, a court will permit evidence of prior or contemporaneous agreements to shed light on the meaning of the ambiguous language. The court will not exclude this evidence under the parol evidence rule, because that rule (1) prohibits only evidence that contradicts the express contractual terms and (2) does not prohibit evidence that shows the true meaning of the language.

Parties' Own Interpretation

The interpretation that the parties have placed on their contract, as shown by their subsequent conduct, has great weight for determination of the meaning of doubtful terms. The parties know best what they meant by their words, and their actions under the agreement are some of the best indications of what they meant.

A contract for the sale of goods may involve repeated occasions for a party's performance along with the other party's knowledge of the nature of the performance and opportunity to object to it. The second party's acceptance or acquiescence concerning the performance can help determine the agreement's meaning.[20] The U.C.C. thus recognizes that the parties' actions are strong evidence of their intentions.

However, if there is no ambiguity in the agreement and the meaning of its terms is clear, the parties' subsequent conduct placing an unreasonable and erroneous interpretation upon the agreement does not prevent a court from enforcing the contract according to the contractual terms. A court will not remake the agreement for the parties because they have acted contrary to its provisions.

Lawful and Fair

If both a lawful and an unlawful interpretation of a contract are possible, the courts assume that the parties intended the lawful interpretation. If there is a choice, a court will interpret a contract as reasonable and fair rather than unreasonable and harsh to one of the parties. Under that approach, courts adopt interpretations that avoid forfeitures of property when possible. If the terms of the contract itself leave its meaning in doubt, courts ascribe to the parties the intent to enter into a fair agreement and therefore interpret the contract equitably.

The U.C.C. "unconscionable contract or clause" section enunciates this approach clearly. That section, which applies to the sale of goods, provides that a court may find all or any part of a contract "unconscionable" and either may refuse to enforce it at all or may apply it in a way that avoids "any unconscionable result."[21] This approach transcends and ignores interpretation and means that a harsh and one-sided sale of goods agreement is not enforceable. The parties' intention is not material. Courts are incorporating this approach slowly into areas of law other than the sales of goods.

Trade Usage, Course of Dealings, and Performance

In interpreting contracts, courts give common words their ordinary meanings and technical terms their technical meanings, and they consider local, cultural, and *trade usage* meanings. In attempting to establish the parties' intent, courts also consider their prior *course of dealings* and their *course of performance* under the contract. The U.C.C. recognizes that these considerations can make interpretation difficult. The U.C.C. attempts to define and distinguish "trade usage," "course of dealings," and "course of performance" and establishes an order of priority among the three concepts to resolve conflicts among them.

The U.C.C. defines "trade usage" as "...any practice or method of dealing having such regularity of observance in a place, vocation or trade as to justify an expectation that it will be observed with respect to the transaction in question."[22] Mercantile law has used this standard for centuries, and it differs from the common law "custom" applied in nonmercantile cases, which generally required universal observance from the beginning.

A "course of dealings" relates to similar transactions between the parties prior to the contract in question. "Course of performance" involves the actual performance of the contract in question that has been rendered without either party's objection.

The U.C.C. has established priorities to use when these four considerations are in conflict. The order of priority is as follows:

1. Express terms of the agreement
2. Course of performance
3. Course of dealings
4. Trade usage[23]

If a court seeks to determine the parties' intent, and the express terms of the agreement do not indicate that intent, the prior course of dealings by the parties should have preference over usage of the trade to establish the meaning of the agreement. Courts admit evidence on these questions.

Parol Evidence Rule

The parol evidence rule provides that, once the parties have reduced an agreement to writing, no oral evidence may contradict its terms. The rule assumes that all the parties' negotiations and agreements are in the final agreement, which may consist of one or more writings. Any evidence, therefore, that contradicts or upsets that integrated agreement is not admissible evidence if the other party objects to it. The other party's failure to object waives the right to exclude the evidence.

The parol evidence rule does not apply to the introduction of evidence to explain ambiguities. The purpose of this evidence is to clarify what the parties intended the final agreement to mean. Evidence to clarify ambiguities explains but does not contradict. Therefore, evidence of the course of performance under the contract, or of the parties' prior course of dealings, or of the usages of trade, is all admissible to assist the court in determining the meaning of the contract.

THIRD-PARTY RIGHTS

The general rule of contract law is that only the parties have rights under a contract. Although a third party may expect to benefit under another's contract, the third party ordinarily does not have any rights. The law recognizes, however, two situations in which third parties have rights and in which the law permits them to enforce a contract others have made:

1. An *assignment* of a contract, by which one party transfers rights arising under a contract to a third party
2. *Third-party beneficiary contracts,* in which one party contracts with another party to confer a benefit upon a third party

In each of these situations, a third party may enforce the contract.

Assignments

Assignment of contracts is common. A creditor often assigns the right to receive money from a debtor to a third party, such as a bank. Assignments involve transfers to other persons of rights of performance under a contract. The party to the contract who makes the assignment is the *assignor,* and the party to whom the rights of contract are assigned is the *assignee.* If the nonassigning party does not honor the assignment, the assignee may sue the nonassigning party just as though the assignee were a party to the original contract.

Rights Assignable. Most contract rights are assignable. Thus, a seller can assign the right to receive payment for the sale of goods to a third person, the assignee. The party owing the obligation to pay for the goods, the *obligor,* then must pay the assignee. Ordinarily, any right to collect a debt may be assigned because it is usually no more difficult for a debtor, or obligor, to pay the assignee the amount owed than it would have been to pay the original creditor, or assignor.

Rights Not Assignable. Notwithstanding the general rule that contract rights are assignable, certain contract rights are not assignable without the obligor's consent. The most common situations in which contract rights are not assignable are as follows:

1. *Law restricts.* A statute may prohibit assignment of specified contract rights. The law often restricts prior assignment of veterans' disability benefits, government pensions, wages, inheritance, and workers compensation benefits. An assignee cannot enforce attempted assignments of these rights.

2. *Contract prohibits.* The parties to an agreement may specify that they cannot, under the contract, assign the rights. These agreements are valid and enforceable. Thus, the standard fire insurance policy prohibits its assignment to new owners of the property insured without the insurer's consent. An insured's attempt to assign the standard fire insurance policy to a new owner of the insured property and to impose an obligation on the insurer to pay the assignee in the event of loss is ineffective.

3. *Contract is personal.* When a lawyer, for example, contracts to provide services, such as representation in court, the lawyer legally cannot delegate those personal duties to another. Personal rights also are not assignable. Personal service contracts require an obligor's actual performance, and courts do not permit attempts to shift that performance to a third party unless the original parties to the contract agree to the change.

4. *Assignment alters performance.* When the assignment materially alters or varies the obligor's performance, a court usually will not uphold it. For example, if Bob contracts to deliver oil to Nancy's house, Nancy may not assign the right to receive delivery of the oil to Dan, who lives in a distant location. The assignment would materially alter Bob's performance.

5. *Personal satisfaction contracts involved.* When the contract provides that the goods or services are to be satisfactory to the purchaser, the agreement is subject only to the buyer's judgment. The buyer may not substitute a third-person assignee's judgment.

6. *Personal injury involved.* When a personal injury is involved and a judgment is pending, the general rule is that a claim against another for damages resulting from personal injury is not assignable, and a final judgment, however, is assignable. For example, in Bob's suit against Nancy, Bob can assign his final judgment to someone else. If, however, the damage is to property, the right to sue for damages is assignable. As an example of this, a property owner whose property is damaged by a wrongdoer receives an insurance payment to cover the damage. The property owner can assign the right to sue the wrongdoer to the insurance company that paid for the damage. These assignments involve the right of *subrogation,* which enables the insurer to "stand in the shoes" of the insured to obtain damages.

U.C.C. The U.C.C. provides for delegation of the duties of either party to a sale of goods contract (1) unless the parties have agreed otherwise or (2) when the nondelegating party has a substantial interest in having the "original promisor perform or control the acts required by the contract."[24] Thus, a seller usually can delegate to someone else the duty to perform the seller's obligations under the contract.

The U.C.C. also provides that rights are not assignable "where the assignment would materially change the duty of the other (nonassigning) party, or increase materially the burden or risk imposed on him by his contract, or impair materially the chance of obtaining a return performance."[25] Under the U.C.C., "unless the circumstances indicate the contrary," a provision prohibiting assignment restricts only the delegation of duties and does not prohibit the assignment of rights.[26]

Forms. To be effective, an assignment needs neither formality nor writing. Any words or conduct that indicate the assignor's intention to transfer contractual rights effects a valid assignment. Assignments are transfers and need not be contracts. Therefore, assignments made as gifts are nevertheless enforceable against the obligor.

However, if an assignment involves subject matter that a statute of frauds covers, such as an assignment for rights under a contract for the sale of land, the assignment must be in writing to be enforceable. Statutes of frauds in all states require that transfers of interests in land be in writing.

Consideration. Although an assignment is a transfer and not a contract, a promise to make an assignment must be a valid contract to be enforceable. Therefore, if Al promises to assign a contract right to Bob, all of the requirements of a valid contract, including consideration, must be present. If, however, Al makes the assignment as a gift, the assignee, Bob, can enforce the assigned contract right against the obligor even though the assignee has given no consideration to the assignor for the assignment. This result is consistent with the general law of gifts, which does not require consideration.

A promise to give a gift is not enforceable, but once the gift is delivered the gift is legally effective and irreversible. An assignor who has not received consideration for a gift from an assignee can rescind the assignment at any time before the obligor has performed the contract without liability to the assignee.

Assignee's Rights. As a general rule, the assignee's rights do not exceed the assignor's. The legal maxim applicable here is that "the rights of the assignee can rise no higher than those of the assignor." If the other party, or obligor, has a defense to the original contract, that party can assert the defense against the assignee. Thus, if the assignor obtained the original contract through fraud or duress, this defense may be valid against the assignee.

Consumer sales contracts often provide that, if the seller assigns the contract, usually to a finance company or bank, the buyer agrees not to assert against the assignee any defenses that may be valid against the seller-assignor. Adding such provisions to a sales contract makes the contract more marketable because it places the assignee in a favored position. For the most part, however, people who receive assignments of sales contracts today accept them subject to any defenses good against the assignor.

Assignee's Duties. Although the assignee usually obtains rights under an assignment, the assignment also may impose duties. The assignor who undertook performance is not, however, relieved of those duties simply by delegating them to the assignee. A primary obligation to perform usually remains with the assignor. In the event the assignee fails to perform in keeping with the terms of the original contract and the assignor is called upon to perform, the assignor has a right to sue the assignee for failure to perform. Whether the assignee is also liable to the nonassigning party for the faulty performance is a question that a court can determine only by careful examination of the entire transaction.

In general, if an assignor assigns rights and delegates obligations to the assignee, the courts permit a third party's enforcement against either the assignee or assignor, but not against both of them. For example, in construction contracts the prime contractor typically delegates performance of all or a portion of the construction to subcontractors. These delegated duties are usually routine, and the other parties to the agreement expect that subcontractors will be involved. If a subcontractor fails to perform properly, either the assignor or the third party (obligee) may sue the assignee (subcontractor). If, however, there was an attempt to assign the duty, as in personal service contracts, for instance, and that duty was not properly delegable, the assignor alone remains liable for faulty or improper performance unless the other party (obligee) has agreed to accept the assignee's performance.

Under the U.C.C., an assignment general in its terms, such as "all my rights under the contract," is both an assignment of rights and a delegation of obligations under the agreement. The assumption is, absent an indication to the contrary, that the assignee promised to perform the contract obligations. Either the assignor or the nonassigning party may enforce the promise.[27]

Notice. A valid assignment takes effect immediately, even though the assignor has not advised the obligor of the assignment. The assignee, however, should immediately notify the obligor of the assignment. In the absence of notice, the obligor may pay the assignor without knowing of the assignee, thus defeating the assignee's right to demand payment or performance from the obligor.

Notice of assignment also protects additional parties who may take subsequent assignments from the assignors. An assignor would not have the right to make the second assignment but would have the power or ability to do so. Thus, the original obligor might make payment to the second assignee.

Which of the two assignees has superior rights against the obligor is a question with different answers:

- The common law view was that, once the assignor had assigned the rights, a second assignment was impossible because the assignor had nothing left to assign. The second assignee merely had rights against the assignor.

- Another view, simple in operation, is that the first assignee to notify the obligor of the assignment has superior rights, and the tardy assignee merely has rights against the assignor.

- The third view is that the first assignee has superior rights regardless of notice unless the second assignee receives payment from or a judgment against the obligor and has no knowledge or notice of the prior assignment.

If the obligor has received notice from both assignees or notice from one assignee and a demand for payment from the other, the obligor should go to court with both assignees as defendants, pay the money into court, and have the court determine which assignee is entitled to payment. If the obligor pays one or the other, it is still possible that the wrong party is being paid.

Third-Party Beneficiaries

At common law, only the parties to a contract could enforce it. Those parties were those who gave or received consideration or those who were in *privity* (in a direct contractual relationship). Today, however, contracts may benefit third parties who may have enforceable rights under those contracts.

Types of Beneficiaries. *Third-party beneficiary contracts* are contracts between two parties that benefit third parties, either directly or indirectly. They are of three types: *creditor beneficiary, donee beneficiary,* and *incidental beneficiary.* The donee and creditor beneficiaries have enforceable rights against the original promisor, but the incidental beneficiary has no enforceable rights.

Creditor Beneficiaries. If the purpose of a contract is to discharge an obligation a party owes, the person to be paid is a creditor beneficiary. For example, Henry owes Chuck $500. Henry sells his car to Jeremy for $1,000, including $500 in cash to Henry and Jeremy's promise to pay $500 to Chuck in discharge of Henry's debt to Chuck. Chuck becomes a creditor beneficiary and after the sale has an enforceable claim against Jeremy. Unless Chuck agrees otherwise, Chuck still can sue Henry until the original debt is paid. Chuck thus has two possible remedies:

1. To proceed, as a creditor beneficiary, against Jeremy
2. To proceed against Henry under the original $500 debt

If Henry's intent in obtaining the promise from Jeremy was to discharge some obligation to Chuck, either due or supposed to be due from the promisee to a third party, the third party is a creditor beneficiary. It is the promisee's intent as the party obtaining the promise that is all important in these situations. The promisor's or the third-party beneficiary's intent is not the decisive factor.

Donee Beneficiaries. If the promisee's intent in obtaining the promise was to make a gift to a third party, to confer a gratuity on that third party, the third party is then a donee beneficiary. To illustrate, Henry wishes to make a gift to Chuck of $500. Henry sells his car to Jeremy for $500 and obtains Jeremy's promise to pay Chuck the $500 price for the car. Chuck is a donee beneficiary of Jeremy's promise for $500, and Chuck can sue Jeremy for $500.

Incidental Beneficiaries. An incidental beneficiary has no rights under the contract. For example, City X contracts with Y Water Company to maintain sufficient water pressure at City X's hydrants for

Exhibit 4-1
Relationship Between Parties to a Beneficiary Contract

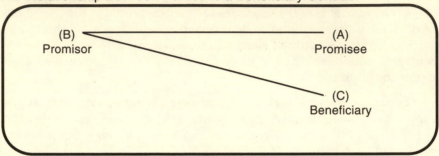

fire protection. A citizen of City X has a house that burns down because of insufficient water pressure. The citizen is an incidental beneficiary and has no enforceable rights under the contract. No performance is due the citizen under the contract. The duty to the citizen is, at best, indirect.

When a person claims beneficiary status, the court must decide whether the contracting parties intended to confer a benefit upon that person. Unless the person making the claim can show a direct interest in the performance of the contract that is known to the contracting parties, the third party is an incidental beneficiary only.

Characteristics of Beneficiary Contracts. Exhibit 4-1 shows the relationship between the parties to a beneficiary contract. The elements of a third-party beneficiary contract are as follows:

1. There must be a binding contract between the promisor and promisee.
2. The parties to the contract must intend that the third party be benefited by and acquire rights under the contract.
   - If the intent is to discharge an existing obligation, the contract is a creditor beneficiary contract.
   - If the promisee's intent is to make a gift to a third party, the contract is a donee beneficiary contract. Some cases hold that the promisee's intention merely must benefit the third party.
3. Care is necessary in each case to clarify to whom the performance is due. If the performance is owed to a third party, then there is a third-party beneficiary contract, either creditor or donee, and the third party can sue to enforce it. If, however, performance is due to the promisee only, then only the promisee can sue and a third party has no rights against the promisor.

4. The beneficiary is always subject to defenses the promisor may have against the promisee. Thus, the beneficiaries' rights are subject to the usual defenses in contract actions, such as lack of consideration, illegality, fraud, and so on.

Legal Trends. The distinction between creditor and donee beneficiary contracts is becoming less important in the law, which today often treats them as one class, *intended beneficiaries*.

Suppose, for instance, that Chuck enters into a valid and legal contract to purchase land from Jeremy, breaches the contract, and forfeits the deposit to Jeremy. Then suppose that Henry expresses an interest in the land, but finds out that Chuck, whom he does not know personally, has forfeited a deposit. Believing that if Jeremy obtains the same purchase price from himself (Henry), and that this would not be fair to Chuck, Henry agrees to purchase the land only if Jeremy will promise to repay Chuck's deposit. Jeremy agrees, and a contract between Henry and Jeremy incorporates those terms. On the theory that Henry intended to benefit Chuck by obtaining Jeremy's promise, and regardless of Henry's motive in obtaining that promise, Chuck would have a right to obtain the forfeited deposit from Jeremy under some modern cases.

Beneficiaries' Rights. In general, beneficiaries under contracts, whether creditor, donee, or intended (but not incidental), may enforce the contract. Suppose, however, that the original parties, the promisor and the promisee, agree to annul or change the contract and to eliminate or reduce the rights of the beneficiary.

The contract between the original parties may provide either that they retain or do not retain the right to eliminate or modify the promisor's duty to the third-party beneficiary. The modern legal trend is to permit the original parties in all cases to cut off the beneficiary's rights unless the beneficiary can prove that his or her position has changed materially in reasonable reliance on the contract or that he or she has already sued on the contract.

DISCHARGE OF CONTRACTS

When contract obligations end, the contract is *discharged*, terminating the parties' duties under the contract. There are many ways to discharge a person's contractual obligations. The usual and intended method of discharge is the parties' complete performance of their obligations under the agreement. Once the parties have completely performed their obligations, the contract is terminated. Also, both parties may agree to the discharge of a previous contract by substituting a new agreement, by the legal processes of waiver, novation, and accord and satisfaction, or by other agreements.

Discharge also arises from the impossibility of performance. Thus, the destruction of the subject matter of the contract may result in discharge through impossibility. A discharge of contract also may occur by *operation of law,* as by bankruptcy or a change in the law that makes performance illegal.

Performance

Performance discharges most contracts. When each party fulfills all promises made, no obligations remain and the contract ceases to exist. Performance under a contract can occur in a number of ways.

Payment. Payment of a money debt discharges a contract. If a person owes several separate debts to another and makes a part payment, which debt is discharged? As a general rule the debtor can specify the debt to be discharged, and the creditor must apply the payment as directed. If, however, the debtor does not indicate the specific debt, the creditor may use his or her discretion in applying the payment. The creditor even may apply the payment to a debt barred by the statute of limitations, or to payment of an unsecured, rather than a secured debt. "Secured" means that the creditor has a right to take a debtor's property if a debt is not paid. For example, a mortgage on a house is a secured debt because the creditor/mortgagee can seize the house upon failure of mortgage payments.

Tender of Performance. A *tender* is an offer to perform one's duties under a contract. Tenders may be either offers to perform a promise to do something or offers to perform a promise to pay something. Depending on whether an act or a payment is tendered, the rejection of that tender has different results. Rejection of a tender to do something discharges that obligation. Rejection of a tender of payment of a debt does not discharge the debt.

Thus, in a contract for the sale of goods, if the seller attempts to deliver the goods, and the other party refuses delivery, the seller is discharged from performance. However, refusal to accept permits the tendering party to sue for breach of contract and to defend a later action for breach of contract. Moreover, if the performance due is the payment of money, an offer to pay the money and a refusal to accept will not discharge the debt. A valid tender, however, stops the running of interest on the obligation, and the most the creditor can collect is the amount due on the date of the tender. For the tender to be valid, it must include the entire amount of the debt, not merely a part.

Substantial Performance. Many contractual obligations are most difficult to perform entirely. A major construction contract, for example, likely will result in some deviation of performance as the building progresses. Rather than permit the promisee to escape liability completely on the ground of nonperformance, courts consider whether the performance actually given was substantial and was made in good faith. If so, a court will permit a plaintiff to win recovery notwithstanding a minor deviation from contract specifications.

Courts carefully compare the nature of the performance expected with the performance given and determine whether the deviation was willful. Failure to perform substantially, or intentional deviations in performance, likely will result in a court's finding that the contractual obligations have not been discharged. If a court finds substantial performance, the party receiving performance must pay the contract price, with possible allowance for variance in the value of the performance. The important result is that the party substantially performing can receive the contract price minus damages for nonperformance, rather than nothing at all for failure to perform.

Personal Satisfaction Contracts. If a contract provides that the promisee must be "personally satisfied," or that "satisfaction is guaranteed," the promisee's taste or personal judgment must be satisfied. That person's good faith decision controls. After all, that was the agreement of the parties.

In the absence of a clear showing of bad faith on the part of the party making the decision (the promisee), performance in a *personal satisfaction contract* is not adequate unless there is personal and subjective satisfaction. Thus, if an artist is to paint an individual's portrait "to the satisfaction of" the subject, then a good faith rejection of the completed portrait precludes the promisor's recovery. Courts, however, apply an objective standard when personal satisfaction relates to utility, fitness, or value. Thus, if the promise is that a vehicle is to be "fit" for operation, a court determines fitness according to what a reasonably prudent person would expect under the circumstances. If a reasonable person would be satisfied, the performance is adequate.

Agreed Time. Many contracts fail to provide the time of performance. In general, each party has a reasonable time to perform. Whether performance occurs within a reasonable time is a question of fact for the trier of fact. Additional problems arise when the parties specify a time for performance but fail to perform by that date. Assume that a contract requires delivery by November 1, but delivery occurs on November 5. Must the promisee accept the late delivery? Does the date set in the contract establish a condition that creates obligations under the contract?

If it is clear that late delivery decreases or negates the benefit for the recipient, the stated time is a necessary condition and the promisee need not take delivery. If the contract expressly provides that time is of the essence in the agreement, that provision is enforced and delivery on the due date is a necessary condition to recovery unless enforcement of the provision constitutes an undue hardship or penalty on the promisor. If time is not of the essence for the contract, either in actuality or according to the contract terms, the promisor must complete performance within a reasonable time after the time stated. In general, failure to deliver within the required time, either exact or reasonable, is a breach of contract.

Agreement

The parties to a contract may agree in advance that a certain event will discharge their obligations to one another. For example, Henry agrees to paint Jeremy's house unless Jeremy sells the house by June 1. If Jeremy sells before June 1, this discharges Henry's obligation. The occurrence of that contractual condition, sale of the house, relieved the parties of performance. Parties thus may provide in their contracts that the occurrence of an event will discharge their contractual obligations.

Agreements To Rescind. Just as the parties may agree to enter into a contract, they also may agree to rescind a contract. Unless the contract requires any subsequent modification or rescission to be in writing, the rescission may be oral. An attempted oral rescission in which there is a contract requirement that a rescission must be in writing nevertheless may constitute a waiver. A party, however, may retract a waiver in a sale of goods by letting the other party know that strict performance is necessary. This retraction is not effective if the other party has changed position materially in reliance on the waiver.[28]

A rescission of a contract for the sale of land, however, usually must be in writing because the original agreement of sale effected a transfer of the equitable title of the land to the purchaser. To retransfer that equitable interest in the land to the seller, the statute of frauds requires a new writing. In all cases, a rescission must contain all the elements of a valid contract, including mutual promises to surrender future rights under the contract in consideration for mutual discharge from future duties.

If breach of a contract has occurred, which gives a party a right to sue for damages, the contract cannot be rescinded. The breach has discharged the contract. Only rights and duties that no one has executed can be rescinded. The party entitled to sue, however, may waive or renounce that right. In general, a legally binding waiver or renunciation requires consideration or, in some states, a seal. In transactions that the U.C.C. covers, however, "Any claim or right arising out of an alleged breach can be discharged in whole or in part without consideration by a written waiver or renunciation signed and delivered by the aggrieved party."[29]

Substituted Agreements.   Just as the parties may agree to rescind a contract, so they may agree to substitute a new contract for a prior agreement. The decision to replace an old contract with a new one is subject to the same rules that apply to rescission of agreements. In addition, the U.C.C. provides that, in sales of goods, a modification of a written contract must be in writing if the original contract requires a writing.[30]

Novation.   A *novation* is an agreement that replaces an original party to a contract with a new party. For the substitution to be effective, all parties must agree to it. The party that remains when the other has been replaced must agree to accept the new party and must release the withdrawing party. The latter must consent to withdraw and to permit substitution of the new party. If these essentials are present, the withdrawing party is discharged from the agreement.

To illustrate, Harvey contracts to perform certain services for Eileen. Later, Eileen and Harvey agree that Toby will perform Harvey's obligations, and Eileen expressly releases Harvey from the original contract. Toby's agreement to replace Harvey discharges Harvey from the contract. If Eileen does not release Harvey expressly, there is no novation. Harvey merely would have delegated performance to Toby and would remain liable under the contract.

Accord and Satisfaction.   An *accord* is an agreement between contracting parties that one of them is to substitute a different performance for that required by the contract. Completion of performance satisfies this accord. The accord is the agreement to accept a different performance, and carrying out that agreement is the *satisfaction*. For example, if Bill owes John $200, and they agree that Bill will paint John's home in satisfaction of the debt, an accord exists. Bill's painting the home discharges the obligation because the *accord and satisfaction* are complete.

An accord and satisfaction may be useful to obtain the discharge of an agreed debt. If Joe owes Betty $500, Betty's agreement to accept less than $500 in full payment is not binding unless Betty receives consideration for the promise to discharge Joe. However, Betty may agree to discharge the debt for a lesser sum (than $500) in return for payment before the due date or in return for a lesser sum plus an item of value.

The value of the additional item may or may not equal the amount of the unpaid debt. This conduct results in accord and satisfaction. The parties have agreed to performance other than that required under the contract, and performance has occurred.

Problems may arise when a creditor accepts an early partial payment without agreeing that the early payment is consideration for the discharge of the entire debt. Therefore, to avoid a possible assertion that an accord and satisfaction has occurred, parties should avoid acceptance of an amount less than the amount owed under most circumstances.

Impossibility

A promisor's duty to perform is discharged if, after the contract has formed, performance becomes objectively impossible. If the objectively impossible performance was the major undertaking of the contract, both parties are discharged from all duties under the contract.

Objective Versus Subjective Impossibility. *Objective impossibility* means that the performance cannot conceivably be done. *Subjective impossibility* means that the promisor will not perform even though performance is conceivable. Most courts hold that only objective impossibility excuses the promisor's performance. Subjective impossibility does not discharge the obligation because the promisor must assume the chance of personal inability to perform.

Change in Law. If performance of a contract becomes illegal after the time of contracting because of a change in the law, or through some act of government, the promisor's performance is excused. Thus, changes in zoning ordinances or building codes may discharge a builder's duty to build because the specifications have become illegal. Similarly, governmental embargoes on certain exports discharge contracts for exporting the goods. The embargoes make an agreement more burdensome than anticipated.

Death or Incapacity. The death or incapacitating illness of a specific person necessary to perform a promise discharges the duty to perform. The service must be "personal." Thus, when Bill promises to build John's house, Bill's death or illness discharges the contract. Conversely, John's death or illness has the same effect. Ordinary contracts of production and sale of property are not personal, and the death or illness of one or both parties does not affect them. In the event of death, the deceased's personal representatives must perform the contract.

Destruction of Subject Matter. If the specific subject matter of the contract is destroyed or becomes nonexistent after creation of the contract, without the promisor's fault, the promisor's duty is discharged by impossibility of performance. Thus, exhaustion of a well discharges a contract to furnish oil or gas. Similarly, the destruction of an auditorium discharges a contract to use it for entertainment.

In contracts for the sale of goods, discharge by impossibility occurs only if specific, identified goods are the subject matter of the agreement. Thus, failure of a crop on a particular parcel of land discharges a contract to sell so many bushels of wheat grown on that land. If, however, a contract does not identify specific land or wheat, the promisor's duty to supply wheat is not discharged even though the promisor intended to fill the contract from the failed crop. Thus, destruction of goods ascertained or identified in a contract excuses performance. In the absence of specific identification, the promisor's obligation to obtain and deliver identical goods from some other source continues.

Other Party's Act. If the other party's act prevents the performance, performance will be excused because of impossibility. Thus, if a contract requires the promisor to perform certain services on the promisee's land, and the promisee prevents entry on the land, the promisor cannot perform and the contract is discharged.

Whether the party who is temporarily disabled from performance can demand the right to perform after removal of the disability depends on whether the late performance materially affected the other party. If late performance is material, the contract is discharged.

Temporary Impossibility. Temporary rather than permanent impossibility merely suspends, rather than discharges, the promisor's duty while the impossibility continues. After the impossibility has come to an end, the duty to perform reattaches. Thus, when the promisor's illness or entry into the armed services prevents performance of a service contract, the obligation of performance may arise again upon removal of the temporary impossibility.

Partial Impossibility. If the promisor's performance is only partially impossible, the duty to perform is excused only to the extent that it is impossible. The promisor must perform the balance of the duty regardless of added expense or difficulty. For example, Bill contracts to build a house and to use a certain type of pipe for the plumbing. That this kind of pipe is no longer manufactured discharges only the use of that pipe and not the entire contract. Bill must erect the house and substitute pipe of similar quality.

Part Performance. Impossibility of performance often becomes apparent only after partial performance. If a party has performed in part, such as by putting one of two coats of paint on a house before it is destroyed by fire, the painter may recover the reasonable value of the service. If completion of a contract becomes impossible, the recipient of the work must pay the reasonable value of all work and material up to the date of impossibility.

One must, however, differentiate between legal impossibility and a mere additional burden. The destruction of a partially completed building, for example, does not make performance impossible. By starting construction anew, performance is possible, although the cost is greater than anticipated, and the contractor must bear the additional cost.

Frustration of Purpose.   In some cases performance is still possible, but a supervening event destroys the purpose or value of the contract. *Frustration of purpose* may discharge the contract. To illustrate, Richard owns a house along a street that a parade route is to pass. Richard rents a room to Ashley for the day of the parade so that Ashley may view the parade from the room. The parade route does not pass Richard's house, and the frustration of purpose excuses Ashley's performance.

Commercial Impracticability.   The U.C.C. has several provisions for *commercial impracticability,* which is more than commercial frustration. "Impracticability" differs from "impossibility." "Frustration" means that one party cannot obtain the desired object or effect. The contract can be performed, but the prospective parade-watcher will not see a parade. If the identified subject matter of a contract is destroyed, however, the contract is "impossible" to perform.

The standards for impracticability are commercial, compared with actual, impossibility. For instance, impossibility to perform a contract because of a wartime lack of shipping is a hazard a shipper assumes because the parties made the contract on the eve of a war at a time when a shipping shortage was foreseeable.[31] The question of impracticability, therefore, is a factual issue to be decided in each case.

The U.C.C. excuses both delay in delivery and failure to deliver goods "...if performance as agreed has been made impracticable by the occurrence of a contingency, the nonoccurrence of which was a basic assumption on which the contract was made, or by compliance in good faith with any applicable foreign or domestic governmental regulation or order whether or not it later proves to be invalid."[32] However, the seller must allocate production and delivery of available quantities among the customers and must give the buyer reasonable notice of the problem and information as to how much, if any, of the goods the seller can deliver.[33]

The U.C.C. expressly provides that increased cost does not constitute commercial impracticability, but commercial impracticability may exist because of "a severe shortage of raw materials or of supplies due to a contingency such as war, embargo, local crop failure, unforeseen shutdown of major sources of supply or the like, which either causes a marked increase in cost or altogether prevents the seller from securing supplies necessary to his performance."[34] Even in these cases, however, the seller must take commercially reasonable precautions to protect the source of supply.

To refute an old rule that shipment must be made from the place and by the mode of transportation stated in the contract, the U.C.C. provides for substitution of the place of shipment or the mode of transportation if the contract terms become commercially impracticable and if a "commercially reasonable substitute is available."[35]

Statutes of Limitations. *Statutes of limitations* prescribe time limits within which to sue after a cause of action arises. Failure to commence an action within that time is a successful defense to the suit. That is, a plaintiff can lose a case entirely for failure to file within the statute of limitations period.

The times within which actions must start vary among states and among types of agreements. In some states, claimants may have two years to file suits on oral contracts and six years on written contracts. Another state may prescribe periods of four years for oral contracts and fifteen years for written agreements. In any event, failure to commence an action within the prescribed period gives the defendant the right to defend on the basis of the statute of limitations. A defendant who does not argue a statute loses the right to use it.

Fraudulent Alteration. Any material alteration of a contract that one of the parties makes intentionally discharges the contract. The law destroys the right to enforce the contract. Thus, if one party fraudulently alters the amount payable on a check, the material alteration discharges the liability of the maker of the check as to the person who alters it.

Conditions

Although all promises in a contract are conditions, not all conditions are promises. If one party fails to fulfill a promise in a contract, the other party can sue. A party's failure to fulfill a condition, however, alters, limits, or discharges obligations under the contract. The other party may treat a breach of a promise as a mere nonfulfillment of a condition and thereby waive the condition. If a party does not deliver goods on the specific day that the contract requires, for instance, the buyer may treat the nondelivery as a breach of the promise to deliver and sue for damages. The buyer may choose, however, to waive the breach of contract by treating the nondelivery as a breach of condition that extends the duty to pay to a later date.

There are three types of conditions in contracts:

1. Condition precedent
2. Condition concurrent
3. Condition subsequent

Some contracts contain multiple conditions.

Precedent. A *condition precedent* is an event that must occur before a duty of performance arises. Nonfulfillment of a condition precedent may discharge a contractual obligation. For example, filing a notice of loss under an insurance policy is a condition precedent to payment of a claim. Though it is not a promise, until the condition precedent is met, the insurer has no duty to perform its obligation under the contract.

Concurrent. A *condition concurrent* must exist when both parties to a contract are to perform at the same time. Thus, if a contract expressly or impliedly provides that both parties are to perform at the same time, the conditions are concurrent. To illustrate, a sale of goods is conditioned on cash payment upon delivery. When the goods are delivered, the buyer cannot pay. The conditions of delivery and payment are concurrent, and the seller may regain the goods because the buyer cannot perform as the agreement requires. This condition is a promise, and the seller may sue for breach of contract.

Subsequent. A *condition subsequent* is a future event that may possibly occur after the contract becomes legally enforceable. In either case it terminates contractual rights. For example, a lease of a store in a shopping center provides that the lessor is to receive a certain rent plus a percentage of the store's gross sales. If sales drop below a set dollar amount per month, the lease terminates at the lessor's option. If the sales do not reach a set dollar amount per month within a year, the lease terminates at the lessor's option. If the first condition subsequent occurs, the lessor may terminate all rights and duties under the lease. If the second event does not occur, the lessor may terminate all rights and obligations under the lease. Neither condition is a promise.

Multiple. Many contracts contain a number of conditions that may affect the parties' rights. To determine the legal consequences of the conditions, it is important to know whether they exist as conditions precedent, concurrent, or subsequent. The insurance contract is an example of an agreement containing multiple conditions. It is not always easy to determine whether the parties to the contract intended a condition to be precedent or subsequent to liability under the agreement. The payment of the premium is a condition precedent to liability under a policy. Also, a loss is a condition precedent to an insurer's liability under a policy.

A condition that an insured must sue within one year from the date of a loss is a condition subsequent. The requirement that an insured submit a notice of loss within sixty days of the loss is either a condition precedent to an insurer's liability or, depending on the wording of the condition, a condition subsequent to the insured's loss. An example is "The insurer's obligation will be discharged if no notice of loss is given within sixty days." It requires careful scrutiny to determine the intent and legal effect of a condition.

BREACH OF CONTRACT

A *breach of contract* is a party's unjustifiable failure to perform all or part of a contractual duty. A breach may be total or partial and may occur by failure to perform acts promised, hindering or preventing performance, or other conduct indicating an intention to repudiate the agreement.

Types

Types of breach include those made in repudiation or anticipation, and material and minor breaches. The nonbreaching party has legal remedies against a breaching party.

Repudiation. A *repudiation* of a contract—that is, the refusal to go through with the contract—must be positive and unequivocal to constitute a breach. A statement of inability to perform in the future is not a repudiation. For example, it is not repudiation of a contract between Bill and John to be performed on November 1 if, on October 15, Bill says to John, "I doubt that I'll be able to perform the contract, and the way prices are going up I don't think I want to anyway." If, however, on November 1 Bill says, "I cannot perform," he has repudiated the contract.

A positive retraction must be by words as well as by conduct. John may not treat the statement as a repudiation of the agreement and sue for breach of contract. John cannot sue until the time for performance has arrived and Bill has failed to perform.

Anticipatory. *Anticipatory breach* developed to avoid "enforced idleness" on the part of an aggrieved party and to avoid making it necessary for that party to tender performance at the time stated in the contract to prove the other party's breach.

In some cases courts do not require the nonbreaching party to wait until the actual date of performance to determine whether the contract will be breached. Thus, if there is (1) a clear expression of intention by a promisor not to perform, and (2) an executory, bilateral contract entailing mutual and dependent conditions, the aggrieved party may treat the repudiation as a present total breach and may sue immediately. This is an anticipatory breach.

For example, Millie promises to sell, and Tina promises to buy, Whiteacre for $150,000 on December 1. On November 15, Tina says to Millie, "I cannot and will not go through with our contract." Tina's positive statement that she will not or cannot substantially perform the contract is a breach of contract by anticipatory repudiation. Millie need not wait until December 1, but may sue immediately for damages for breach of contract.

Anticipatory breach applies only if there is a clear statement of intention to repudiate a binding promise. It does not apply to a unilateral contract because, in a unilateral contract, the promisee has not made a promise but has the option to perform an act and to become entitled to compensation. If the promisee does not perform the act, the promisor cannot sue.

Material Versus Minor.   Many courts distinguish between material, or major, breaches and minor ones. The materiality of the breach is a question of fact to be determined by a trier of fact. Several circumstances affect the materiality of a breach—the extent to which the breaching party has performed, willfulness of the breach, and the extent to which the nonbreaching party has obtained benefits and can receive adequate compensation.

A material breach by one party excuses the other party's performance and immediately gives rise to remedies for breach of contract. A minor breach causes only slight delay in performance or a slight deviation in quantity or quality. Minor breaches (1) temporarily suspend any duty of performance by the nonbreaching party that would have arisen on proper performance and (2) give the aggrieved party a cause of action for damages for the breach, usually an offset to the agreed price, but not to remedies for breach of the entire contract.

Remedies

If a contract is breached, the injured party can choose one of three following remedies to correct the situation:

1. To bring an action to collect money damages (in a contract for the sale of goods, an action for the price)
2. To request specific performance of the contract
3. To request an injunction

Damages.   Damages in contract actions fall into the following categories: compensation, consequential, punitive, extracontractual, and liquidated.

Compensatory.   The most frequent remedy for breach of contract is an action for money damages arising from the breach. Damages compensate for the breach and are therefore called *compensatory damages*. The injured party should be placed in approximately the same position, through receiving compensatory damages, as if the contract had been performed properly. Thus, a court attempts to give the injured party the "benefit of the bargain."

Compensatory damages consist of the difference between the value of the promised performance and the plaintiff's cost of obtaining that performance elsewhere. They include losses caused and gains prevented by the defendant's breach. In the case of contracts for the sale of goods, the U.C.C. provides that the measure of damages is the difference between the contract price and the market price at the time of breach.[36] The objective is not to punish the party breaching, but to put the injured party in as good a position as he or she would have been in if the other party had performed fully.

Consequential (Special).   In addition to the standard measure of contract damages, a breaching party is also liable for any *consequential* or *special damages*. Recoverable loss thus usually extends to any loss resulting from the breach that the defendant, as a reasonable person, should have foreseen at the time the contract arose. Consequential damages are recoverable only when the defendant was aware of the probable occurrence of the damages.

To illustrate, a manufacturer orders a supply of raw materials for delivery on a certain date. The seller does not deliver until after that date. The manufacturer then demands as part of the damages the loss incurred because of the plant shutdown resulting from unavailability of raw materials unavailable from any other source. Although that loss flowed directly from the breach, the manufacturer cannot sue for them because manufacturers usually order raw materials for delivery in advance of actual need. Also, raw materials are usually available from substitute sources. The seller, therefore, has no reason to believe that delayed shipment will cause a shutdown. If the manufacturer, however, informs the seller of the critical need and the seller, with that knowledge, promises to perform on a given day, delayed delivery makes the seller liable for the foreseeable loss arising from the shutdown.

Punitive.   *Punitive* or *exemplary damages* punish a defendant for a malicious act and need not bear any relationship to a party's actual damages. They are common in tort actions, such as for an unprovoked and malicious assault and battery. The purpose is to deter such conduct.

Punitive damages are not appropriate in most contract cases because the contract objective of damages is to give the plaintiff the benefit of the bargain. If a seller of personal property has committed fraud or misrepresentation, however, punitive damages may be appropriate. The punitive damages here, however, are based on the fraud rather than on breach of contract. An insurer unreasonably delaying payment or contesting a claim without reasonable grounds by statute may be liable for the insured's attorney's fees as a penalty.[37]

Extracontractual. Another development affecting insurance involves the awarding of *extracontractual* damages beyond assuring the benefit of the bargain for the insurer's breach of contract.

Grounds. The grounds for assessing extracontractual damages are as follows:

1. Breach of duty of good faith and fair dealing in contracts of insurance
2. Intentional infliction of emotional distress on the insured by the insurer's extreme and outrageous conduct

If one or both of these occurs, a court may award the insured both consequential and punitive damages. Consequential damages may include compensation for physical and mental suffering and distress, loss of assets, and attorneys' fees. In most cases extracontractual damages far exceed contract damages resulting from the breach.

Mitigation. The nonbreaching party to a contract owes a duty of *mitigation of damages*, which means that, upon learning of a breach, the injured party must take reasonable action to minimize the loss. When the buyer breaches a contract for the sale of goods, the seller must dispose of the goods otherwise at the best price possible. If a seller delivers a defective product and the buyer knows that the product is dangerous and may cause injury, the buyer must not permit its use. Similarly, if an employer fires an employee, the employee must make a good faith effort to seek a similar position and mitigate any damage to be claimed from the employer.

An improperly dismissed employee may not go on a vacation and expect the full remaining salary to be paid if a court awards damages. If, of course, the employee finds a position at a lower salary, the employee's damages are the difference between the higher and lower salaries.

A plaintiff must mitigate damages. If the employee does not try to get another position, for instance, a suit for damages for breach of contract will fail because the employee cannot prove damages. If, however, the employee locates a position for a lower salary and then decides it would be better to take a vacation, the maximum recovery would be the difference between the salary for the new job and the salary under the breached contract. If the seller breaches a contract for the sale and delivery of goods, and the purchaser does not buy the goods elsewhere, damages are appropriate for the difference between what the goods could have been purchased for and the price under the breached contract.

Liquidated. The parties may agree in the contract for the amount of damages to be paid if a breach occurs. These *liquidated damages* are an agreed amount. Courts do not always enforce liquidated damages provisions. If a court finds them to be a penalty, the court will disregard them and the injured party must prove actual damages.

To be a valid liquidated damage clause, the sum specified by the parties must be a good faith effort to estimate actual damages that probably would ensue from a breach. A court considers in each case whether the contract involved subject matter that would make damages difficult to ascertain and whether the amount agreed upon represented a reasonable estimate of the damages that the parties actually might incur.

Action for Price. In a contract for the sale of goods, the seller has two remedies for breach. One remedy, damages, is available if the seller properly resells the goods and receives less than the contract price. The difference is the damages. If the seller receives more than the agreed price, the excess need not go to the buyer and belongs to the seller.

The seller, however, sometimes may sue for the agreed price, but only in the following circumstances:

1. When the buyer has received and kept the goods
2. When the goods are destroyed or damaged after the buyer assumes the chance of loss
3. When the buyer wrongfully rejects delivery, and the goods cannot be sold after reasonable effort to sell at a reasonable price[38]

Equitable Remedies

The burden of loss passes to the buyer in the following situations:

- When the goods are accepted
- When a carrier tenders the goods to the buyer if the contract requires the seller to ship the goods to the buyer
- When the seller delivers the goods to the carrier if the contract provides only for delivery to the carrier and not to the destination

- When a third party holds the goods for delivery without moving them
- When the buyer receives some document indicating the buyer's right to the goods
- When the third party acknowledges the buyer's right to possession[39]

Specific Performance.   Sometimes dollar damages are not adequate for an injured party. The only adequate remedy may be to require the breaching party to perform the contract by performing the promise. A suit in a court of equity for *specific performance* is not appropriate if money damages are adequate. To determine whether money damages are adequate, courts consider the following:

1. The difficulty of valuing the subject matter of the contract
2. The existence of sentimental and aesthetic qualities of the subject matter that make it unique
3. The difficulty or impossibility of obtaining a duplicate or substantial equivalent of the subject matter

Actions requesting specific performance of a contract occur most frequently in contracts for the sale of real estate. Real estate is unique, and a court will order a seller to perform a contract and transfer title to an injured party.

A court will order specific performance of a contract to sell personal property only if the item is in some way unique, such as an antique, painting, or other one-of-a-kind item. Courts do not direct specific performance of personal service contracts. To do so would require the courts to supervise the performance to assure that it is adequate. Courts do not order specific performance of contracts requiring supervision, such as building contracts.

Injunctions.   Although a court will not order specific performance of a personal service contract, if the personal services are truly unique, a court may prevent the promisor from performing elsewhere during the term of the contract by granting an *injunction.* An injunction is a court order that a party must do or not do something. When a court grants an injunction, it is "enjoining," or preventing, an action. A court probably would not grant an injunction against a singer in an opera chorus who broke the contract to refrain from singing elsewhere, but probably would grant such an injunction against an important soloist.

Commercial contracts containing negative agreements are enforceable by injunction. If a business is sold, and the seller promises not to compete with the buyer in a given area for a given time, the restriction is legal. If the seller breaches the provision and starts to compete, the buyer may request an order enjoining the seller from competing.

In both of these cases money damages would be inadequate. There is no way to assess the money value of the soloist's performance, and a series of lawsuits for damages from the illegal competition would be too burdensome on the buyer. Therefore, an injunction is appropriate.

Reformation. Another contract remedy but not necessarily involving breach of contract is a request for reformation of a contract. *Reformation,* or altering a contract, is generally appropriate when a mistake was made in reducing the parties' oral agreement to writing or in contract cases in which one party made a mistake that the other party induced. The court reforms, or changes, the contract to conform to the parties' true intention.

Courts require that the evidence of the mistake be clear and convincing before ordering reformation. The court corrects the formal contract to reflect the parties' actual agreement. Thus, if an insurance policy issues and does not contain the coverage the parties orally agreed upon, a reformation action may be appropriate to change the contract to conform to the parties' true intent.

SUMMARY

The statute of frauds requires written contracts in the following situations:

1. Contracts involving the sale of or interest in land
2. Agreements that cannot be performed within one year
3. Promises to answer for the debt of another
4. Promises in consideration of marriage
5. Executors' promises to pay decedents' debts personally
6. Contracts for personal property sale for $500 or more

Otherwise, oral contracts usually are valid, even for most insurance contracts.

The parol evidence rule limits contractual terms to those terms the parties chose to commit to writing. Parol, or oral, evidence is admissible only to complete incomplete contracts; to clarify ambiguities; to bring justice to contracts involving fraud, accident, illegality, or mistake; to show that a condition was necessary for contract to take effect in the first place; or to effectuate transactions under the Uniform Commercial Code.

Courts interpret contracts by using several rules or maxims. They strive to give words their plain and ordinary meaning and attempt to effectuate the parties' intent. They also must examine parties' prior courses of dealings and apply trade usage of terms where necessary. Courts decide in some cases whether contracts are entire or divisible. They correct clerical errors and omissions and will invoke implied terms in addition to those terms the parties have expressed. Courts often must reconcile contradictory terms and ambiguities. In the end, a court must determine what is lawful and fair in each situation.

Third parties obtain rights under contracts either by assignment or by their status of third-party beneficiaries. Some rights are assignable and some not, and the U.C.C. has provisions directly applicable to assignments. Third-party beneficiaries include creditor, donee, and incidental beneficiaries. This chapter examines the differences in these categories and the relative rights of third-party beneficiaries under contracts.

Discharge of contract can occur by the parties' performance or agreement, but contract performance can become impossible because of unanticipated events. Performance can come about legally through payment, tender of performance, or substantial performance. Parties can agree to rescind a contract, or they can substitute new agreements, create novations, or discharge a contract via accord and satisfaction.

Impossibility of performance involves questions of objective versus subjective impossibility, changes in law, a party's death or incapacity, destruction of the subject matter of a contract, the other party's acts, temporary or partial impossibility, partial performance, frustration of purpose, commercial impracticability, statutes of limitations, or fraudulent alterations. The U.C.C. also applies to performance in specific situations.

Contractual conditions affect discharge, and in any given contract they can be either precedent, concurrent, or subsequent conditions, or any combination of the three. Breach of contract can occur by repudiation or anticipatory breach and can be either material or minor. The remedies for breach of contract include compensatory, punitive, extracontractual, and liquidated or unliquidated damages. Equitable remedies include specific performance, injunction, or reformation.

This has been the final chapter on basic contract law. Chapter 5 will focus on contract law as it applies to insurance and will conclude the contract law component of this text.

Chapter Notes

1. U.C.C. § 2-107.
2. U.C.C. § 2-201.
3. U.C.C. § 2-201(2).
4. U.C.C. § 2-201(3c).
5. U.C.C. § 2-201(3a).
6. U.C.C. § 8-319.
7. U.C.C. § 9-203.
8. U.C.C. § 1-206.
9. U.C.C. § 2-202.
10. U.C.C. § 2-202-a.
11. U.C.C. § 2-202-b.
12. U.C.C. § 2-307.
13. U.C.C. § 2-612(2).
14. U.C.C. § 2-612(2)(3).
15. U.C.C. § 2-204(3).
16. U.C.C. § 2-305(1).
17. U.C.C. § 2-309(1).
18. U.C.C. § 2-306(1).
19. U.C.C. § 2-306(1).
20. U.C.C. § 2-208.
21. U.C.C. § 2-302.
22. U.C.C. § 1-205(2).
23. U.C.C. § 1-205(4) and 2-208(2).
24. U.C.C. § 2-210(1).
25. U.C.C. § 2-210(2).
26. U.C.C. § 2-210(3).
27. U.C.C. § 2-210(4).
28. U.C.C. § 2-209(5).
29. U.C.C. § 1-107.
30. U.C.C. § 2-209(2).
31. Madeirence Do Brasil, S.A. v. Stulman-Emrick Lumber Co., 147 F.2d 399 (2d Cir. 1945), cited in U.C.C. §615, comment 8.
32. U.C.C. § 2-615(1).
33. U.C.C. § 2-615(2)(3).
34. U.C.C. § 2-615, comment 4.
35. U.C.C. § 2-614(1).
36. U.C.C. § 2-708 and 2-713.

37. Robert Keeton, *Basic Text on Insurance Law* (St. Paul, MN: West Publishing Co., 1971), n. 14, at pp. 455-458.
38. U.C.C. § 2-207.
39. U.C.C. § 2-509. *See also* U.C.C. § 2-510.

CHAPTER 5

Insurance Contract Law

The last three chapters have provided a basic understanding of American contract law. This chapter applies those concepts to insurance contracts and examines their distinctive features.

FEATURES DISTINCT TO INSURANCE CONTRACTS

The insurance contract provides protection if specified losses occur. Conditions, limitations, and exceptions become part of the insurance agreement because they define and limit those losses. Creating a contract that defines covered losses and is also comprehensible is a challenge that has troubled both insurers and insureds since the inception of written policies. Shortcomings in this area have resulted in public criticism, restrictive legislation, and adverse court rulings.

"Flood of Darkness"

In reviewing the language of a fire insurance policy in 1873, a court stated as follows:

> Whether [people] ought to be what they are, or not, the fact is, that in the present condition of society, men in general cannot read and understand these insurance documents. . . . Forms of applications and policies, of a most complicated and elaborate structure, were prepared, and filled with covenants, exceptions, stipulations, provisos, rules, regulations, and conditions, rendering the policy void in a great number of contingencies. . . . The compound, if read by [an insured], would, unless he were an extraordinary man, be an inexplicable riddle, a mere flood of darkness and confusion. . . . [I]t was printed in such

175

small type, and in lines so long and so crowded, that the perusal of it was made physically difficult, painful, and injurious. Seldom has the art of typography been so successfully diverted from the diffusion of knowledge to the suppression of it. There was ground for the premium payer to argue that the print alone was evidence, competent to be submitted to a jury, of a fraudulent plot. . . .[1]

In another court case, in 1975, the court decided that the holders of an insurance policy were not bound by its provisions because its printing was of "a size type that would drive an eagle to a microscope." The court added the following:

It cannot be reasonably assumed that the insured having average sight of a human being would be aware of the content of the questioned clause, at least in the absence of special optical equipment. . . . It should not be necessary for the insured to provide himself with a microscope in order to inspect the small print contained within his insurance policy. Neither should it be necessary for an insured to provide himself with an insurance policy to protect himself against the provision to be found within such small print of his insurance policy.[2]

A state insurance department study of the readability of insurance policies measured the standard automobile policy by the Flesch Readability Scale.[3] This scale assesses the readability of written documents by assigning point values for length and complexity of sentence structure. The higher the total score, the more readable the document. For the passages selected for this particular study, the Bible received a readability score of 66.97, and Einstein's Theory of Relativity scored 17.72. Both scored higher as to readability than the standard automobile policy at 10.31.

Current trends in insurance policy construction are toward more simplified language. Any new language in insurance contracts, however, requires interpretation by the courts. Therefore, the success of efforts at clearer expression remains to be seen.

The insurance contract has the same basic requisites as other contracts. There is a need for an agreement, competent parties, consideration, and a legal purpose. However, the insurance contract also has other distinctive features. Insurance contracts cover fortuitous events, are contracts of adhesion and indemnity, must have the public interest in mind, require the utmost good faith, are executory and conditional, and must honor reasonable expectations.

Fortuitous Events

While most contracts involve an exchange of money for goods or services, insurance contracts provide protection upon the occurrence of an uncertain, or fortuitous, event. The event is the insured peril. If the peril does not occur, no obligation of performance arises; therefore, the contract does not have to be carried out.

Not Wagering Agreements. An insurance contract is not a wagering agreement. Insurance is not a contract of chance, but a contract under which some of the rights of the parties are contingent upon certain events. Gamblers can experience either gain or loss through their wagers. In the insurance contract, the parties seek to replace loss caused by fortuitous events with no gain resulting on either side. Insurance is a device to reduce uncertainty, to maintain the status quo. Gambling, on the other hand, creates or increases uncertainty and will almost always effect a loss on one side.

Protection Afforded. It is not true that, if the peril does not occur, the insured receives nothing. The insured has received the protection of the insurance coverage. The insured is free to participate in the activities exposing him or her to peril, with the assurance that the insurer will make good any loss. The existence of insurance coverage can give the insured an advantage in transacting business with third parties. Thus, the insured receives something of value regardless of the amount the insurer ultimately must pay.

Contract of Adhesion

Courts recognize insurance contracts as *contracts of adhesion,* which are contracts one party draws up. The other party simply adheres, or assents, to the terms of these contracts. The insurer prepares the insurance contract and offers it to the insured, who has little opportunity to alter its words or terms.

Strict Construction. The hallmark rule for interpretation of the contract of adhesion is the so-called *rule of strict construction.* Under this rule, a court interprets any doubt or ambiguity in the contract against the insurer who wrote it. A court assumes that the insurer had every opportunity to serve its own best interests and that the insured, on the other hand, simply adhered to the agreement without understanding or reading its terms. Consequently, the insurer must pay the penalty for any ambiguity it creates.

Ordinary Meaning. If there is ambiguity, a court will interpret a contract against the party who drew it up. However, courts interpret insurance contract terms according to terms the parties have used. These terms have plain, ordinary, and popular meanings. As one justice stated, "Insurers who seek to impose upon words of common speech an esoteric significance intelligible only to their craft must bear the burden of resulting confusion."[4]

Application.   Courts often find ambiguity in insurance contracts and interpret contracts to mean what reasonable insureds would expect them to mean, thus protecting insureds' expectations.

For example, one court case involved an insured's death resulting from inhalation of carbon monoxide, a cause of death excepted from the policy's double indemnity rider, which guarantees a double payment in the event of death in many cases. The company, in an attempt to comply with a state requirement to print a brief description on the front page of the policy, had stamped, "DOUBLE INDEMNITY FOR FATAL ACCIDENT" in purple ink on the policy. The court allowed the insured recovery for double indemnity benefits even though the death had occurred by inhalation of carbon monoxide. The stamped writing superseded the printed rider, and the court resolved the conflict in the insured's favor.[5]

Indemnity

Indemnity, the most basic principle of property insurance, is reimbursement for loss. An insured is entitled to indemnity only to the extent of loss sustained. Property and liability insurance policies often provide that indemnification cannot place an insured in a better position than before a loss. If gain is possible, a contract is actually a gambling transaction.

Moral Hazard.   *Moral hazard* refers to any condition, other than a physical one, which increases the likelihood for destruction of the insured property. For example, the possibility of profiting from a property loss can lead to the temptation to destroy property. If property worth $5,000 could be insured for $10,000, the owner might be tempted to destroy the property and obtain double its value. This hazard is not a physical one, but an "intangible," or moral, hazard.

Valued Policy Laws.   Many states have passed *valued policy laws,* under which the value of real estate stated in the policy is the amount paid for total destruction of the property. These laws apply even if the amount paid is more than the property's actual value at the time of loss. Other valued policies fix values for personal property such as jewels and furs.

Valued policy laws are not contrary to the principle of indemnity because the parties established the amount of insurance beforehand with an eye toward the true value of the property. Valued policy laws encourage insuring parties to value property correctly and to avoid unnecessary disputes concerning property values in case of total destruction.

Insurable Interest. A person may not insure a property or a life in which he or she has no *insurable interest*. In other words, unless a person stands in some relation to property that would result in economic loss to him or her upon its destruction, then no insurable interest exists and that person cannot obtain coverage. A person cannot insure a neighbor's property, for example, and then collect for its later destruction.

Public Interest

Insurance contracts are different from other commercial contracts because insurance is more a necessity than a matter of choice. Therefore, insurance is a *business affected with a public interest,* as reflected in legislative and judicial decisions.

State laws restrict contractual rights for insurers in the public interest. For example, insurers cannot consider an applicant's race or religion in determining acceptability or rate classification. Many jurisdictions have adopted legislation limiting the insurers' rights to reject, cancel, or refuse to renew certain types of insurance. This legislation usually requires prescribed notice periods to cancel, nonrenew, or increase premiums on insurance contracts.

Utmost Good Faith

The insurance contract is a *personal contract requiring the utmost good faith* between the parties. In other words, neither party is concealing or misrepresenting anything. The parties' character, credit, and conduct are very important. Either party's failure to disclose vital information, dishonesty, or fraud can result in a court's declaring a contract voidable if the innocent party so chooses. Depending on the type of fraud, the contract might also be completely void.

Fiduciaries. *Fiduciaries* are those who serve in confidential capacities, such as agents, trustees, or guardians, and whose positions involve trust and confidence. They owe a duty of full disclosure to the principal beneficiary in all contractual and other dealings. Even when there is no fiduciary relationship, and no duty to advise the other party of all information possessed, a person may not actively misrepresent or defraud the other person under any circumstances.

Personal Nature. Because of the personal nature of the insurance contract, courts have established certain rules of interpretation for them. Thus, the property insurance contract does not "run with the land." For example, a fire insurance contract issued to a property owner to cover specific property will not, after sale of that property, extend the policy's protection to the new owner. The insurer granted the policy because of the applicant's character, reputation, and occupation. To permit the policy to pass as part of the sales transaction would require the insurer to assume loss possibilities that the insurer did not bargain for, but that the new owner presented. A new owner must apply for a new policy based on new information. The same rule applies to property other than real estate.

Assignability.   Although the rights in insurance contracts generally are not assignable, there are exceptions. In these cases, other factors, such as business necessity or the nature of the policy, outweigh the personal nature of the contracts.

Marine Insurance.   A marine policy may be assigned to someone else in the chain of transportation and ownership because goods are frequently transferred in distant ports under circumstances that would make obtaining new coverage very difficult. The coverage therefore follows the goods or cargo. The marine policy may be assigned to the insured's successor in ownership without an insurer's agreement or assent, avoiding delays that otherwise might be experienced in transporting the insured cargo. Parties can still expressly forbid assignment of a marine policy.

Life Insurance.   An owner of a life insurance policy may assign it. The owner may be someone other than the insured or a beneficiary. While the life insurance contract is a personal contract, it also can be an investment because many of these policies actually involve investment of funds for future use. These interests are therefore assignable.

Assignment transfers all ownership rights under the life policy. The assignee of a life insurance policy becomes the owner with or without the insurer's consent although a specific policy provision may restrict assignment without the insurer's or beneficiary's consent. The transfer of a life policy to a new owner may occur as the result of a contract, an assignment, or as a simple gift. The new owner has all rights of ownership and may borrow against the policy, cash it in, change the beneficiary, transfer it to another owner, or do any acts the owner of property may usually perform.

Executory and Conditional Contract

The insurance contract is both an executory and conditional contract. It is executory in that it is not executed fully until a loss occurs, and it is conditional simply because it contains many conditions.

The number of conditions and special language required in conditions have led to court rules of interpretation for insurance contracts that are often favorable to insureds. As a result, many policy forms and conditions have become highly standardized. Laws often require the use of standard policy language, which can limit the number of conditions in a policy. For example, identical language exists in many modern automobile policies. The definition of an insured, the circumstances for use of a vehicle, and the policy exclusions are identical or similar in various automobile policies.

Executory. Although an insured performs an insurance contract by paying the premium, the contract remains executory on the insurer's part. If it becomes necessary, one of the parties, the insurer, still must perform some act called for in the contract. The insurer does not execute its part of the agreement until a specified event occurs.

Conditional. The insurance contract is also subject to numerous conditions, including the occurrence of the insured event. Until that event occurs, the insurer need not perform.

Policies spell out the various conditions of the insurer's promise and settlement, as well as the insured's obligations. The insured must usually give notice of a loss within a specified period of time or as soon as practicable following the loss. For a fire insurance policy, an additional "proof-of-loss" statement may also be necessary to provide loss itemization.

Most liability policies also stipulate that the insured must cooperate with the company in the investigation and settlement of the case. An insured's failure to fulfill the duties of notice and cooperation may result in loss of policy protection. The insurer can usually make decisions regarding settlement of a case without the insured's consent and assumes duties in liability policies to investigate occurrences, make settlements, and defend any actions instituted.

Reasonable Expectations

Under the *doctrine of reasonable expectations,* courts interpret policies to include coverages that an average person would reasonably understand them to include, regardless of policy provisions. Insurers cannot enforce limitations and exceptions inconsistent with insureds' reasonable expectations.[6] This doctrine has resulted from the complexity of insurance policies, as well as from the facts that most policyholders do not read their policies; if they do, they fail to understand the terms. Additionally, an insured usually relies on an agent's knowledge and ability. The doctrine has spurred insurers to greater efforts to define coverages carefully, to indicate conditions and exceptions clearly, and to inform insureds of policy provisions that might bear on their expectations.

FORMATION OF INSURANCE CONTRACTS

To be enforceable, an insurance contract, like any other contract, must have an agreement consisting of a legally binding offer and an acceptance. The parties to the agreement must be competent, and there must be legally sufficient consideration and lawful purpose. The parties must have given genuine assent, but an insurance contract need not be in writing. This section focuses on the need for a binding agreement.

Agreement

Agents handle insurance almost exclusively. Insurers rely on agents to solicit business, take applications, and sometimes issue policies. Agents can create contract liability for insurers even though the insurer intended not to be bound. Commitments by insurance agents are binding on insurers if agency law imposes liability. Chapters 11 and 12 discuss agency law, which courts also apply to an agreement to determine whether it is binding on an insurer.

Insurance company agents vary as to the type of insurer they represent, degree of specialization, and authority to act for insurers. Some insurance companies employ their own exclusive agents and give them varying degrees of authority. Other companies employ independent agents who represent several insurers and have varying degrees of authority to bind insurers for coverages.

The insurance agent is the legal intermediary between the insurer and the insured. When parties purportedly enter into an insurance agreement, or some claim for benefits arises under an insurance contract, establishment of the following is necessary in evaluating the parties' liability:

- The existence of a contract
- The existence of an agency relationship
- The nature of the agent's representation
- The extent of the agent's authority
- The type of coverage involved
- The circumstances surrounding the agreement

Offer and Acceptance. When an agent contacts a prospective insured to sell an insurance policy, is the agent making an offer to contract or merely soliciting offers? As a general rule, the agent's selling efforts are merely a solicitation of offers that the insurer may not accept and are not offers themselves.

The application for insurance that the applicant signs and sends to the insurance company through the agent is the offer. The insurance policy issued later is the acceptance. If the policy the insurer issues does not conform to the application, or initial offer, the policy is a counteroffer requiring the applicant's specific acceptance.

Policy as Offer. Often the insurance applicant does not make an offer but merely invites the insurer to make an offer. For example, if an applicant has definitely not decided to take the insurance but submits an application with a premium to determine whether the insurer will accept the risk, the applicant has not made an offer. In that case, when the insurer issues the policy and the insured accepts it with payment of the premium, they have concluded an offer and acceptance. Similarly, if the policy the insurer issues does not comply with the coverage or rates the applicant requested, the policy is a new offer that the applicant may then accept or reject.

When a policy issued is merely an offer, the person named as insured does not have to accept it. To help avoid litigation in these cases, an agent should not deliver the policy to a proposed insured until receipt of a premium. When the agent mails a policy to an insured before receipt of a premium, it is possible that the insured may pay no premium for a considerable time. The status of the contract is questionable throughout that period. While no contract exists, the possibility of dispute over validity of the contract and alleged promises to pay the premium may be grounds for a lawsuit.

Communication of Offer. As with contracts in general, the communication of the offer to the offeree is essential in an insurance contract. One who does not know about an offer cannot accept it. Thus, when a policy is merely an offer, it is not binding as a contract until actual communication to the offeree or the offeree's agent, who can accept offers. Only the person to whom an offer is addressed can accept an offer. For example, if a proposed insured died before taking action to accept a policy, the widowed spouse could not accept the offer.

The mailing of an acceptance, if mailing is permitted as acceptance, binds an insurance contract at the time the acceptance is mailed, whether or not the other party receives the mailed acceptance. Thus, if the insurer's issuance of a policy is the offer, the insured's mailing of the premium in response to that policy (offer) is the binding acceptance.

Oral Contracts. Oral insurance contracts are as binding as written ones. When the insurance agent has authority to enter into oral agreements to bind coverage, the parties' words and conduct govern the offer and acceptance just as with any other contract. Generally, acts or words of intent to offer and accept establish a binding insurance contract. In the field of property and liability insurance, oral applications and contracts are common. On the other hand, in life insurance, written applications and contracts are necessary.

Property and Liability Insurance. The requirements of modern commercial life have necessitated immediate insurance coverage in many situations. For example, a person who enters into a contract to purchase property may assume the risk of loss for destruction of the property. It is therefore necessary to obtain insurance coverage without delay. In property and liability insurance, agents usually have authority to bind insurance companies immediately.

For example, Judy telephones agent Kathy and asks for "immediate fire insurance coverage on my home in the amount of $100,000." Kathy replies, "You're covered." The fire insurance company Kathy represents must provide fire insurance protection under this oral agreement.

Immediate Coverage. When the insurance agent and the prospective insured have not agreed to immediate property and liability insurance coverage, it is necessary to examine the parties' conversations, as well as the agent's authority, to determine when the policy becomes effective. If an agent obtains a prospective insured's fire insurance application without any assurance that the coverage would take effect immediately, the application is an offer that the insurer may accept by issuing a policy conforming with the offer. The prospective insured and the insurance agent may agree that coverage is effective immediately or may not refer to the effective date. In the latter situation, the coverage may not be effective until the insurer issues the policy.

Time Acceptance Takes Effect. Unless the parties agree otherwise, an acceptance made in the manner requested completes the agreement as soon as the offeree accepts. Thus, when an agent, Kathy, offers to insure Judy's house against fire with the insurance effective upon premium payment, and requests that Judy mail the premium check, coverage is effective when Judy mails the check. If the house burns while Judy's check is in transit, the insurer must pay benefits.

Life Insurance. The life insurance contract differs from the property insurance contract in several important ways:

1. A potentially long period of coverage, the life of the insured, is involved.
2. The parties often agree to a very large amount of coverage.
3. Specialized underwriting considerations regarding such factors as medical history and life expectancy enter into the insurer's consideration.

These factors have made insurers cautious in extending authority to insurance agents to enter into life insurance contracts. In the life insurance contract, the prospective insured offers to contract by submitting an application. Acceptance of the offer and formation of the contract are not effective under most life insurance policies until actual delivery of the policy to the insured and payment of the first premium. If the insurer does not accept the original application with the coverage and rate offered, the insurer is making a counterproposal, or counteroffer, that the prospective insured may accept or reject.

In the absence of a specific policy provision or agreement to the contrary, the life insurance contract is effective under the usual contract rules of offer and acceptance. For example, if Judy applies to the X Insurance Company for a life insurance policy and pays the first premium with the understanding that the insurance must be approved at X's home office, X's notification of approval is effective as an acceptance when mailed, without regard to whether Judy actually received the acceptance.

When Judy applies in writing for life insurance to the X Insurance Company, pays the first premium, and is given a receipt that states, "This insurance shall take effect on the date of approval of the application," subsequent approval at the home office is an acceptance of Judy's offer even though X Insurance Company does not notify her of the approval. The parties have agreed that acceptance will occur upon approval, and actual notification to the offeror, Judy, is not essential for an acceptance. The offeree, X Insurance Company, has performed its part of the bargain sufficiently to create a binding contract upon approval of the application.

Other Types of Coverage. Offer and acceptance of accident and health insurance policies are generally subject to rules applying to life insurance agreements. The parties understand that the application for coverage requires examination and approval in the insurer's home or regional office. There, an underwriter considers the special risk factors in the applicant's employment and health history before making any final decision to accept. Then, as in the case of most life insurance policies, the coverage becomes effective upon delivery of the policy to the insured and upon the insured's payment of the first premium.

In group insurance coverages, the insurance policy is issued to a group policyholder, which may be an employer, labor union, or some other association. The agreement is binding when the insurer accepts the group policyholder's application following the registration of the required number of certificate holders, or individual insureds. These agreements usually provide that the group policy is effective on a specified date, provided a certain percentage of eligible group members agree to accept the coverage and to become certificate holders under the policy.

Once the group policy is effective, individual certificate holders may obtain coverage automatically by applying to the plan, subject to the group policyholder's approval. If the plan requires underwriting individual certificate holders, coverage must await underwriting approval.

For example, travelers may obtain air terminal insurance through machines in airports. The insurer's forms for travelers' completion are the insurer's offer that the prospective insured may accept by completing the forms and mailing the application. The offeree's mailing of the acceptance creates a contract even if the insurer never receives the mailed acceptance.

Effective Date of Insurance Contracts. Determination of the exact moments insurance contract coverage begins and ends is of crucial importance. Unless a loss occurs within the policy coverage period, no benefits are payable.

The general rules of contract law concerning the time when acceptance becomes effective are also applicable to the insurance contract. Frequently the policy itself specifies the date and time when the insurance contract is effective. *Binders* and *conditional receipts* have both aided and complicated the law with respect to the effective dates of insurance contracts. Binders frequently apply to property and liability insurance, and conditional receipts apply to life insurance.

Binders. The binding slip, or binder receipt, is very important in insurance. They are of a temporary nature and provide evidence of insurance and interim coverage until an insurer approves and issues a policy to an insured. Binders are informal written contracts providing memorandums of the basic coverages and terms of the insurance agreement. They meet the requirements of modern business by providing evidence of immediate and temporary protection. Binders frequently provide extension of coverage for thirty days, pending issuance of the policy.

Even though a binder is usually evidence of a contract of insurance, the insurer may still prove that there was an oral understanding that the insurance was not to take effect until the happening of some condition. For instance, the condition might be that temporary coverage is not effective until another insurer assumes part of the risk. An insurer's cancellation of a binder must be according to the methods the policy prescribes. All policy provisions are effective the moment the binder is issued. The binder is effective until actual notice of cancellation or until issuance of a policy.

In property and liability insurance, binders provide immediate coverage when authorized agents issue them. A written policy that the insurer issues customarily in a similar situation controls the actual coverage of the binder. While the binder is a brief document, it must contain the basic information needed for an agreement and must indicate types of coverage so that the events insured against can be determined.

If an object such as an automobile is insured, the binder should describe the vehicle briefly and indicate the insured's name and the insurer's identity. The amounts of coverage must also be clear to establish policy limits. With agreement on these basic points, the more detailed policy provisions may be determined by reference to the policy to be issued. Exhibit 5-1 is a typical binder receipt for automobile insurance.

Conditional Receipts. Insurance companies do not use the word "binder" in life, health, and accident premium receipts. Instead, they call them "conditional receipts" and clarify that these receipts do not provide immediate coverage. Many legal disputes have arisen over the question of whether these receipts bind insurers to coverages, and courts have reached different decisions in these cases.

Most disputes about temporary insurance contracts concern life, health, and accident insurance. The long periods of policy coverage, the potentially large amounts of benefits involved, and the need for highly specialized underwriting regarding health history cause insurers to be cautious in binding these types of insurance, even temporarily. Insurers attempt to phrase the premium receipt in life insurance to avoid immediate coverage to the applicant and do not wish to be bound before learning whether the applicant is insurable.

While property and liability insurance binders have relatively standard form and content, the life insurance conditional receipt has at least three major forms: binding, approval, and insurability receipts.

Binding Receipts. A few life companies use *binding receipts* in much the same way as property insurance companies do. These receipts provide coverage on the date of the receipt and continue the coverage until a specified time or until the company disapproves the application. The customary practice, however, is for insurers to issue some form of conditional receipt.

Approval Receipts. *Approval receipts* reflect the insurer's intention not to be bound by a receipt until it actually gives approval. The approval is a condition precedent to the existence of coverage.

Most courts have upheld the condition where it is clear, permitting suspension of coverage until approval is given. Other courts hold that the applicant in these cases pays for a period of coverage that is never actually received. Courts hold that the insurers are collecting premiums while giving little more coverage than if they had received no premium. Thus, courts have interpreted approval receipts as expressing a

Exhibit 5-1
Binder Receipt

BINDER RECEIPT

The undersigned Company agrees to extend the following coverages as are indicated by the mark ☒ as respects the described automobile for a period of 30 days from the effective date indicated, pending the issuance of an automobile insurance policy. This extension of insurance shall be in accordance with the terms of the Company's auto insurance policies and manual of rates and classifications applicable in the state on the effective date of this agreement. This agreement may be cancelled by the Company by mailing written notice to the applicant stating when in accordance with any applicable statutes or policy terms such cancellation shall be effective.

Applicant: _____

COVERAGES: | A – Comprehensive ☐ ACV less $ _____ ded. | B – Collision ☐ ACV less $ _____ ded. | C – Property Damage ☐ $ _____ 000 |

D – Bodily Injury ☐ $ _____ 000 ea. person, $ _____ 000 ea. accident/occurrence | E – Med. Pay. ☐ $ _____ ea. person Loss _____ ded.

F – Fam. Comp. ☐ | G – C. Fam. Liab. ☐ $ _____ 000 ea. occurrence, and Med. Pay ☐ $ _____ ea. person | H – ☐ UMC

Pers. Inj. Prot. ☐ Less $ _____ ded. Add. or Excess Pers. Inj. Prot. ☐ $ _____ | Loss of Use ☐ T & L ☐

Insurance to apply on: Automobile _____

_____ _____ _____
Year Trade Name Identification Number

Receipt of $ _____ Cash ☐ Check ☐ is hereby acknowledged; Balance of $ _____ due

Effective date: _____, 19 ____. Date remittance received _____, 19 ____.

Lienholder and Address: _____ Date Lien Expires _____
                                                                              Month   Day   Year

$ _____ premium pays for Coverage ☐ A and ☐ B

If marked ☒ to _____
                     Month   Day   Year

The right of any refund during the encumbrance period is hereby assigned to the Lienholder named herein ☐ Yes ☐ No

CHECKS AND DRAFTS ARE RECEIVED SUBJECT TO COLLECTION ONLY

Agent _____ Institute Insurance Company

condition that afforded insurance coverage as of the date of the receipt but subject to later determination of insurability. These interpretations have led to the more extensive use of a third type of conditional receipt, the insurability receipt.

Insurability Receipts. *Insurability receipts* are the most frequently used life, accident, and health receipts. The typical language of insurability receipts stipulates that the insurance is effective on the date of the receipt or on the date of the medical examination, provided the applicant is insurable on that date. Under these receipts, even though the insurance is not effective unless the applicant is found insurable, the applicant's insurability on a specific date can still be determined even after the applicant's death. If the applicant dies after the issuance of the receipt, and it is found, by applying the company's objective underwriting standards, that the applicant would have been insurable on the date of the receipt, the coverage exists. Here are two examples:

- In the first example, Judy applies for life insurance and receives an insurability receipt dated May 1. The insurer's home office finds Judy insurable, but a car hits her before the insurer actually issues the policy. Because Judy was insurable on the date of the receipt, coverage is effective even though she was killed before the policy was issued.

- In a second example, Judy applies for life insurance and receives an insurability receipt dated May 1. This time, the insurer finds her uninsurable by application of objective underwriting standards. If a car hits and kills Judy before a rejection of the application has issued, there still is no coverage because she did not meet the company's insurability standards.

Exhibit 5-2 is a typical example of an insurability receipt in the life, accident, and health field.

Court Interpretation. The variety of conditional receipts and the complexity of their language have led some courts to view them as "instruments of confusion" that they interpret strictly against insurers. Some courts find the receipts ambiguous and interpret any doubts against insurers, because insurers prepare them, by holding that the conditional receipt provides immediate interim coverage. Most courts, however, find no life insurance in force until determination of an applicant's insurability.

When an applicant is determined insurable, the effective date of the insurance is retroactive to the date of the receipt. An insurer that has not determined insurability, or lack of it, at the time of an applicant's death must make that determination later. The evaluation must be in good faith, using the insurer's usual underwriting stan-

Exhibit 5-2
Conditional First Life Premium Receipt

This receipt must not be detached unless settlement of the first full premium has been made by the Applicant at the time of application and such premium amount meets the Company's minimum Premium rules.

CONDITIONAL FIRST LIFE PREMIUM RECEIPT: NO INSURANCE WILL BECOME EFFECTIVE PRIOR TO POLICY DELIVERY UNLESS THE ACTS REQUIRED BY THIS RECEIPT ARE COMPLETED. NO AGENT OF THE COMPANY IS AUTHORIZED TO CHANGE ANY ACT REQUIRED.

Received from _____ this _____ day of _____, 19____, the sum of _____ Dollars ($ _____) in connection with an application for Life Insurance in Institute Insurance Company which application bears the same date and printed number as this receipt.

If the sum indicated above equals the first full premium on the premium payment basis selected in the application for the insurance applied for and if the following acts are completed: (a) receipt by the Company of a fully completed application and amendments thereto, if any, which includes fully completed medical examinations if required by published underwriting rules because of the age of the Proposed Insured, the amount of insurance applied for or because of the Proposed Insured's past medical history or current condition and (b) completion of all investigation by the Company and the Company is satisfied that the Proposed Insured and (without prejudice to the Proposed Insured) each person proposed for coverage under the Family Rider or the Children's Rider (whichever is applicable and if applied for) is insurable and qualified under the Company's established rules, limits and standards on the plan and for the amount applied for and at the premium specified herein, the said insurance shall take effect and be in force subject to the provisions of the policy applied for from the date of the application or the last medical examination, whichever is later, or if no medical examination is required, the insurance shall take effect on the application date. Unless all acts required are completed, no insurance shall take effect nor be in force under the application or this receipt unless and until a policy has been manually delivered to and received and accepted by the Applicant and the full first premium specified in the policy has actually been paid to and accepted by the Company during the continued insurability of the Proposed Insured and (without prejudice to the Proposed Insured) during the continued insurability of each person proposed for coverage under the Family Rider or the Children's Rider (whichever is applicable and if applied for). Insurance under the Family Rider or the Children's Rider (whichever is applicable and if applied for) shall take effect at the same time and under the same conditions as the insurance on the Proposed Insured.

In any event, the amount of insurance becoming effective under the terms of this receipt is hereby limited to the extent that in the event of the death of the Proposed Insured the total liability of the Company shall not exceed $150,000, said amount to include any life insurance then in force with the Company and any benefits payable by the Company as a result of accidental death.

If the application is declined, the amount evidenced by this receipt shall be refunded.

_____
(Agent must sign here)

_____ Agent

NOTICE: This receipt is not valid for any premium for the insurance applied for except the first full premium thereon which in no event shall exceed one annual premium for such insurance together with the premium for interim term insurance, if any.

dards. If the company does not make the decision or makes an incorrect decision, a judge or jury must decide what insurability finding the company should reasonably have made.

Silence or Delay. The law of contracts requires unequivocal manifestation of both parties' mutual assent, either by words or conduct. At common law, courts consider either party's silence or delay as equivocal and insufficient acceptance to create a contract. This rule was subject to the qualification that if a prior course of dealings indicated that silence was acceptance, then those prior dealings would control. For example, for years an agent has insured Mike's property against fire under annual policies. At the expiration of one policy, and consistent with prior practice, the agent sends Mike a renewal policy and a bill for the premium. Mike holds the policy for two months, remaining silent, and then refuses to pay the premium on demand. Mike is liable for the premium accruing before his rejection. In the example, the course of prior dealings between the parties gave the offeror agent a basis for concluding that silence would constitute acceptance.

By contrast, the agent may direct a letter to Mike indicating, "Your fire insurance policy will be renewed for another three years unless I hear from you to the contrary." Mike does not reply. Because there was no prior course of dealings indicating that acceptance by silence may be inferred, continued coverage does not result automatically. Mike's silence is not an unequivocal promise to accept the agent's promise to renew and is not sufficient for acceptance.

Unsolicited Offers. Another reason for the contract rule that mere silence is not an acceptance of an offer involves unsolicited offers. If silence could be acceptance of an offer, those who sell goods or services could flood the country with offers that recipients would have to reject or otherwise be bound by contract to buy.

The law does not permit a seller to force on a prospective buyer the obligation of rejecting or returning offered goods or services. The enterprising insurance agent who mails policies to everyone in the area advising, "Unless I hear from you in a week, I will assume that you accept this coverage," imposes no duty to respond on the recipients of the offers. Similarly, if a merchant mails an unsolicited item to a person's home, that person has no duty either to respond or to return the item.

Delay in Acting on Insurance Applications. When an applicant gives an insurance company an application for coverage, and the company fails to act within a reasonable time, the insurer's silence or delay is not acceptance of the application. An insurer, however, may be liable under its contract if it negligently delays to act on an application within a reasonable time. Courts apply the rationale in this situation that insurance is a business affected with a public interest. Because insurers have generally solicited these offers, and because applicants have frequently paid premiums in advance, the insurer must act promptly in accepting or rejecting the offer. The insurer can also spread the risk of harm from delay in acting on the general public's applications.

The special nature of the insurance business imposes the duty of action on the insurer' part when considering applications for insurance. Some courts refer to the obligation as an "implied contract," while others assert that the insurance company should be estopped, or prevented, from claiming that the application was not accepted after the lapse of a reasonable time. Most courts, however, base recovery on the theory that the insurance company has been negligent and impose a duty on the insurer to act on the application, either by acceptance or rejection, without unreasonable delay. If the insurer has breached the duty, and the applicant suffers a loss, then liability should be imposed on the negligent insurer. Recovery thus rests on the tort of negligence instead of on contract law.

What constitutes unreasonable delay is a matter of fact. Among important facts are the distance of the insurance office considering the application from the office where the application was made, any special difficulties in underwriting the risk, any seasonal or other workload problems of the insurer, and the type of coverage involved.

Some state statutes prescribe the reasonable time limits within which an insurance company must act on an application. The problem of unreasonable delay can arise despite the immediate coverage afforded by property and casualty binders or life insurance conditional receipts. Property insurance binders often stipulate coverage for "thirty days only." Life insurance conditional receipts may be conditional and may not provide any interim coverage. In either case, an unreasonable delay in acting on the application could result in the imposition of coverage.

What Is Included in Insurance Contracts

The insurance contract is generally a result of negotiations. A frequent question is which papers and conversations form the ultimate agreement. Once an insurer writes the policy, courts consider all prior negotiations or agreements, written or oral, as merged into the writing. Every contractual term in the policy at the time of delivery and those written in afterwards as policy riders or endorsements with both parties' consent are part of the written agreement. The policy must refer to conditions, endorsements, applications, and other papers if they are part of the policy.

Advertising materials and circulars that insurers issue are not part of a contract unless the contract expressly states that they are. If these materials contain false representations, an insured may sue the insurer for fraud, but courts do not usually allow the wording of advertising materials to change actual policy terms.

In the insurance business, it is often necessary to add a new term to a policy or to modify or waive an existing term. Insurers issue *policy riders* or *endorsements* for these purposes. They put in writing pertinent information about terms and can be binding on the parties as though they were in the original policy. Courts require evidence that insurers have communicated the addition of riders or endorsements to insureds.

Incomplete Agreements

Even though oral contracts of insurance are valid, written contracts are preferable to oral ones because oral contracts raise too many questions. Oral agreements often give rise to lawsuits. Lawsuits about oral agreements often come down to one person's word against another's, with a judge or jury having the last word. An insured who does not have a written contract may be unable to recall an oral conversation with sufficient accuracy to persuade a jury of its content.

Oral Insurance Contracts. Oral contracts to write property and liability insurance are common, particularly when the application process and binder are completed by telephone with a computer enacting the coverage. The demands of modern commercial life require the ability to obtain insurance coverage instantaneously.

Oral contracts are not as frequent in life and accident and health insurance. In the life and health fields, conditional receipts frequently provide evidence of interim coverage. In all oral insurance contracts, as well as in the case of informal written contracts, such as preliminary binders and conditional receipts, the final contract is the policy form itself. The crucial question is what contract language is in force from the time of the original oral agreement or informal written contract until the insurance contract is written.

Terms That Must Be Agreed On. An agreement to insure must include certain elements. The oral statements or informal written contract must indicate the types of coverage sought.

First, what are the risks or events insured against? Was fire, accident, liability, or life insurance purchased? Second, what object or premises, if any, is to be insured? If liability insurance in connection with ownership of property is involved, what is the address of the premises involved? A reasonable identification is necessary. If reference is made only to "my residence" and the proposed insured has several residences, the identification is ambiguous and can result in no coverage.

Third, the amount of insurance must be agreed upon to establish policy limits and the insurer's liability. Fourth, the insured's name must be known, although it is not necessary to establish the insurer's identity at the moment of the agreement.

It is also desirable that the parties indicate the duration of the coverage, although this may be implied from the parties' past dealings.

Terms Implied. If the parties agree to these basic elements, then the parties and the courts may turn to several other sources, including previous dealings between the parties, customary usage of terms, and legal requirements, to establish what terms to infer from the oral or informal written agreement.

Previous Dealings. Previous dealings between the parties provide the most accurate basis for implying terms of an insurance contract. If an insured requests that an agent "renew my fire policy," the renewed policy implies all the terms of the previous policy, including the amounts of coverage and premium. Provisions of renewal contracts by implication are the same as those of an existing policy.

Customary Usages. An insurer's customary usage of terms provides another important source for establishing terms the parties have not mentioned explicitly. What type of policy does an insurer usually issue in a given situation? What type of policy do most insurers usually issue?

The policy language and conditions set forth in the insurer's other contracts are a good source for supplying implied terms. If the particular insurer does not usually provide a certain coverage, the policy in question impliedly contains the provisions of policies customarily issued for this type of coverage. Where the parties have not specified the amount of premium, and there have been no previous dealings between them, the court implies the rate the insurer has filed with the insurance regulatory authorities or the rate the insurer usually charges others for this type of risk.

Finally, the courts consider the insured's insurance needs and practices by comparing them with those of others engaged in similar occupations. While these needs and practices may bear on the implied terms, an insured's unique situation may not necessarily result in implied insurance provisions.

Legal Requirements. In many lines of coverage, statutory requirements and administrative regulations have prescribed policy language. When an oral contract or a binding receipt for fire insurance is involved, statutory provisions contain the applicable language. State law prescribes many provisions such as definitions of terms, right to convert group life insurance to other types of coverage, and life insurance coverage in the event of suicide.

Insurance Company Designation. An agent representing two or more insurance companies can agree to provide coverage to an applicant without designating the insurer's identity at the outset. In the event of a loss before the time the actual policy has been issued, a question can arise as to which insurance company the agent intended to bind to coverage.

If an agent has placed previous business or oral renewals for an insured with a particular company, there is little dispute about whether that agent's accepting another oral agreement makes the same insurance company liable. The parties' previous dealings imply that company's liability. When, however, there have been no previous dealings between the parties or when the agent has switched companies several times in making renewals, more difficult problems arise.

If the agent has made a note or memorandum indicating the company that will write the coverage, the note is sufficient to bind that company. The agent must have made some outward indication of intent. For instance, dictation into dictating equipment can be a sufficient record. The agent's mere mental resolve to place business with "Company X tomorrow" is not sufficient to bind Company X if the loss occurs before an actual notation.

In one court case, an applicant for insurance requested that an insurance agency president place builders' risk insurance on two properties that the applicant owned, one property on Quincy Street and another on Van Buren Street. The agreement was oral, and the president made an ambiguous note to place the coverage with Ohio Farmer's Insurance Company. The agency later submitted an application for insurance for coverage on the Van Buren Street property, but not for the Quincy Street property.

A tornado damaged the Quincy Street property before Ohio Farmer's issued the actual policy. The court held that the oral binder obligated Ohio Farmer's to provide the requested coverage. While the oral binder was sufficient to bind coverage, the insurance agency was required to designate a company to assume the coverage. Here the agency clearly indicated a choice (Ohio Farmer's), although, through inadvertence, it omitted the Quincy Street property from the actual application.

The needs of modern business require and justify reliance on oral agreements of insurance agents entered into while acting within their apparent authority. Agents have considerable latitude in granting oral binders, and in this case the obvious intent was to bind Ohio Farmer's, which was responsible for the tornado damage.[7]

Thus, an insured may have an insurance policy with a company the insured has never heard of if the agent selects the insurer. An agent who has designated an insurer is no longer liable even though the insurer received no notification. There may be a violation of the agent's duty to the insurer in disregarding instructions, but the responsibility to the insured remains the same.

Failure To Read. A party to a contract is assumed to know about that contract's provisions. Written contract terms bind a party, regardless of whether that party reads and understands the words. However, courts, through the doctrine of reasonable expectations for example, have been reluctant to hold insureds responsible for knowing or for having read insurance policy terms.

It is not realistic to assume that insureds read and understand insurance policies. The doctrine of reasonable expectations is the principle that courts should interpret an insurance contract to provide the coverage a reasonable insured would expect under the circumstances. The insured, however, is still bound by the terms of an insurance contract. Special circumstances, such as mistake, misrepresentation, or fraud, may negate an insured's contractual obligations.

Delivery of Insurance Policies

Delivery is placing an insurance policy in the insured's hands or control. Key legal issues concerning delivery involve the parties' intention that a contract is not effective until delivery of the subject matter of the agreement. This differs from general contract law, which does not require that a contract be delivered to be enforceable.

In most bilateral contracts involving the exchange of promises, delivery is not essential to completion of the agreement. In many unilateral contracts involving an offeree's performance of an act, delivery of goods or services may be required as acceptance.

In the case of insurance contracts, there is no common law or statutory requirement that an insurance policy be delivered before the formation of an insurance contract. Still, in cases where there is no oral agreement, binder, or other written memorandum, the contract does not usually bind the insurer until delivery of the policy and payment of the first premium.

Delivery provides evidence of creation of the contract and communication of the insurer's acceptance of the insured's offer. The insurance policy is binding only upon delivery and the meeting of all conditions precedent.

Property and Liability Insurance. In property and liability insurance, delivery is rarely in dispute. The wide use of preliminary oral agreements and written binders gives rise to effective dates of policy coverage that seldom involve the question of policy delivery. However, policy delivery has been the subject of litigation in life insurance. It is customary in life insurance applications, as well as in some life policies, to provide that coverage is not effective until delivery of the policy and payment of the first premium.

Life Insurance. The life policy conditions precedent of delivery and payment of premium make it clear that no coverage exists until actual delivery of the policy to the insured. Delivery of the life insurance policy is clear evidence of the insurer's intent to be bound. Even so, courts have interpreted "delivery" broadly.

Courts interpret *constructive delivery,* which is an intended but not an actual delivery, as equivalent to physical delivery, even in absence of actual physical delivery of the policy. For example, Y Insurance Company mails a life insurance policy to its agent with a letter stating, "This policy is effective when you physically deliver it to Mike." Y also writes a letter to the applicant, Mike, stating, "We have mailed your policy to the agent, and it will be effective when the agent hands the policy to you." Mike dies in an accident after the letters and policy are mailed, but before they are received. Under these circumstances, Mike's beneficiary can recover the life insurance proceeds, notwithstanding the expressed intention requiring actual physical delivery. When no other decision or act remains to be performed other than the mere physical handing-over of a policy, a court will decide that a constructive delivery has been made.

On the other hand, when delivery is required under the life insurance policy, the delivery may be subject to a condition. For example, Y Insurance Company mails a life insurance policy to Mike with a letter stating, "This policy will become effective when you pay $100 to the agent." Mike is killed in an accident after receipt of the letter and policy, but before paying the $100. Y is not liable under the policy. Delivery of the policy was subject to a condition, and that condition was not met. Evidence may show that the policy was placed in Mike's possession, subject to the condition of premium payment.

Conditional Receipts. Although conditional receipts in life insurance may provide interim coverage, the delivery requirement is also significant. If delivery actually occurs, courts view it as communicating the insurer's acceptance of the insured's application. If the conditional receipt gives the insurer the right to refuse to deliver a permanent policy, actual delivery or the insured's declination of delivery has strong impact on the question of whether the policy became effective.

Clauses relating to delivery of life insurance policies, inserted in both policies and applications for life insurance, are thus valid and enforceable. The increased use of conditional receipts has lessened the significance of delivery, and some courts have applied the concept of constructive delivery broadly enough to impair the effectiveness of the requirement. Still, the requirement continues in most life policies and remains the subject of litigation in cases of death before actual delivery of the policy.

First Premium Payment.   As in the case of policy delivery, the parties to an insurance contract may stipulate that the policy is not effective until payment of the first premium. In the absence of an express (clear) agreement, it is generally understood that payment of the first premium is not necessary to the validity of an oral preliminary contract, but that payment will occur upon delivery of the policy.

Even in the absence of an express promise to pay a premium, an implied promise to pay a reasonable premium is sufficient consideration to support an insurance contract. If, however, it is clear that the parties intend that no contract arises until the first premium payment, then no contract is complete until that payment occurs.

INSURANCE AS THIRD-PARTY BENEFICIARY CONTRACT

Insurance contracts provide many examples of third-party beneficiary agreements. The life insurance policy is one of the best-known examples. The contract between the insured and the insurer is for the benefit of a third person, the beneficiary, who seldom gives consideration for this benefit and is usually a donee beneficiary. The rights of beneficiaries under life insurance policies may usually be altered or eliminated during the insured's life if the policy provisions permit.

Third-Party Interests in Liability Insurance

Liability insurance protects an insured against loss caused by the insured's doing something wrong, usually by negligence, to a third person. Although a named insured obtains the policy, the protection may extend to others, such as additional drivers of the insured's car.

The victims of the insured's negligence also benefit from that liability coverage. In recent years some states have adopted *direct-action statutes,* which permit injured persons to sue the defendant's insurance company directly, or at least to join the insurer in an action against the insured. In most jurisdictions, however, the purpose of liability insurance is to indemnify the insured who is required to pay a loss he or she negligently causes, so the third party cannot sue under the insurance policy until the claim has been reduced to judgment against the insured. Only after a favorable judgment, and after the insurer has declined payment of benefits, may the third party sue the insurer.

Sellers and Buyers of Real Estate

Though frequently unaware of it, sellers of real estate are exposed to loss. A buyer of real estate obtains an equitable interest in it at the moment both parties sign the agreement of sale. *Equitable* means reasonable, just, and fair. The real estate is the buyer's, subject to the payment of the purchase price, under the *doctrine of equitable conversion*. One result of this equitable ownership is that the buyer bears the chance of loss. If the property is destroyed before legal transfer, the buyer must still pay the full purchase price.

The buyer may eliminate this problem by having the contract provide that the burden of any loss shall be on the seller until actual transfer of title. After that time, of course, the loss exposure lies with the buyer, and the seller's responsibility terminates.

There are three possible situations in which the loss exposure could be on the buyer:

1. Only the seller has insurance coverage on the property sold.
2. Both the seller and buyer have separate coverage.
3. The seller and buyer purchase an insurance policy together.

The first arrangement, that the seller alone has insurance, is the most common in sales of residences. If fire damages or destroys the property, the sale still goes through.

The second arrangement, that the seller has insurance and the buyer purchases insurance on the property to protect their respective interests, is usual in commercial transactions and in some sales of residences. This is a good arrangement for the buyer, who then controls the type of coverage, the amount, and the insurer. Both recover to the extent of their respective losses. If the loss is total, both recover completely.

The third arrangement is the most sophisticated. If the seller and buyer together have obtained fire insurance on the property covering their respective interests, any insurance proceeds are distributed to make each party whole. For example, the seller collects policy proceeds to the extent of the unpaid purchase price, and the buyer collects to the extent of the deposit.

Mortgagor's and Mortgagee's Interests

Both the mortgagor and mortgagee have separate and distinct insurable interests in mortgaged property. The *mortgagor* is the buyer of property who gets a mortgage, and the *mortgagee* is the lender who provides the mortgage. Although it is customary for the parties to stipulate in the mortgage who will obtain insurance on the property, the provision is sometimes omitted. If the parties make no provision for insurance, one of three situations may exist:

1. The mortgagor may obtain separate insurance on the property. If so, the policy is only for the mortgagor's benefit.
2. The mortgagee may obtain separate insurance on the property. If so, money paid by the insurer in the event of loss does not accrue to the mortgagor's benefit (is not payable to the mortgagor).
3. The mortgagor may obtain insurance for the mortgagee's benefit. The mortgagee may receive an assignment of the policy, or the policy may contain a standard mortgage clause making the policy payable to the mortgagee "as the mortgagee's interest may appear."

Limited Interests in Realty

Legal issues often arise with respect to limited interests in real property. Limited interests are any interests in real property short of legal ownership, such as lease interests or life estates.

Lease Interests.   Courts are divided with respect to the lessor's and the lessee's rights to recover under insurance policies covering insured property. The *lessor* is the owner of the leased property, and the *lessee* is the tenant. Some courts uphold the principle of indemnity and subscribe to the theory that the total insurance payment cannot exceed the loss, while other courts permit a profit from an insured loss.

Until relatively recently, fire insurers of lessors did not make subrogation claims against lessees for the lessees' liability in causing fire damage to insured property, but that has changed. Protection may take the following forms:

1. Endorsement of the lessor's fire policy by which the insurer waives its subrogation rights against the lessee
2. Inclusion of a provision in the lease placing "all-risks" loss on the lessor
3. Inclusion of the lessee as an additional insured on the lessor's policy

4. Purchase of an insurance policy by the lessee protecting him or her against liability for causing damage to the lessor's property
5. Purchase of a separate fire policy by the lessee covering the leased premises

Life Estates. A *life estate* is an interest in real property for the duration of a person's life. The person having that interest is a *life tenant,* and the person who has an interest in the property after the life tenant's death has a *remainder interest.*

The general rule is that if a building has been insured before, and is destroyed after, the creation of a life tenancy, the destruction converts the interests in the property to personal property, and the life tenant has only a life estate in the insurance contract proceeds. This arrangement is not satisfactory from the life tenant's or the remainder-person's standpoint, and both would be better off if specific arrangements were made in advance for insurance coverage to apply towards repairs.

A life tenant, holding a policy in his or her own name without designating the remainder-person as an additional insured, may recover the entire value of the property in case of a loss, even if it exceeds the cash value of the life estate. However, insurers often choose to overlook this deviation from the principle of indemnity. Otherwise they would be asserting a position inconsistent with having collected the premium corresponding to the full value of the property. Furthermore, the amount saved by resisting the life tenant's claim might not be worth the cost of defense in expense and loss of good will. Also, the life tenant could be "insured," possessing a representative insurable interest in part on behalf of the remainder-person. If so, however, some of the proceeds should be held for the remainder-person's benefit.

Generally, in the absence of specific provisions to the contrary, the life tenant need not keep the premises insured for the remainder-person's benefit or to repair accidental damage to the property not due to his or her fault.

Sellers and Buyers of Goods

The doctrine of equitable conversion applies only to real estate, and not to sales of goods. Even after full payment of the purchase price, a seller of goods who keeps possession of them until the buyer comes to get the goods assumes the chance of loss until the buyer either receives the goods or refuses to accept them.[8] The seller, having control of the goods, must take care of them and, to protect against possible casualty or theft loss, should insure them.

REPRESENTATIONS AND WARRANTIES IN INSURANCE

Statements on an insurance application are called *declarations* and are usually classified as either (1) *representations* or (2) *warranties.*

Representations are oral or written statements that an applicant for insurance makes concerning the loss exposure and that induce an insurer to make the insurance contract. Representations precede and accompany the contract and are not matters about which the parties contract. In other words, a prospective insured may represent on an application that he or she has no history of traffic violations or accidents to induce an insurer to issue a policy, but the representation is not the subject matter of the contract.

Representations

False representation, or *misrepresentation,* makes an insurance contract voidable. The following are the elements required to establish false representation:

- There must be misrepresentation.
- The misrepresentation must be of a material fact.
- The insurer must rely upon the misrepresentation.

These elements are the same as those for fraud, except that intent is not a necessary element of false representation. An insurer's detriment is presumed in cases of false representation because the insurer issued a policy in reliance on false information.

That there was neither intent to deceive nor reckless disregard for the truth is the most crucial difference between fraud and misrepresentation. Even an innocent misrepresentation, if material and the insurer relied on it, makes the contract voidable. The loss that an insurer may be asked to indemnify is a different likelihood of loss from that which the insurer assumed.

Representations and misrepresentations refer only to conditions at the time the contract is made. Promises of conditions to exist after the completion of the contract do not involve representations. Thus, conditions represented must exist at the time the contract is made, but not necessarily later. An applicant may withdraw representations found untrue at any time before the completion of the contract, but not afterwards.

Misrepresentation. Misrepresentations are misstatements of a past or present fact. While an insurer may verify some facts easily, such as the kind of building construction, the make of a car, or the location of property, an insurer cannot verify some facts so easily and must rely on the applicant's word. Although the rule permitting avoidance of an insurance contract because of misrepresentation originated in the concept of fraud, something less than fraud is sufficient to establish misrepresentation.

Misrepresentation of Opinion and Belief. Misrepresentation is the making of any untrue or misleading statement, intentional or not. Some cases involving expressions of opinion qualify this rule, and statutory language sometimes specifies that the misrepresentation must be willful or intentional.

Statements of opinion and belief involve matters of judgment, possible inaccuracy, and personal viewpoint, rather than objective fact. Because an insurer should recognize subjectivity, courts frequently require evidence of fraudulent intent before they permit avoidance of the policy. In insurance law, therefore, it is important to determine whether the misrepresentation was of fact or of opinion. If the insured did not actually hold the opinion but said so, the misrepresentation is grounds for avoidance of the policy.

Most of the confusion in law regarding misrepresentation has arisen in life insurance cases. For example, in completing an application for life insurance, the applicant must answer the following questions:

1. Have you ever had any ailment or disease of the stomach?
2. Have you had medical consultation within the last five years?

The insured answers both questions, "No," although at the time of the application the insured had experienced a spasm of the esophagus and had undergone a physician's treatment for the ailment within the last five years. The insurer would not have issued the policy if it had known these facts, so the representations were material. The response to the question regarding "ailment or disease of the stomach" is an opinion because a layperson may not understand whether an ailment of the esophagus was an ailment of the stomach.

If the applicant answers in good faith, the insurer cannot avoid the policy. However, the statement regarding prior medical consultation was a representation of fact. A statement indicating no medical consultation would permit avoidance of the policy, even without fraudulent intent. Even innocent misrepresentations of material facts permit avoidance of an insurance policy.[9]

Statements of opinion are false only if the person did not have that opinion. Thus, the nsured's intent is important, and the insurer must establish that the insured spoke fraudulently and did not have the alleged opinion. An insured's opinion of his or her health or the value of his or her home may be mistaken. Still, if the insured honestly holds the opinion, it may be valuable to the insurer's estimate of the loss exposure. If the insured misrepresents the opinion, the insurer is induced to accept a loss exposure other than that agreed to and may avoid the contract.

As another example, a person owns a building with an actual value of $150,000, carrying a mortgage of $75,000. In applying for insurance on the building, the owner represents that the building is worth $175,000, and the outstanding mortgage is $50,000. The representation of the value of the building is an opinion and, although the amount estimated was far from accurate, that fact alone does not justify the insurer's avoidance of the policy. The insurer must show that the applicant actually did not hold this opinion but fraudulently misrepresented its value.

The question of intent is vital when the representation concerns opinion and belief. The representation regarding the amount of the mortgage, by contrast, represents an external fact and not a question of opinion or judgment. The fact is material and would permit avoidance of the policy even though the misrepresentation was innocent. The question of the insured's intent is immaterial in the case of objective or descriptive representations.

Material Fact. The second element for an insurer's defense of misrepresentation is that the false statement must relate to a material fact. As in concealment, the test of a material fact is whether the insurer was influenced or induced to enter into the contract in reliance on the representation. If so, the fact was material.

Mere silence on the insured's part is not a representation. A representation requires an active statement or conduct, even just shaking one's head. Mere silence can, however, give rise to the defense of concealment. There is a duty to speak in many cases involving concealment, but there is no such duty in misrepresentation. Concealment requires fraudulent intent.

For example, that a fire insurance application represents a house to be "brick" when the house actually is wood involves misrepresentation of a material fact. The insurer assumes a much different loss exposure than represented. The insurer could avoid the policy, assuming that the insurer's reliance on the representation was reasonable. If, however, the applicant says the house is white when it is blue, the statement involves a false representation but it does not relate to a material fact.

Insurer's Reliance. An insurer must have relied upon a misrepresentation for that misrepresentation to be grounds for avoiding a contract. An insurer's investigation of facts the insured reported affects the insurer's right to avoid the policy because of misrepresentation. An insurer, however, who discovers the falsity of the representations cannot claim reliance on them. If the investigation discloses facts that place on the insurer the duty of further inquiry, then it is difficult for the insurer to show reasonable reliance.

For example, suppose Mary received notice of revocation of her driver's license four days after she applied for an automobile policy. The insurer knew Mary had been previously insured with an insurance company specializing in substandard automobile insurance business. Mary's application reported two tickets for traffic violations in an eight-month period before the application. The insurer hired an independent investigative agency to check Mary's background, but the insurer made no check regarding motor vehicle records. The application itself showed facts that placed a duty upon the insurer to investigate further than it did. The insurer had no right to rely on Mary's representations. An insurer may not avoid a policy for misrepresentation if its reliance on representations was not justified.

Statutory Qualifications. State statutes limiting an insurer's defense based on misrepresentation often require that misrepresentation be intentional or may require materiality, meaning that the misrepresentation had a substantial effect on the insurer's decision whether to issue a policy.

Statutory Requirement of Intent. The New York Standard Fire Policy of 1943, adopted as the standard fire policy in nearly every state, provides as follows:

> This entire policy shall be void if, whether before or after a loss, the insured has *willfully* concealed or *misrepresented* any material fact or circumstance concerning this insurance or the subject thereof. . . .[10]

Therefore, insurers cannot avoid the fire insurance policy or policies that contain fire insurance coverage such as the homeowners policy because of innocent misrepresentation. Many states have similar provisions for life insurance, and many set forth alternative requirements that the misrepresentation must have either (1) been made with the "intent to deceive," or (2) affected or materially increased the likelihood of loss.

Determination of Materiality. A statement of fact is material if it may have influenced the insurer's appraisal of the risk or influenced the premium rate.

In automobile liability insurance, misrepresentations are material when they relate to the insured's previous driving record, moving violations, and prior cancellations. For example, a failure to disclose previous policy cancellations is material to the insurer's acceptance of the risk. An insurer would not accept a risk in such a circumstance.

A court may determine materiality on two different bases. The first is the *objective reasonable insurer's standard,* which asks, "What would a reasonable insurer have done with knowledge of the true facts?" The court would examine what most insurers would have done in a similar situation. The second test the court might apply is the *subjective individual insurer's standard,* which asks, "What should this insurer have done with knowledge of the facts misrepresented?"

Statutory Modification. To prevent insurers' use of immaterial or technical defenses, many states have enacted statutes modifying the insurers' defenses as to the effect of insureds' representations. These statutes fall basically into two groups with respect to evidence of materiality, requiring proof of (1) an increase of risk or (2) contribution to the loss:

- *Increase-of-risk statutes* are more common and may set either an objective or a subjective standard for determining materiality. One state statute may express a choice for the subjective individual insurer standard, while another state statute may provide that no misrepresentation is material unless the misrepresentation increased the risk of loss. Another statute may use the phrase "materially affected the risk," which probably conveys the same meaning as increasing the risk of loss.

  An example is a case in which, contrary to the insured's representation, there was a driver under twenty-five years of age in the household. Automobile insurers customarily charge higher premiums to younger insureds because they increase the risk of loss. The representation here was material.

- *Contribute-to-loss statutes* modify the law more radically and are not as common as increase-of-risk statutes. The rule under most of these statutes is that, regardless of materiality, the breach of a provision does not avoid the contract where, from its very nature, it could not contribute to the destruction of the property. On this theory, a court may find, for example, that a contribute-to-loss statute prevents avoidance of a fire insurance policy if the breach relates to the following:

  1. A representation that the insured had never been refused other insurance
  2. A provision requiring the insured to install mechanical fire extinguishers
  3. A requirement that the insured furnish a certificate of a magistrate or notary public as a part of the proof of loss
  4. A provision against other, concurrent, or additional insurance

Misrepresentation of Age. One of the most common misrepresentations is that of age, with applicants usually saying they are younger. If an insurance application asks about age, it may be a material fact. In the case of life insurance, the age of the applicant is crucially important to underwriting and rating.

Most state statutes require that all life and health insurance policies issued in the state contain an *age-adjustment clause,* typically stating as follows:

Age and Sex

If the Insured's age or sex has been misstated, any amount payable by the Company under this policy shall be such as the premium paid would have purchased on the basis of the correct age or sex.

Under this provision the amount payable upon the insured's death is adjusted if the insured misrepresented his or her age. Insurers set different premium rates for different ages. The amount payable upon death is the amount of insurance the premium paid would have purchased for an applicant of the actual age of the applicant at the time the insurance was taken out. Understatement of age is a material misrepresentation and is a ground for avoidance of a life insurance policy if there is no age-adjustment clause.

Construction of Representations. Misrepresentation of facts, ideas, and circumstances can assume many forms. The problem of when a representation becomes a misrepresentation sufficient to justify avoidance of an insurance policy can be difficult. Courts often interpret representations in favor of insureds. Even when a representation is not literally true, it is not a misrepresentation if it is "substantially" true, which means that it is more true than it is false.

To illustrate, an application for an accident and health policy may ask whether the insured has ever experienced a "serious injury." In a lawsuit based on the policy, the insurer shows that the applicant had fallen forty feet from a tree as a child. Whether that injury was serious is for the jury to determine. If failure to mention all injuries sustained in life can be the bases for policy avoidance, few policies would stand.

Whether an inaccurate objective fact is substantially true depends upon its materiality to the agreement. The test of materiality, in turn, is whether the contract would have been made had the truth been told.

Warranties

In general contract law, a *warranty* is a written or oral statement that a certain fact is true. In insurance law, warranties are statements or promises in a policy that, if untrue, would render the policy voidable, whether or not they are material. Strict application of this common law definition too often resulted in insurers attempting to escape liability for reasons not material to the person or property involved.

Because of the harshness of the warranty doctrine, courts, whenever possible, have interpreted statements as representations rather than as warranties. For a promise to be a warranty, (1) the parties must have clearly and unmistakably intended it to be a warranty, and (2) the statement must form a part of the contract itself. Absent either of these requirements, the stated fact or promise is a representation, rather than a warranty.

An insurer may require that an applicant agree to a policy provision that statements of fact or promises in the application are warranties. Therefore, if the facts the applicant stated are wrong in any respect, the insurer may avoid the policy.

Distinguished From Representation.   The different legal requirements and consequences of warranties and representations make it important to distinguish them clearly. Exhibits 5-3 and 5-4 clarify these distinctions, which are as follows:

1. Warranties are part of the final insurance contract. Representations are merely collateral, or indirect, inducements to the contract.
2. Warranties are presumed to be material, and their breach makes the contract voidable. Representations must be material. That is, the insurer must prove that the representation induced it to enter into the contract for the misstatement to permit the insurer's avoidance of the contract.
3. Warranties are either written in the policy expressly or incorporated by reference. Representations may be oral, written in the policy, or written on another paper and need not be incorporated by reference expressly.
4. Warranties require strict compliance. Representations require substantial truth only.

Incontestable Clause.   The *incontestable clause,* required by all states in life, accident and health, and group life insurance policies, is unique. In insurance it is customary for the parties to agree that they will not contest the validity of the contract after a certain period.

This unique clause is contrary to one of the basic maxims in contract law, that fraud vitiates [negates] consent." Genuine assent cannot be based on fraud. In life and accident and health insurance, the maxim is that "fraud vitiates consent, except in a life insurance contract after the contestable period has expired. Thus, an insurer cannot

Exhibit 5-3
Insured's Statements Pertaining to Risk Upon Application for Insurance

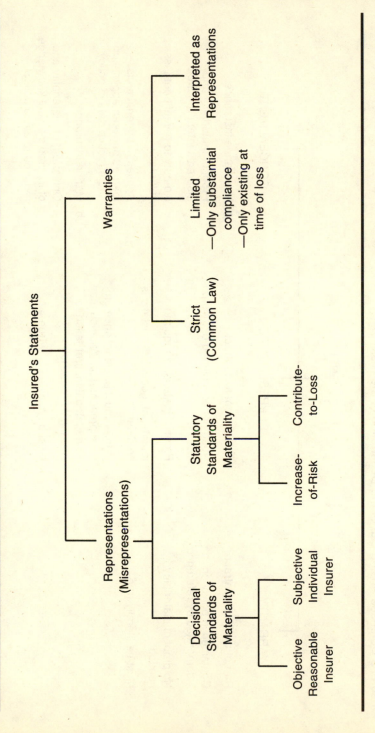

Exhibit 5-4
Insurer's Defenses Arising Out of the Description of the Risk

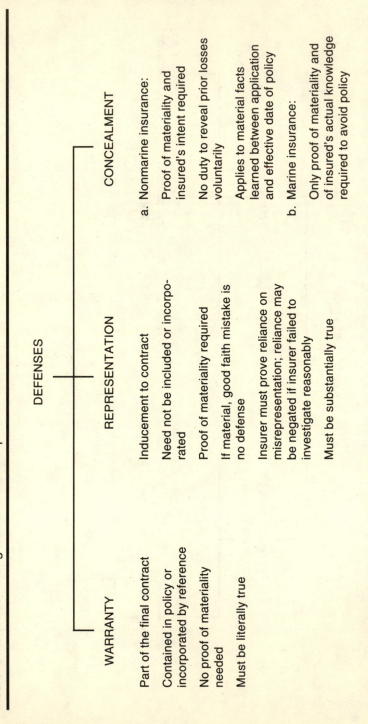

DEFENSES

WARRANTY

Part of the final contract

Contained in policy or incorporated by reference

No proof of materiality needed

Must be literally true

REPRESENTATION

Inducement to contract

Need not be included or incorporated

Proof of materiality required

If material, good faith mistake is no defense

Insurer must prove reliance on misrepresentation; reliance may be negated if insurer failed to investigate reasonably

Must be substantially true

CONCEALMENT

a. Nonmarine insurance:

Proof of materiality and insured's intent required

No duty to reveal prior losses voluntarily

Applies to material facts learned between application and effective date of policy

b. Marine insurance:

Only proof of materiality and of insured's actual knowledge required to avoid policy assert material misrepresentation, concealment, or fraud in connection with life insurance applications when the policy has been in force longer than the *contestable period,* usually two years, during the insured's life. The insurer agrees to waive these defenses after this time period.

The incontestable clause assures policyholders that their beneficiaries will receive payment. In the past, cases in which policies had been in force many years, only to be challenged by insurers on the insureds' deaths, created many difficult problems for beneficiaries and insurers. The beneficiaries were denied policy proceeds, and people were reluctant to purchase policies that might be found invalid after their deaths. The insurer has reasonable opportunity to investigate an applicant's statements during the contestable period.

Contest. For an insurer to be able to raise a defense and avoid an incontestable clause, the insurer must institute a "contest." A "contest" means a formal court action, such as a suit to cancel the policy. An insurer's mere denial of liability is not a contest.

The date of issue of the policy or the date the coverage attached, whichever is earlier, controls the period within which an insurer must commence the contest. The usual incontestable clause requires that the policy must have been in effect for two years during the insured's lifetime. Thus, an insurer can contest a policy if the insured dies during the two-year contestable period.

Application. The incontestable clause does not extend coverage. If a policy excludes death resulting from flying an airplane, the policy will not cover death from flying an airplane even though two years have elapsed. Nor does the incontestable clause preclude showing that the person who took out the policy had no insurable interest in the insured party's life. The strong public policy requiring insurable interest when a person buys a life insurance policy and against wagering on human life prevails over the public policy favoring the incontestable clause.

Although the incontestable clause applies to fraud, if the fraud is particularly vicious, a court may find the policy was invalid at the outset and may permit the fraud to be shown even after the contestable period has expired. For example, when one purchases a life insurance policy to profit from the murder of the beneficiary, or when another person takes the insured's medical examination, the incontestable clause will not prevent the insurer from legally refusing to pay insurance proceeds. The public policy against these flagrant wrongs outweighs the reasons for the incontestable clause.

Classification. Warranties may be either affirmative and continuing (promissory), or they may be implied.

Affirmative and Continuing (Promissory). An *affirmative warranty* states that specific facts exist at the time the contract is made. A *continuing* or *promissory warranty* states that certain things shall be done or that certain conditions shall continue to exist during the policy term.

Because they relate only to conditions that existed at the time of the contract, affirmative warranties are less harsh than continuing warranties, and courts prefer to interpret warranties as affirmative. This approach is consistent with the general rule that if an insurance policy has two interpretations, a court will apply the interpretation favorable to the insured. If an insurer wants a continuing warranty, the policy language must state clearly that the warranty is to apply to future and continued use.

For example, a fire insurance application asks, "Who sleeps in the store?" The applicant writes, "A guard on premises at night." This is an affirmative warranty of conditions at the time of the contract. If a guard slept on the premises at the time of the application, but not later, the affirmative warranty is not breached. If the insurer wants a guard on the premises at night during the term of the policy, the language must say so clearly. Language referring to the future (continuing), such as that a guard "will be on the premises at night," is necessary.

Implied. *Implied warranties* are warranties the law implies to render transactions reasonable and fair. They are very important in sales of goods transactions. All warranties in insurance law, however, are generally expressed in the policies or incorporated by reference.

Lessening Warranty Effects. Insurers prefer that courts interpret insureds' statements as warranties rather than as representations because, for a representation to be grounds for an insurer's avoidance of a policy, it must be material. Insurers also prefer that warranties be continuing and therefore extend through the policy period. State laws, however, usually require that life insurance statements by insureds be representations.

Although the doctrine that insured's statements are usually warranties applies to property and liability insurance, courts have decreased the harshness this doctrine can cause by interpreting statements as representations of fact and not as warranties whenever possible. They also prefer to interpret warranties as affirmative rather than as continuing.

When possible, courts also interpret policies as *severable*. This means that if one provision is invalid, it may not invalidate the entire policy but can be "severed" or separate from other provisions. Therefore, noncompliance with a warranty concerning one type of covered property will not defeat coverage for another type of property to which the warranty does not relate.

The parties' intention determines whether a statement in the policy is a warranty or representation. A court interprets a policy as a whole, including the hazards insured, the language employed, and the situation of the parties. The use of the word "warranty" or "representation" is not conclusive. For instance, a declaration that statements of fact are warranties may have no effect if other provisions or circumstances do not indicate that this was the parties' intention. A statement is a representation rather than a warranty unless the language unequivocally states that it is a warranty. When any doubt exists, the statement is not a warranty.

Although warranties are legal, they are often unfair and harsh. Some state statutes make a breach of warranty no more burdensome for the insured or beneficiary than a material false representation. A typical statute may provide that no oral or written misrepresentation or warranty by the insured will be material or defeat or avoid a policy unless there is an actual intent to deceive, or unless the matter misrepresented or made a warranty increased the risk of loss. Some states employ a contribute-to-loss statute to eliminate the distinction between representations and warranties.

Some state statutes prevent insurers from specifying that representations have the same effect as warranties. Other statutes relate to the strict compliance aspect of warranties and specify that only substantial compliance is necessary. Still other statutes relate to the time in which the breach of warranty existed and prevent avoidance of the policy unless it existed at the time of the loss.

WAIVER, ESTOPPEL, AND ELECTION

An insurer may be unable to defend a lawsuit on the bases of fraud, concealment, mistake, misrepresentation, or breach of a condition because the insurer has done one of the following:

1. Waived the defense
2. Become estopped from asserting the defense
3. Elected not to take advantage of the defense

The doctrines of waiver, estoppel, and election are used more frequently in insurance law than in any other field of the law. The terms are often confused or are used incorrectly as synonyms. These three doctrines apply to almost every ground on which an insurer may deny liability.

Whenever an insurer asserts a policy defense, such as lack of notice, failure to sue within the prescribed time, fraud, or concealment, the insured usually responds by alleging waiver, estoppel, or election. In essence, if the insurer has forfeited a defense in some manner, it should not be allowed later to revive that defense.

Waiver

Waiver is the intentional relinquishment of a known right. It requires knowledge of the facts and relinquishment of a right based on knowledge of those facts. Waiver involves conduct of an insurer or its representative that has the legal effect of relinquishing a defense based either on the insured's noncompliance with a condition or misrepresentation. A waiver may be expressed or implied from the circumstances.

For example, a life insurance company issues a policy to an insured providing that, if the insured enters the military service, the company may declare the policy void. The insured subsequently enters the service and is killed in battle. A representative of the company, learning of the death, writes the beneficiary stating that, because the insured died in the country's service, the company waives its defense that death occurred in military service. Later, the company writes another letter stating it has changed its position and is declaring the policy void.

Under these circumstances, the first letter was an express waiver of a defense and of the power to declare the policy void. That letter is binding even though it was not based on consideration and even though the beneficiary had not experienced any change in position in reliance on the letter. The company knew the facts and intentionally relinquished its rights when it sent the first letter.

Waiver Inapplicable. For waiver to occur, there must be a policy. A statement made before the contract comes into existence is not a waiver of a known right, but an attempted waiver of a future right.

For example, suppose that in the case of a clause in a life insurance policy enabling the insurer to declare the policy void if the insured entered the military service, the insured upon application expressed an intention to join the service at some later date. Suppose further that the agent told the insured that the company did not intend to enforce the clause. The attempted waiver is ineffective because the parol (oral) evidence rule would exclude evidence of the conversation and the policy itself would represent the entire contract.

The doctrine of waiver does not apply to a peril that a policy does not cover. An excluded peril differs subtly, but importantly, from a condition. It is one thing to state that the policy does not cover a given peril and quite another to say that the company has the right to cancel the policy under certain conditions. The insurer may waive the right to cancel, and the full policy remains in force except that the insurer cannot enforce that right. A peril excluded expressly, however, is not the insured's right, but a duty that the insurer has not assumed. Thus, if a homeowners policy excludes earthquake damage, the insurer has no duty to pay for that damage.

An insurer should not have to pay for a loss when the insured did not pay a premium for the insurer's assuming the loss exposure. For example, an insurance agent tells an insured that an automobile liability policy covers the insured while driving an employer's automobile. Actually, the policy contains a nonowned automobile clause excluding coverage while the insured drives an automobile furnished for the insured's regular use but not owned by the insured. There would be no coverage for this excluded situation, regardless of the agent's representation. The agent might be liable for the misrepresentation, but the insurer would not be liable.

What May or May Not Be Waived. A party may waive almost any right or privilege under a contract. Thus, an insurer may waive the benefit of any policy provision, even though it is a standard legal form. A party may even waive a provision in the policy that specifically prohibits waivers. Agents may waive provisions with respect to notice or proofs of loss, stipulations that the policy is not effective until inspection of the property or a medical examination, provisions concerning suspension of the policy for premium nonpayment, and provisions concerning occupancy and nature of the insured property.

A few matters cannot be waived. For example, an insurer may not waive privileges that further public policy, such as the requirement that the insured have an insurable interest in the insured's property or life. An insurer cannot waive actual facts. An insurer's agent remains the insurer's agent, even though the insured may believe that the agent is his or her agent. Attempts to have the agent considered the insured's agent are ineffective on this ground.

Consideration. The law of waivers in insurance law is different from that of general contract law. In general contract law, voluntary waivers are not binding. In insurance law, however, they are binding.

In general contract law a binding waiver requires some form of consideration, but some waivers are binding in insurance law without any consideration. An example is the waiver of a right to a proof of loss after the time for filing a proof of loss has lapsed. Other waivers arguably have consideration in the insured's reliance on a promised waiver. An example is a promise not to enforce the occupancy clause of a fire insurance policy, followed by the insured's extensive absence. Consideration does support some waivers, such as a promise to reinstate a forfeited policy upon the payment of the next premium.

The formation of a substitute contract requires consideration. Assume that an insured desires coverage for a specifically excepted peril. Any language by the insurer that purports to be a waiver is ineffective to afford the coverage unless consideration supports it. The insured must pay an additional premium to make the attempted waiver enforceable.

To illustrate, the New York Standard Fire Policy excludes theft loss. A waiver could not accomplish an agent's attempt to cover theft under the policy in the absence of additional consideration. Only an agreement to cover the loss upon payment of an additional premium would make the waiver, now supported by consideration, effective. This agreement is a "contractual waiver," but, more accurately, a new contract.

Another example of a "contractual waiver" is a policy waiver of premiums during the period of an insured's total disability. The consideration for this waiver is that part of the policy premium covers this waiver. It is therefore a contractual waiver.

Knowledge Requirement.   An insurer must know of a breach of condition under the policy before it can waive that breach. Once it has such knowledge, however, the insurer must act immediately to waive the breach. Failure to act is a waiver of the breach. Whether the insurer has waived a right depends upon the facts of each case. Thus, when the insurer requests information regarding a loss after the expiration of the twelve-month suit clause in the policy, the inquiry is not a waiver of the suit clause. But when an insurer denies liability and refuses to pay a claim, the refusal is a waiver of the policy requirement regarding filing a proof of loss.

Only pertinent knowledge qualifies as a waiver. For example, an agent knows that an insured is constructing an addition to an insured plant that has a sprinkler system for reducing the spread and impact of fire. The agent, however, does not know that the sprinkler system will be shut off temporarily during construction. The agent's failure to act is not a waiver of the automatic sprinkler clause. Once an insurer has denied liability on one ground, it may not defend later on a different ground and has waived the other grounds.

When a liability insurer defends an action brought against an insured, with knowledge of facts that take the case outside the coverage of the policy (and without taking a reservation of right or nonwaiver agreement), the defense will preclude the insurer from denying liability because of noncoverage.

Policy Provisions.   Courts generally do not enforce policy provisions requiring written expression of waivers. Permitting insurers to negate the defense of waiver simply by inserting provisions in the policies would defeat the law of waivers entirely. Waiver is based on the contract rule that valid contractual provisions should be enforced. Therefore, a nonwaiver provision should be enforced just like any other contractual provision. Even that view, however, has loopholes. Suppose an agent can make written changes in a policy. Does it necessarily follow that the agent may make oral changes?

By way of illustration, an insurance agent tenders Ed a life policy containing the condition that the policy not take effect unless the first premium is paid in cash. The policy also provides that any waivers must be in writing. Ed, who is out of funds, offers a ninety-day note, which the agent accepts. This is a waiver, even though it appears to be an agreement contradicting one of the contractual terms. An agent may waive the condition requiring prepayment in cash orally if the agent is authorized otherwise. This is true even though the policy contains a nonwaiver provision.

Acts Constituting Waiver. Any words that express, or acts that imply, an intention to give up the privilege to assert a known defense can constitute a waiver. The insurer must know of the breach before it can be waived. Acts that may show an intent to continue a contract in force and that therefore constitute waivers include the following:

1. Receipt of a premium with knowledge of a breach of policy conditions.
2. Demand for appointment of appraisers or submission of a dispute to arbitration pursuant to policy provisions, or any other demand by the insurer that it is entitled to only if the policy is in force.
3. Waiver in open court during court proceedings.
4. Request for proof of loss after knowledge of a breach without a nonwaiver agreement.
5. Insurer's silence for an unreasonable time. Thus, where a defect exists in the proof of loss, the insurer's silence concerning the defect for an unreasonable time constitutes a waiver.
6. Delivery of a policy to the insured with full knowledge of facts that would permit avoidance of the policy, such as knowledge of the falsity of representations made in the application, is a waiver of the right to avoid. When the insurer knows at the time of delivery of the policy that the insured suffers from asthma, it cannot later claim the insured was not "in good health" at the time of delivery.

Parol Evidence Rule. The parol evidence rule prohibits, among other things, the introduction into evidence of oral agreements made before or contemporaneous with the execution of a written contract. Waivers, which are agreements, are subject to the parol evidence rule.

Thus, oral evidence preceding or accompanying the written contract or policy cannot prove a waiver.

Waiver agreements alleged to have arisen from words or acts before or contemporaneous with the inception of a policy are assumed to be merged in the final policy, and parol evidence to establish them is not admissible. Waiver agreements made after the inception of the policy, if properly authorized, are provable by parol testimony. In the case of waivers, an agent's oral promise to waive future breaches before, or at the time of issuance of, the policy is ineffective as a waiver because of the parol evidence rule and is not admissible as evidence.

Parol evidence does not apply to estoppel, which is collateral to the contract. Parol evidence is admissible to prove estoppel, and it is immaterial whether the words or acts occurred before or after the making of the written contract.

Estoppel

Estoppel is a broad, general principle of law found in many areas: the law of agency, contracts, partnerships, corporations, and others. As a concept, it is familiar to everyone: someone makes a statement to another person, the other person in some way relies on that statement, and then the maker of the statement does not want to abide by it. This is the common social problem of the broken promise. In law, however, to constitute estoppel, a situation must meet strict requirements. A promise that is broken and results in bad feelings is not necessarily one that is legally subject to the doctrine of estoppel in law.

Insurance Law. Estoppel in insurance law is one party's representation of fact that is relied upon by the other so that it would be unfair to allow the first party to refuse to be bound by the representation. The elements of estoppel are as follows:

1. False representation of a material fact
2. Reasonable reliance on the representation
3. Harm or prejudice resulting if the representation is not binding

For example, a fire insurance policy is issued to an insured on a building located on leased land, a fact the insured disclosed on the application. The agent delivers the policy to the insured, saying, "Here is the policy, and it fully covers your building." The policy expressly provides that it is void if the building insured is located on leased ground. The insured accepts the policy without reading it and puts it with other valuable papers. When the building later burns, the insured learns of the policy provision and the company denies the claim.

All the elements of estoppel are present. The company, through its agent, made a false representation by stating that the policy covered the building. The insured reasonably relied on the representation by accepting the policy. The insured's failure to read the policy does not mean reliance is not reasonable. For the insurer to defend its actions based on the policy would harm the insured, who would have no insurance coverage. The insurer is prevented, or "estopped," from denying that coverage exists. There is no waiver because the insurer does not intend to give up any right under the policy.

Distinguishing Estoppel From Waiver. In insurance law the distinction between waiver and estoppel is often blurred. Although the legal effect of the two defenses is the same, they are different and involve distinct elements:

1. Waiver is contractual in nature and rests upon agreement. Estoppel is equitable in nature and rests upon a false representation.
2. Waiver gives effect to the intention of the waiving party. Estoppel defeats the inequitable intent of the estopped party.
3. Waiver is subject to the parol evidence rule. The parol evidence rule does not apply to estoppel.

Factors Establishing Estoppel. When an insurer is aware of a breach of condition, any of the insurer's words, acts, or other defenses under the policy that the insured can reasonably interpret as representations that the contract is valid will prevent the insurer from claiming the contract is not valid. The insured must not be guilty of fraud or bad faith and must come into court with "clean hands."

The insured's actions must have been in good faith and in reasonable reliance on the insurer's representation. The estoppel rule does not punish fraud or falsehood but establishes, for the sake of justice, that the one who caused the loss should bear the loss.

In one case a man was insured under a group life insurance policy. The insured said at the outset that he was not interested in the coverage unless he could obtain $50,000 in life insurance. A manager advised him that he was eligible for only $30,000. However, after negotiations it was agreed that a $50,000 policy would be issued, and a certificate was issued in that amount. The insured was killed accidentally. His widow submitted a claim, and the insurer found that the insured had been eligible, under an established credit-point system, for only $30,000 in life coverage. The insurer paid $30,000 and refunded the premium for coverage over that amount. The court held that all the elements of estoppel were present. There was a false representation of a material fact, a reasonable reliance, and harm resulted. The company had to pay the additional $20,000.[11]

If an insurer's agent misinterprets questions or falsifies answers in an application and misleads the insurer into thinking that the answers are truthful when they are not, estoppel applies. The insurer's agent made the misrepresentation. Therefore, the insurer cannot deny the truth of the statements.

For example, a woman insures her son, who plays high school football and also works during vacations as a salesperson. The agent describes the son on the life insurance application as a salesperson. The son is later killed in a football game. The insurer attempts to avoid the policy obligation on the ground of the false representation of the nature of the loss exposure, proving that the premium charge would have been higher had it been known that the boy played football. In this case, the insurer cannot dispute the truthfulness of the answers on the application. Unless there is evidence of wrongful collusion between the insured and the agent, coverage exists under the policy as issued.

Similarly, if an insurer's agent states that acts an insurer's policy requires, such as including a certain policy endorsement, have been done when they have not, the representation creates estoppel. Thus, if an agent states that an endorsement will be added to a policy to permit a building to be vacated for certain periods, and the policy is delivered without the endorsement, the insurer cannot deny the validity of the intended endorsement. That the insured failed to check the policy does not negate the element of reasonable reliance. Oral evidence is admissible in court to prove the facts. In all of these cases, the insurer may have a right to sue an agent for wrongful acts, but the innocent insured is protected.

Election

Election is the voluntary act of choosing between two alternative rights or privileges. If the insurer or insured chooses between two available rights, this choice may imply a relinquishment of the right not chosen.

Application. Application of the doctrine of election, a cross between waiver and estoppel, limits a party's range of choices. The concept may be useful to the party asserting it because it softens both the waiver requirement of voluntary relinquishment of a known right and the estoppel requirement of detrimental reliance. Waiver, estoppel, and election are not interchangeable doctrines.

The thrust of the election doctrine is that an insurer or insured may not adopt a "heads I win, tails you lose" position. The insurer may not treat the contract as valid for the purpose of collecting premiums, but invalid for the purpose of indemnity.

Examples of election are evident whenever one party has two or more alternatives and chooses one of them. Very frequently an insurer must decide between rejecting a tender of premium and affording coverage. If the insurer elects to accept the premium, it is bound by that choice and is not permitted later to reverse its position and declare that no coverage exists.

Another example in which election is a more accurate term than waiver or estoppel involves a choice between alternative rights under a policy. The standard fire policy gives the insurer the option to repair or rebuild instead of paying monetary compensation in case of loss. When the insurer's words or acts lead the insured to believe that it will pay a loss in money, the insurer has elected that method of discharging its duty under the policy. The insurer had reserved the right to elect between two alternative duties and, having elected one, has lost the right to choose the second alternative. The insurer cannot pursue the course most advantageous to itself in each instance and is bound by its election. This is the result even though the insurer did not relinquish a known right voluntarily (waiver) and there was no detrimental reliance (estoppel).

Insured's Election. The doctrine of election also applies to choices the insured makes. In many instances the insured must choose between two inconsistent legal remedies. Having elected one course of action, the insured may not pursue the other.

For example, a life insurance company cancels a life insurance contract including provisions for the payment of disability benefits. The insured elects to sue the company for fraudulent breach of the contract and receives damages, but not reinstatement of the policy. Later, the insured attempts to sue to recover disability benefits that would have accrued before the previous suit, had it not been for the insurer's cancellation of the contract.

In the first suit, the insured alleged a breach of contract and a right to damages. In the second suit, the insured demanded benefits that would have been payable absent breach of contract. The second cause of action is inconsistent with the first. Election of the first remedy bars the insured's right to use the second remedy. The insured is bound by the first choice, the award of damages, and cannot proceed with the second action for the payment of disability benefits. The insured elected to treat the contract as canceled in the lawsuit, and that election barred the right to pursue the second inconsistent remedy that assumes no cancellation of the contract.

Choosing Among Waiver, Estoppel, and Election

While the doctrines of waiver, estoppel, and election are available to either party to the insurance contract, in most cases insureds use them. Insureds are usually more successful when they rely on the doctrine of estoppel in lawsuits.

The central element of estoppel is that the insured has changed his or her position and suffered detriment in reliance on the insurer's position. The reliance and detriment requirements of estoppel are usually easier for the insured to establish than the insurer's intentional relinquishment of a known right (waiver) or the insurer's choice between two remedies (election). Exhibit 5-5 summarizes waiver, estoppel, and election.

Insurer's Protection Against Waiver, Estoppel, and Election

When someone sues an insured for a covered loss, the insurer has three main alternatives:

1. To refuse to defend the insured
2. To investigate or defend under a reservation-of-rights notice or nonwaiver agreement or both
3. To investigate or defend without any reservation or both

Exhibit 5-6 illustrates these alternatives.

Justified Refusal. The insurer's justified refusal, if the claim is outside the policy coverage, presents no problem. All cases agree that an insurer who justifiably refuses to defend has not breached the contract. The insurer is not liable for its action and has no obligation under the policy concerning any claim arising out of the noncovered loss.

Unjustified Refusal. If the insurer wrongfully refuses to defend an action against the insured, and the claim is within the policy coverage, the insurer is liable for breach of contract even if the refusal is based on an honest mistake. In such a case, the insurer is liable for the amount of the judgment against the insured or of a reasonable settlement by the insured. In addition to a possible judgment that may exceed the policy limit, all reasonable expenses, such as court costs and attorney fees, are recoverable.

An obvious result of an insurer's refusal to defend is the release of the insured from the contractual obligation to leave the management of the suit to the insurer. In such a case, the insurer cannot complain later

Exhibit 5-5
How Insureds Use the Doctrines of Waiver, Estoppel, and Election

	Waiver	Estoppel	Election
Defined	— Insurer's voluntary and intentional relinquishment or abandonment of known right	— Insured's detrimental reliance upon insurer's representation, express or implied in words or conduct	— Insurer's voluntary action or choice of inconsistent alternatives; precludes subsequent selection of different alternative
Relative Advantages for Insured	— No proof of insured's reliance to detriment required	— No proof of voluntary relinquishment of known right	— Softens the respective requirements of voluntary relinquishment and detrimental reliance
Relative Disadvantages for Insured	— Requires proof of voluntary relinquishment of known right	— Proof of detrimental reliance required	—Difficulty of proof
Other Distinguishing Characteristics	— Insurer's act or conduct required	— Proof of act or conduct of both parties to the contract required — Insurer: representation of a fact — Insured: reliance on the representation only to suffer disadvantage	—Insurer's act or conduct

Exhibit 5-6
Insurer's Post-Loss Alternatives When Coverage Is Questionable

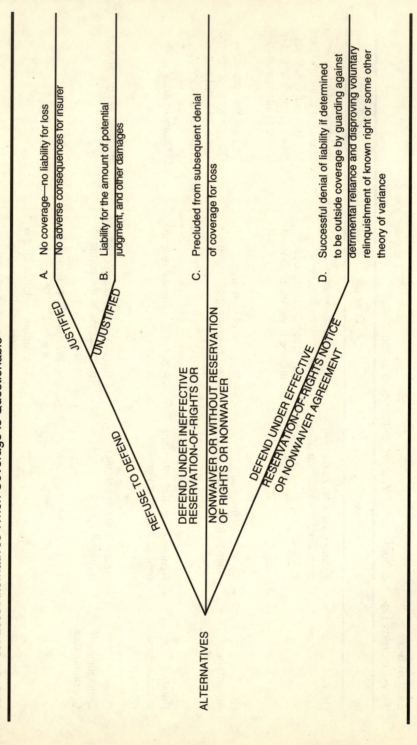

ALTERNATIVES

REFUSE TO DEFEND

JUSTIFIED

A. No coverage—no liability for loss
No adverse consequences for insurer

UNJUSTIFIED

B. Liability for the amount of potential
judgment, and other damages

DEFEND UNDER INEFFECTIVE
RESERVATION-OF-RIGHTS OR
NONWAIVER OR WITHOUT RESERVATION
OF RIGHTS OR NONWAIVER

C. Precluded from subsequent denial
of coverage for loss

DEFEND UNDER EFFECTIVE
RESERVATION-OF-RIGHTS NOTICE
OR NONWAIVER AGREEMENT

D. Successful denial of liability if determined
to be outside coverage by guarding against
detrimental reliance and disproving voluntary
relinquishment of known right or some other
theory of variance

about the conduct of the defense. Similarly, the insured is released from other affirmative policy provisions such as proof of loss, notice of suit, and provisions requiring cooperation, aid, and assistance. The insurer by unjustified refusal waives any possible defense based on such noncompliance.

Reservation-of-Rights Notice or Nonwaiver Agreement. *Reservation-of-rights notices* and *nonwaiver agreements* are instruments insurers use to prevent claims by insureds for avoidance of certain defenses against liability that the insurers may have under the terms of the policies. Claims personnel frequently use them when investigation of a loss reveals the possibility that, for one reason or another, the insurer may deny coverage under the policy. Exhibits 5-7 and 5-8 are illustrations of a nonwaiver agreement and a reservation-of rights notice.

This possibility poses a dilemma for the insurer. If it continues to investigate the loss on the merits without deciding whether it has a coverage defense, it may have prejudiced the insured's rights and brought about a waiver, estoppel, or election, forfeiting its policy defense. If it does not investigate, it may forfeit all defenses. In addition, the loss may increase.

Nonwaiver agreements and reservation-of-rights notices help solve this dilemma. They allow an insurer to advise an insured that the company's activities regarding the loss are not the relinquishment of the insurer's rights to stand on policy provisions, which may establish its nonliability, and thus prevent waiver, estoppel, or other rights that vary with the policy. The insurer can continue to investigate and evaluate the loss on its merits, an activity beneficial to the interests of the insured and the insurer. Simultaneously, the insurer can investigate and determine the question whether the insured has violated policy terms and whether the insurer will accept liability under the contract.

Nonwaiver is a written contract under which the insured and the insurer agree that neither will waive any of its rights under the policy as a result of the investigation or defense of an action against the insured. It is bilateral in that both parties execute it. A reservation-of-rights notice differs from this in that it is unilateral, usually an insurer's letter to an insured.

The insurer should attempt to enter into a nonwaiver agreement with the insured as soon as the potential coverage question surfaces. The nonwaiver agreement requires both the insurer's and insured's signatures. When the insurer with knowledge of a ground of forfeiture or noncoverage manages the defense of an action brought against its insured without giving timely notice of its reservation of rights, it cannot assert the grounds of forfeiture or noncoverage.

Exhibit 5-7
Nonwaiver Agreement

It is hereby agreed by and between the (insurance company) and (insured) that no action heretofore or hereafter taken by the (insurance company) shall be interpreted as a waiver of any of its rights and defenses under a policy number issued to (insured) with respect to any claim or suit arising in connection with an accident or loss which occurred on or about (date) and at or near (place).

It is further understood and agreed that, by the execution of this agreement, (insured) does not waive any rights which he or she may have under the policy.

Signed (Insured)

Signed (Insurance Company Representative)

Difficulties.   Occasionally some practical difficulties arise in the attempt to secure the insured's consent and signature:

1. Even if the claim representative clearly explains the significance of the nonwaiver agreement, the insured still may become alarmed and refuse to sign. This can delay the investigation of the loss, which the agreement is supposed to expedite.

2. If the claim representative does not explain the importance of the agreement fully and fairly to the insured, the binding force of the nonwaiver agreement becomes questionable, even if the insured signs it. It may create a claim of lack of contractual intent, of misunderstanding, duress, or other defenses that may jeopardize its validity on the theory of disallowing unconscionable advantage.

In the first case, the only way the company can protect itself against later claims of variance is to resort to the reservation-of-rights notice. This is a unilateral declaration and a notice to the insured that the insurer intends to safeguard its rights to dispute liability under the terms of the policy and that its conduct in investigating the loss should not be interpreted contradictory in this respect.

Both the reservation-of-rights notice and the nonwaiver agreement prevent subsequent claims not only of waiver, but also of estoppel, election, and other theories of rights at variance with policy provisions.

Exhibit 5-8
Reservation-of-Rights Notice

To: (Insured's name)

Subject: Accident or loss on (date) at or near (place)

Your letter reporting the above accident was received on (date). In view of the delay in reporting this matter and for other reasons which may become evident as a result of our investigation, this investigation is being made with full and complete reservation of all rights afforded to the (insurance company) under policy number_____ issued to you.

Signed (Insurance Company Representative)

Elements. Certain elements must be present for a reservation-of-rights notice or nonwaiver agreement to be effective.

First, the reservation-of-rights notice must be communicated to the insured, usually by letter and seldom by oral notice because it would be difficult to prove oral notice.

Second, the notice must be timely. A reservation-of-rights or nonwaiver notice prevents estoppel because it gives the insured an opportunity to hire counsel to take over the defense from the insurer if the insured so desires. Because the notice must give reasonable time to assume the defense, the insurer's safest course is to give notice as soon as it obtains knowledge of the policy defense.

The reservation-of-rights notice must inform the insured fairly of the insurer's position. It should include the policy provisions the insurer relies on and the facts that would result in a denial of liability if proved.

For example, a liability insurer who questions coverage under an automobile policy writes six letters to the insured informing her that it would defend an action against her but with express reservations of its rights to contest the policy. The insured contends that she never received the letters. Because the letters were addressed to her both at her residence and place of employment, a presumption arises that she received the letters.

If an insurer acts in good faith and uses every reasonable method to contact the insured, the insurer is not precluded from asserting its policy defense.

The following is an example of the rule that an insurer must disclaim liability within a reasonable time. The insured is involved in an automobile accident. The application and the policy provide that the use of the car is for "pleasure and business." In accordance with the policy provisions, the insurer investigates the claim, and seven months after the accident the insurer discovers that, at the time of the accident, the automobile was used to carry passengers for hire, an exclusion from coverage. Upon learning this fact, the insurer disclaims liability. The insurer is not estopped from raising the policy defense in spite of the seven months between the accident and the date of the disclaimer because of the following:

1. The insurer could rely upon the insured's report of the accident, which did not disclose that he was carrying passengers for hire at the time.

2. The insurer disclaimed liability as soon as it learned of the true facts.

3. A year and a half elapsed before the case went to trial, so the insured had ample time to prepare his own defense.

SUMMARY

This chapter concluded the examination of contract law by focusing specifically on insurance contracts and discussing their distinctive features and formation. Then it examined insurance third-party beneficiary contracts, representations and warranties in insurance contracts, and, finally, waiver, estoppel, and election.

Insurance contracts involve the utmost good faith, cover fortuitous events, are contracts of adhesion and indemnity, and are contracts affected with a public interest. They are executory in that they do not pay benefits until a loss occurs. Policy standardization has occurred in most lines of business, and courts interpret insurance contracts to meet insureds' reasonable expectations.

An insurance contract requires an agreement consisting of an offer and an acceptance. These two elements can involve many legal questions, which often depend on whether a policy is for property and liability insurance or for life insurance.

The effective date of insurance contracts can depend either upon binders for property and liability insurance or on conditional receipts for life insurance. Conditional receipts include binding, approval, and insurability receipts.

Insurance contracts can be oral. Some terms must be in writing, but others can be implied, such as those drawn from previous dealings, customary usages, or statutory requirements. Courts frequently do not require that insureds read their contracts because of the complexity of the contracts. Insurance contracts also provide many situations involving third-party beneficiary arrangements.

Statements on an insurance application are usually classified as either representations or warranties. Warranties are statements or promises in a policy that, if untrue, would render the policy voidable, whether or not they are material. A misrepresentation can make an insurance contract voidable. The elements of false representation are as follows:

- Misrepresentation
- Material fact
- Reliance by the insurer

Some state statutes modify the common law in these situations with either increase-of-risk or contribute-to-loss statutes.

An insurer may be unable to assert the defenses of fraud, concealment, mistake, misrepresentation, or breach of a condition because the insurer has done one of the following:

1. Waived the defense
2. Become estopped from asserting the defense
3. Elected not to take advantage of the defense

A waiver is the intentional relinquishment of a known right and requires knowledge of the facts and relinquishment of a right based on knowledge of those facts. Estoppel is a broad, general principle of law and is essentially the common social problem of the broken promise. In insurance law, estoppel is one party's representation of fact that is relied upon by the other so that it would be unfair to allow the first party to refuse to be bound by the representation. The elements of estoppel are as follows:

1. False representation of a material fact
2. Reasonable reliance on the representation
3. Harm or prejudice resulting if the representation is not binding

Election is voluntarily choosing between alternative rights or privileges. An insurer's or insured's choice between available rights may imply a relinquishment of the right not chosen.

Either party to the insurance contract may use the doctrines of waiver, estoppel, and election. In most cases, however, insureds use them. They are usually more successful when they rely on the doctrine of estoppel in lawsuits.

Insurers use reservation-of-rights notices and nonwaiver agreements to prevent claims by insureds for avoidance of certain defenses against liability that the insurers may have under the terms of the policies. They allow an insurer to advise an insured that the company's activities regarding the loss do not waive the insurer's rights to stand on policy provisions. They prevent waiver, estoppel, or other rights that vary with the policy. An insurer can continue to investigate and evaluate the loss on its merits.

Chapter Notes

1. Delancy v. Insurance Company, 52 N.H. 581 (1873).
2. Drake v. Globe American Casualty Company, Ohio 10th Circuit Court of Appeals, unreported case No. 74AP-472, March 11, 1975.
3. Pennsylvania State Insurance Department press release, February 23, 1973.
4. Gaunt v. John Hancock Mutual Life, 160 F.2d 599 (2d Cir. 1947).
5. New York Life Insurance Co. v. Hiatt, 140 F.2d 752 (9th Cir. 1944).
6. See Standard Venetian Blind Co. v. American Empire Ins. Co., 469 A.2d 563 (Pa. 1983), and its predecessor, Hionis v. Northern Mutual Ins. Co., 322 A.2d 363 (Pa. Super. Ct. 1974), for the development and limitation of this doctrine.
7. Julien v. Spring Lake Park Agency, 166 N.W.2d 355 (Minn. 1969).
8. U.C.C. § 2-509(3), and comment 3.
9. Jeffries v. Life Ins. Co., 89 U.S. 47 (1874).
10. New York Standard Fire Policy of 1943, lines 1-5.
11. Clauson v. Prudential, 195 F.Supp. 72 (D.Mass. 1961).

CHAPTER 6

Commercial Transactions

This chapter provides an overview of five areas involving commercial transactions:

- Sales contracts
- Negotiable instruments
- Secured transactions
- Consumer law
- Bankruptcy

The first three subjects—sales contracts, negotiable instruments, and secured transactions—are governed by the Uniform Commercial Code (U.C.C.), which most states have adopted to regulate commercial transactions generally. Therefore, this chapter refers frequently to the U.C.C. and often to particular articles, or sections, of the U.C.C. Federal and state statutes regulate consumer matters, and federal law regulates most bankruptcy matters.

The chapter is an "overview" because each of these subjects involves a complex web of terminology, definitions, and statutory law. Out of necessity, these areas of law have been extensively simplified to give the reader only a general understanding of basic principles. Law schools generally treat these subjects in four or five individual courses, which reveals the complexity of these subjects.

SALES CONTRACTS

The law of sales, governed by Article 2 of the U.C.C., applies only to sales of goods. This discussion employs many of the contractual terms and concepts discussed earlier in Chapters 2 through 4. In general,

231

goods means things that are movable and does not include such things as investment securities and rights to sue. Growing crops and timber are considered goods. Minerals, oil and gas, structures, or parts of structures are goods if the sales contract provides that a seller is to sever them from land.

One unique characteristic of the law of sales is its many special rules for *merchants*. A merchant is a person who deals in the kind of goods being sold, or a professional, including an agent, who purports to have special knowledge or skill concerning those goods.

Contract Terms

The general rules of contract law apply to contracts for the sale of goods, except that a sales contract need not state the price of the goods to be enforceable. If the price is open or if some method of fixing the price is provided, the price is the reasonable price at the time for delivery. Statutes of frauds apply to sales contracts under the same rules that apply to other contracts.

Offer and Acceptance. The general principles of offer and acceptance apply to contracts for the sale of goods. In the law of sales, however, a formal acceptance is often not necessary. Instead, the offer will call for a shipment of goods as the acceptance, particularly when the transaction is between merchants.

Article 2 defines *conforming* and *nonconforming goods.* Conforming goods are goods that are in accordance with the contract or that fall within trade usage or the prior course of dealing of the parties.[1] All others are nonconforming goods. Although theory would indicate that the shipment of nonconforming goods is a breach of the contract, Article 2 provides two exceptions to that general rule:

1. A shipment of nonconforming goods is not an acceptance or a breach of contract if the seller notifies the buyer that the shipment is only an accommodation to the buyer.

2. If a buyer rejects goods because they are nonconforming, the seller may notify the buyer of an intention to "cure" the nonconformity by the shipment of conforming goods, so long as the time for performance has not expired. Even so, if the seller had reasonable grounds to believe that the goods conformed to the contract because, for instance, the buyer had accepted them as conforming goods in prior transactions, and the buyer still rejects the goods as nonconforming, the seller still has a reasonable time to substitute conforming goods.

An offeree may accept an offer of a bilateral contract by tendering or giving the completed performance within the time allowed for accepting the offer by giving a promise to perform. Additionally, an offeree may accept an offer to buy goods for prompt shipment either by prompt shipment or by a prompt promise to ship. Also, if an offeree accepts a contract by a promise to ship the goods, the offeree may make the promise in any reasonable manner unless the offer clearly indicates that only one method is acceptable.

If a definite expression of acceptance of an offer to buy or sell goods contains additional or different terms, the offeree still accepts the original offer unless the acceptance is expressly conditional on the offeror's consent to those new terms. Whether the new terms go into the contract depends on two variables:

1. If one of the parties is a nonmerchant, the new terms will not be part of the contract unless the offeror expressly agrees to them.
2. If both parties are merchants, the proposals become part of the contract if they do not materially alter the contract and if the offeror does not object within a reasonable time.

If a proposal materially alters the contract, it will not become part of the contract unless the offeror expressly agrees to the alteration.

A proposal "materially alters" a contract if its inclusion in the contract without the other party's knowledge would result in hardship. For example, a proposal to negate certain standard warranties would alter a contract materially, but a proposal to limit the time for complaints would not.

Consideration. Consideration is essential to sales contracts. Contrary to general contract law, however, an agreement by the parties to modify a contract for the sale of goods is binding despite the lack of new consideration.

Unconscionable Contracts or Terms. The general rules of fraud, mistake, duress, and undue influence apply to contracts for the sale of goods. In addition, the U.C.C. provides that if a contract was unconscionable when made, it is unenforceable.

Warranties

Contracts for sales of goods may contain warranties created by statute as well as the seller's implied or express warranties. A *warranty* is a promise that something is true.

Warranty of Title. The seller gives a *warranty of title* to the goods assuring that the sale is rightful. *Title* is legal ownership, so warranty of title is a promise that the seller has legal ownership of the goods. The seller also warrants that he or she knows of no security interest or other lien on the goods, other than those disclosed to the buyer.

The contract may exclude the warranty of title, and the warranty is not present if the buyer has reason to know that the seller does not have full title. For example, a sale of goods by an agent alerts the buyer that the agent does not have title. A merchant warrants, in addition, that the goods do not infringe a patent.

Implied Warranties. The implied warranties in sales of goods are those of merchantability and fitness for a particular purpose.

Merchantability. A *warranty of merchantability* is implied only when the seller is a merchant. This warranty requires that the goods meet the following tests:

1. The goods will pass without objection in the trade under the contract description.
2. Fungible goods (indistinguishable and interchangeable goods, such as grain) must be of average quality for the kind of goods sold.
3. The goods must be fit for the ordinary purpose for which they are used.
4. All goods in a lot shall be of approximately like kind and quality.
5. The goods must conform to the specifications on the container or label, if there is one.

In addition, implied warranties may arise from the course of dealings between the parties, or from the usages of a particular trade.

Fitness for a Particular Purpose. When any seller, whether a merchant or nonmerchant, has reason to know that the buyer requires the goods for a particular purpose, and that the buyer relies on the seller's skill or judgment to furnish suitable goods, an implied *warranty of fitness for a purpose* arises.

For example, suppose that John has never been deep-sea fishing but wants to fish for marlin. He asks a sporting goods dealer to recommend suitable equipment. The dealer recommends certain equipment as suitable and John buys it. Without negligence on John's part, the equipment breaks under ordinary and usual marlin fishing circumstances. The seller has made and has apparently breached a warranty of fitness for a particular purpose.

Exclusion or Modification of Implied Warranties. The only implied warranty that can be excluded or modified orally is the warranty of merchantability, and then only if the contract itself is oral and if the word "merchantability" is used in the disclaimer.

All implied warranties, however, are excluded by expressions such as "as is," "with all faults," or other language that means there are no implied warranties. The warranty of title can be excluded expressly and specifically and is automatically excluded if the buyer has reason to know that the seller does not claim title or is selling on a third party's behalf.

If the buyer inspects, or refuses the opportunity to inspect, the goods at the time of making the contract, there is no implied warranty with regard to nonlatent defects that an inspection would have revealed. If, however, the seller's statements concerning the article cause the buyer's failure to inspect, it is excused, and the seller's statement may be an express warranty.

Past practice between the parties, or usages of trade, can also result in the exclusion of these implied warranties, just as they can result in the creation of implied warranties. If a contract contains both one or more express warranties and a general exclusion of "all warranties, express or implied," the express warranty prevails.

Express Warranties. If a statement is the basis of the bargain, it is an *express warranty*. The law infers implied warranties, but a seller gives express warranties voluntarily in the following ways:

1. An affirmation of fact concerning the goods, or the seller's promise that the goods conform to a certain standard. For example, a statement about a car's gas mileage is a warranty that the statement is true, even without the words "warranty" or "guarantee."

2. Any description of goods in a contract is a warranty that the goods conform to the description. For example, a contract to sell a "new hay baler" is an express warranty that it is new.

3. If the contract is based on a sample or model, there is a warranty that the goods will conform to the sample or model.

Third-Party Beneficiaries of Warranties. Products liability involves the tort (noncontractual) liability of a contractor, manufacturer, or vendor for injury to a third party. Article 2 of the U.C.C. deals with sales of goods from a contractual point of view and with a seller's contractual liability on express or implied warranties to third parties who are not immediate buyers.

Article 2 provides that a seller's warranty extends to any person who is in the buyer's family or household or who is a guest in the buyer's home, and who suffers injury resulting from breach of the warranty, if it is reasonable that the person use or be affected by the goods, and who suffers injury resulting from breach of the warranty. An express or implied warranty concerning a ladder, for instance, would extend to the buyer's child or to a house guest. A seller may not limit the operation of the express or implied warranties that extend to any person who is in the buyer's family or household or who is the buyer's guest.

Types of Sales Contracts

There are several specialized categories of sales contracts:

1. *Sale on approval*—sale to a consumer who wants to try the goods before buying them. If the goods do not satisfy the buyer, they may be returned at the seller's risk. Title remains with the seller until acceptance. Risk of loss remains with the seller, who should insure them.

2. *Sale or return*—sale to a person who intends to resell the goods but who has the right to return the goods if they are not sold. Even though the seller purports to retain title until payment or resale, the buyer's creditors may attach the goods. They may not do so, however, if the buyer is a person who sells other persons' goods, or if they are otherwise on notice of the seller's interest in the goods. Return of the goods is at the buyer's risk.

3. *Auction sales*—public offering in which the highest bid is the acceptance of an offer. If the auctioneer wishes to surrender the option to withdraw the goods if the bids do not go high enough, the sale must be advertised as "without reserve." In such cases, the highest bidder must get the article. In any type of auction sale, however, the bidder may retract the bid at any time before the auctioneer announces completion of the sale, and the bidder's retraction does not revive any prior bid. Therefore, bidding begins again.

Delivery Terms

The following are common delivery terms in sales contracts:

1. *F.O.B. (Free on Board) Place of Shipment.* The seller need only deliver the goods to the carrier at the seller's risk and expense and give the buyer the shipping papers. If the sale is F.O.B. place of destination, the seller must transport the goods to the destination at the seller's risk and expense.

2. *F.A.S. (Free Alongside) Vessel.* The seller must deliver the goods alongside a shipping vessel at the seller's risk and expense. If F.O.B. vessel, the seller must also load the goods on board the vessel at the seller's risk and expense.

3. *C.I.F. (Cost-Insurance-Freight).* The price includes the cost of the goods, of insurance, and of the freight charges to the destination. Again, all necessary documents must be forwarded to the buyer.

4. *C.A.F. (Cost and Freight).* The same as C.I.F. above, but the seller does not bear the cost of insuring the goods.

Inspection. The buyer generally has the right to inspect the goods as a condition to acceptance and payment. The inspection may include reasonable testing at the buyer's expense, but if the goods fail to conform and are rejected, the buyer may recover the testing cost from the seller.

There is generally no right to inspect in two instances:

1. When the goods are delivered *C.O.D. (collect on delivery)*

2. When payment must be made at the time the document of title is delivered, unless payment is due only after the goods are available for inspection

Time for Delivery. If the time for delivery is not set in the contract or implied from past practice of the parties, delivery must occur within a reasonable time. Unless a seller assumes a greater obligation, as by agreeing that "time is of the essence" in the contract, delay in delivery or nondelivery is not a breach of contract if performance becomes impracticable by some event that the parties had assumed would not occur.

Title and Risk of Loss

As a practical matter, under the U.C.C., risk of loss (that is, liability) follows title except when identified goods are at the seller's residence or place of business and the buyer is to pick them up. If the seller is a merchant, risk of loss does not pass to the buyer until the buyer receives the goods. If the seller is not a merchant, risk of loss passes to the buyer when the seller tenders delivery.

When the goods delivered or tendered do not conform to the contract and the buyer has the right to reject them, the risk of loss remains with the seller until the deficiency is remedied or the buyer accepts the goods. The parties may agree that the risk of loss will pass at some other time than specified by the U.C.C., and prior practice of the parties, trade usages, or the circumstances of the case also may change the time that risk of loss passes.

One can transfer to another person only such title as one has. A person, for instance, who unwittingly holds stolen goods has no legal title at all and can transfer no title, even to a good faith purchaser.

There are two exceptions to this rule under the U.C.C.:

1. A person who holds a "voidable" title can transfer good title.
2. A person to whom goods have been "entrusted" can transfer valid title even though he or she has no title to the goods.

Voidable Title. A sales transaction is voidable, and the seller can regain the goods from the purchaser when one of the following situations exists:

1. The buyer has criminally defrauded the seller.
2. The buyer has deceived the seller by pretending to be someone else.
3. The check for payment is dishonored.
4. The transaction was to be a "cash sale," but delivery occurred without payment.

Entrusting. If one *entrusts* goods to a merchant who deals in goods of that description, the merchant can transfer whatever title the entruster has to a buyer in the ordinary course of the merchant's business. For example, Mary takes a watch to a jeweler who repairs and sells watches, new and used. If the jeweler sells that watch to John, who is unaware of Mary's interest in the watch, John will get the full title that Mary had. Mary, of course, can sue the jeweler.

Breach of Sales Contracts

If goods do not conform to the contract, the buyer may accept them, reject them, or accept part of them and reject part of them. To sue for breach of contract, the buyer must give reasonable notice of rejection. The buyer must state the particular defect or lose the right to sue if the seller could have cured the defect with timely notice, or if, between merchants, the seller had made a written request for a written statement of the defects the buyer claims.

If the seller has no agent or place of business in the buyer's market area, the buyer must follow the seller's instructions on what to do with the rejected goods and can demand indemnity for necessary expenses in holding or shipping the goods. If the goods are perishable, the buyer may sell them on behalf of the seller. If the goods are not perishable, and the buyer does not receive instructions within a reasonable time, the buyer may sell them, store them, or reship them to the seller. The buyer's acceptance of nonconforming goods does not waive or forfeit any rights to sue for the breach. The buyer, however, must notify the seller of the nonconformity within a reasonable time and must prove that the goods were nonconforming.

Revocation of Acceptance.   A buyer may revoke his or her acceptance later under the following circumstances:

1.   The buyer reasonably assumed that the defect would be cured and it was not cured.
2.   The buyer accepted the goods before discovering the nonconformity.
3.   The buyer accepted the goods in the first place because it would have been difficult to discover the defect, and because the seller gave assurances about the quality of the goods.

Excuses for Nonperformance.   The following circumstances provide excuses for nonperformance:

1.   *Loss of identified goods.* If specific and identified goods are destroyed or damaged before the risk of loss passes to the buyer, and if the loss or damage was not either party's fault, the contract is avoided if the loss is total and may be avoided if the loss is partial. The buyer may accept damaged goods with an allowance in the price for the deficiency. In neither case, however, can the buyer sue the seller.
2.   *Agreed shipping unavailable.* If the agreed carrier becomes unavailable, or if the agreed berthing, loading, or unloading facilities become unavailable, without either party's fault, any offer by the seller to use a commercially reasonable substitute must be accepted.
3.   *Failure of a presupposed condition.* A seller of goods is excused from performance if the performance becomes commercially "impracticable" or if performance is halted by a domestic or foreign governmental regulation. The "impracticability" must be caused by an unexpected contingency that affects a condition that both parties assumed would continue undisturbed. The outbreak of war, for instance, might make shipping impossible between two points. If, however, the outbreak of war were "foreseeable," the contingency would have been expected. A severe shortage of materials caused by an embargo or by a natural disaster may be commercial impracticability.

Seller's Remedies.   The seller's remedies for breach of contract depend on whether the breach occurred before or after delivery of the goods.

Before Delivery.   If the buyer declares an intent not to perform the contract before delivery, an anticipatory breach, the seller may resort immediately to any remedy for breach. Alternatively, the seller may wait for performance for a reasonable time or may simultaneously pursue a remedy for the buyer's breach of contract. If the buyer revokes the acceptance, repudiates the agreement, or fails to make a required payment, the seller may withhold delivery of the goods.

A seller who, before delivery, discovers that the buyer is insolvent may refuse to deliver the goods except for cash. If the goods are still en route, the seller may stop delivery unless the seller already has delivered to the buyer any negotiable document of title for the goods, or unless a carrier or warehouse operator has notified the buyer that the goods are being held for the buyer.

After Delivery. If the seller discovers that the buyer has received the goods on credit while insolvent, the seller may demand their return within a period of time. If the buyer has previously misrepresented that he or she was solvent, the time period does not apply. When a buyer wrongfully repudiates the contract, fails to make a payment due before delivery, or wrongfully rejects the goods, the seller may sue.

Therefore, if the buyer repudiates the contract, the seller may recover the difference between the contract and the market price at the time and place of delivery and lost profits, if any.

If the goods are still being manufactured at the time of breach, the seller may complete their manufacture or stop their manufacture and sell them for scrap value.

If the buyer fails to pay for goods after they are accepted or the risk of loss passes to the buyer, the seller may sue for the contract price of the goods and also for the full price of the goods even if the seller still possesses them, but only if the goods cannot be sold at a reasonable price.

Buyer's Remedies. If the seller fails to deliver the goods or repudiates the contract, the buyer is entitled to the difference, if any, between the contract price at the time the buyer learned of the breach and the market price.

Alternatively, if the goods that were not delivered are unique, or cannot be obtained from another source, the buyer is entitled to specific performance. Also, a buyer who cannot obtain substitute goods has a right of *replevin,* which means that a court will order the seller to turn the goods over to the buyer.

Because buyers of goods often need those goods immediately, a buyer may, after learning of a breach, purchase substitute goods within a reasonable time and then recover any difference between the cost and the contract price. A buyer who rightfully rejects delivery or revokes acceptance has all the rights that a seller has when the buyer breaches before delivery. The buyer may hold the goods for the seller's instructions or sell them.

If the buyer accepts nonconforming goods and informs the seller of the nonconformity, the buyer is entitled to the difference, if any, between the value of the goods accepted and the value they would have had, at the time and place of acceptance, if they were as warranted. In addition, the buyer can recover any loss resulting from the nonconformity that the seller had reason to know might follow from a breach and that the buyer could have prevented.

NEGOTIABLE INSTRUMENTS

In face-to-face trade or commerce, a buyer need only strike a bargain with the seller, take possession of the goods, and give something in exchange. When trade and commerce, however, are conducted at a distance or over a period of time, written legal documents ensure that payment will be made at the distant place or at some future time. Article 3 of the U.C.C. governs *negotiable instruments,* which are the written documents that meet the need to pay at a distance or at a future time.

Types of Commercial Paper

Article 3 covers the following types of commercial paper, the two most common of which are the draft, or check, and the promissory note:

1. *Certificates of deposit* (CDs). A document issued by a financial institution acknowledging receipt of money and promising to repay it, with interest, at a definite time.
2. *Notes.* A promise to pay money on demand or at a definite future time.
3. *Drafts and checks.* A paper containing an unconditional order by the drawer, or person making out the draft or check, requiring the drawee, or bank, to pay a certain sum ("sum certain") in money to the payee or to bearer.
4. *Trade acceptance.* A two-party draft used when a seller wants cash immediately, but the buyer cannot provide it until resale of the goods.

A basic requirement of commercial paper is that it be readily salable because the person to receive payment, the seller, may not want to await payment and may want to sell the paper to another person. If the document were an ordinary assignable contract, a buyer of the instrument would take two initial steps before purchasing it:

1. Check the credit rating of the person who is to make payment
2. Find out whether that person has any defenses against the seller, such as full or part payment

Exhibit 6-1
Draft (in the form of a check)

```
                                          (Date) June 1, 199X

   Pay to the
   order of    (Payee)      Peter Payee             $ 10.00

   _____
   Ten and ───────────────────────────── ⁰⁰/100 Dollars

   Bank/Drawee

                            (Drawer)    Dorothy Drawer
```

A negotiable instrument avoids these time-consuming steps. The person who buys a negotiable instrument has the personal liability of the seller of the instrument and therefore only needs to know the seller's credit rating. In addition, the purchaser of the instrument may sometimes be in a position to take it free and clear of virtually all defenses that the drawer or maker may have against the payee, such as poor quality of delivered goods. This expedites the transaction and meets the needs of commerce. The instrument becomes freely transferable, almost like cash.

Drafts. The modern *draft,* or *check,* is a three-party instrument. The buyer prepares a document that orders a person, bank, or another company to pay a given sum to the seller. Both the buyer and the seller have access to the party who will make the payment. The instrument is delivered to the seller, who may present it at the appropriate time to the person who is to make the payment and get the money. A simple form of draft is a check, shown in Exhibit 6-1.

The three parties to a draft are the drawer, drawee, and payee. The drawer draws on the credit he or she has with the drawee, who is then to pay the amount stated to the payee.

Promissory Notes. The *promissory note* is a simple two-party transaction, and Exhibit 6-2 is a simple form of the promissory note. In this transaction, one party promises to pay a certain amount of money to a second party.

Elements of Negotiability

To be negotiable, an instrument must be in writing and must meet the following requirements under Article 3:

Exhibit 6-2
Promissory Note

$10,000   Anytown, June 1, 199X

One year after this date I promise to pay to the order
of Peter Payee Ten Thousand Dollars ($10,000)

Due June 1, 199Y   (Signed) Mary Maker

1. Be signed by the maker or drawer
2. Contain an unconditional promise or order to pay a certain sum in money and contain no other promise, order, obligation, or power on the part of the drawer or maker except as otherwise provided by Article 3
3. Be payable on demand or at a definite time
4. Be payable to order or to bearer

Transfer and Negotiation

If an instrument is merely transferred, the transferee obtains only such rights as the transferor had. The transferee takes rights subject to any defenses good against the immediate transferor. For example, if goods were never delivered, payment would not be due. The transferee is subject to this defense. If, of course, the transferor was free of defenses, the transferee is also free of defenses. Delivery alone negotiates a bearer instrument. Endorsement plus delivery negotiates an order instrument. Only an assignment can transfer a nonnegotiable instrument.

Primary and Secondary Liability.   A person who is absolutely required to pay the instrument according to its terms has *primary liability*. A person whose liability on the instrument depends on someone else's refusal to pay or accept the instrument has *secondary liability*. Therefore, only the maker (of a note) and the acceptor (of a draft) are primarily liable. Even the drawer of a draft is not primarily liable, because a drawer's liability is not incurred unless and until the drawee refuses to accept or pay the draft. An endorser's secondary liability does not arise until the maker or drawee dishonors the instrument.

Endorsements. An *endorsement* must be written in some form, even a rubber stamp, on the instrument, usually on the back, and must transfer the entire sum. As long as there is a signature, other words do not affect the endorsement. For example, an endorsement stating that "I hereby assign my interest in this note to AB—signed CD" is an effective endorsement. If the payee's or transferee's name is not correct, that person may (1) endorse the instrument in the name in which it was made out, (2) endorse it with the correct name, or (3) endorse it in both names.

A *special endorsement* specifies the person to whom or to whose order the instrument is payable. If the payee of a check, for instance, does not wish to deposit the check but to negotiate it to another person, that payee will write "Pay to the order of Richard Roe," or "Pay to Richard Roe," above his or her signature on the back of the check. Once delivered to Richard Roe, the instrument may be further negotiated only with Richard Roe's endorsement.

A *blank endorsement* is solely the signature of the payee or holder. The most common *restrictive endorsement* is "For deposit" or "For collection," followed by the depositor's signature. Such checks are clearly intended to go through the bank collection process.

The usual endorsement is unqualified. That is, the endorser contracts to pay the instrument according to its terms at the time of endorsement to any subsequent endorser or to the holder if he or she is properly notified that the instrument has been dishonored. This is called the *endorser's secondary liability*. Secondary liability can be avoided by adding words such as "without recourse" or words of similar meaning to the endorsement. The instrument remains negotiable, but the endorsee does not have the secondary liability of the "qualified" endorser.

Holders in Due Course

A basic feature of an instrument that is only assignable, and not negotiable, is that an assignee is subject to any defense that the obligor has against the obligee. Therefore, an assignee should find out, before purchasing an instrument, whether there are any defenses. For a negotiable instrument, however, anyone who purchases it from the payee may achieve a special status, that of *holder in due course,* and not be subject to most defenses.

A holder in due course can sell and transfer that status to a transferee. Therefore, even if one is not a holder in due course, one may have the rights of a holder in due course if the transferor of the instrument to the holder also was a holder. This *shelter provision* gives a mere holder the "shelter" of the transferor's freedom from defenses. The shelter privilege, however, does not apply to a holder who previously was a party to any fraud or illegality affecting the instrument or who, as a prior holder, had notice of a defense against or claim to the instrument.

A holder in due course is free of *personal defenses,* which are all claims to the instrument by any person and defenses that would be effective in a simple contract transaction, such as lack or failure of consideration, misrepresentation, or fraud. *Real defenses* go to the very existence of the obligation, such as the maker's, drawee's, or drawer's defense of incapacity and the defenses of duress, illegality, or discharge in bankruptcy.

To be a holder in due course, one must first be a "holder," a person who possesses an instrument drawn, issued, or endorsed to him or her or to his or her order or to bearer. Therefore, the instrument must have been issued properly, and, if the holder is not the payee, must have all the necessary endorsements. A holder in due course is a holder who has taken the instrument under the following circumstances:

1. For value
2. In good faith
3. Without notice that it is overdue or has been dishonored or of any defense against or claim to it on the part of any person

A payee who meets these requirements may be a holder in due course. It is often essential that a party establish qualifications as a holder in due course to attain maximum rights on the paper. The party must meet each element, and the absence of any one element bars a person from being a holder in due course. However, the failure of a holder to succeed to the rights of a holder in due course is only important if there is a legal defense to the instrument. Thus, to be a holder in due course, it is always necessary to be a holder, which is one who possesses the instrument drawn, issued, or endorsed to him or her, to his or her order, or to bearer.

A holder who obtains the instrument does not become a holder in due course in the following situations:

1. The instrument was purchased at a judicial sale or taken under legal process.
2. The instrument was acquired in taking over an estate.
3. The instrument was purchased as part of a bulk transaction (such as the purchase of all the assets of a business) not in the regular course of the transferor's business.

Checks

Checks are the most familiar negotiable instruments. A bank depositor is a creditor of the bank to the extent of the balance in the account. When a checking account is established, the bank becomes the depositor's agent in making disbursements from that balance. The following summarizes common check transactions:

1. *Failure to honor checks.* A bank is liable for all damages caused by its failure to honor a check when there are sufficient funds in the depositor's account.

2. *Overdrafts.* A bank can honor a check not covered by the depositor's balance, thus creating an overdraft and making the depositor the bank's debtor.

3. *Altered checks.* A bank may charge an altered check to the depositor's account to the extent of the check's original terms.

4. *Stale checks.* A bank need not pay an uncertified check presented more than six months after its date. It has the right, however, to do so and to charge the customer's account.

5. *Stop payment orders.* An oral stop payment order is effective for only fourteen days. A written stop payment order is effective for only six months, unless renewed in writing.

6. *Certified and cashier's checks.* Certification equals acceptance. Therefore a *certified check* is one that a bank has accepted. A *cashier's check* is a check the bank draws on itself. The purchaser of such a check is secondarily liable on it only if the check is payable to the purchaser and he or she endorses it.

7. *Drawer's death or incompetence.* When a drawer dies or becomes legally incompetent, the bank can pay outstanding checks until it knows or should know of the death or incompetence. Even with knowledge of the death, a bank may pay or certify a check drawn by the deceased for ten days after the date of death.

8. *Forged signatures.* A bank may not charge a check with a forged drawer's signature, a forged signature of a necessary endorser, or a materially altered check for more than its original amount, against the customer's account. The customer, however, must use reasonable care and promptness to notify the bank of such defects, so that the bank can avoid payment on future frauds by the same parties.

SECURED TRANSACTIONS

The buyer of goods may pay for the goods in the buyer's own cash, in cash borrowed from an outside source, or on open credit granted by the seller. The seller or a third-party lender may require that the buyer agree to give the seller or lender a *security interest* in the article sold, which means that the seller or lender can take the goods or otherwise prevent the buyer from disposing of them. If the buyer defaults on payments, the seller or outside lender, or *secured party,* can retake the article sold, or the *collateral.* The security device only affects recovery of the article. Even if a security device is ineffective, contract common law still provides relief in the form of damages.

Security devices in the sale of goods include pledges, suretyship, and guaranty. A *pledge* is a device by which a person who borrows money delivers an article of value to the seller. If the borrower does not repay the money, the seller can retain the article. For example, Kathy borrows money from Nancy and gives Nancy her diamond ring as security for the loan. The transaction is a pledge.

A *surety* or *guarantor* agrees to be responsible for the performance of another person's contract to repay money borrowed or to perform a certain duty. The party who must perform is the *principal.* A surety joins the principal in making the promise, and both are primarily liable to the third party, who is the *obligee.* A surety who must perform a promise is entitled to reimbursement from the principal. A guarantor promises to perform only if the principal does not perform and has secondary liability. The guarantor who performs is entitled to reimbursement from the principal.

Definitions

Article 9 of the U.C.C. treats all security interests in personal property under the single concept of a *secured transaction.* A security interest gives the seller or creditor a security interest in the collateral that will be good against third persons, as well as against the buyer or debtor. In other words, if the buyer or debtor fails to pay the seller or creditor, the latter has not only ordinary contract remedies but also the ability to recover a piece of property to sell. The following are definitions of terms necessary for an understanding of secured transactions.

- *Perfection*—the steps to be taken to achieve a security interest
- *Secured party*—the seller or creditor
- *Security interest*—an interest in personal property that secures payment or performance of an obligation
- *Collateral*—the property subject to a security interest
- *Debtor*—the person who owes payment or other performance, whether or not that person owns or has an interest in the collateral

- *Security agreement*—the agreement that creates the security interest
- *Financing statement*—the instrument filed in a public records office that gives the public notice of a security interest in the collateral

Rights of Perfected Security Interests

A *perfected security interest* is superior to a later perfected security interest and to most subsequent lien creditors, with limited exceptions, such as the following:

1. A holder in due course takes a negotiable instrument free of any perfected security interest in it.
2. An artisan's lien for services or materials with respect to the collateral takes priority over a perfected security interest in that collateral.

Perfecting a Security Interest

There are three basic methods of perfecting a security interest, depending on the type of collateral:

1. Filing a *financing statement* in a public records office is the most common method and is notice to the world of the secured party's interest.
2. *Transferring actual possession* of the collateral from the debtor to the secured party perfects the interest.
3. *Perfection by attachment* applies in sales of consumer goods to gain priority over conflicting security interests, does not require filing when the security interest is created, and occurs when a legal interest "attaches" to the goods.

The nature of the collateral controls the method to be used. For example, possession is the only method of perfecting a security interest in a negotiable instrument, because mere delivery can transfer ownership. Possession, however, is not practical for perfecting a security interest in equipment, consumer goods, and farm products that the buyer wants to use.

Consumer Goods. Filing a financing statement is not necessary to perfect the seller's security interest in consumer goods. However, a person who buys the consumer goods from the first buyer for personal purposes buys the goods free of the seller's security interest.

Financing Statement. The financing statement, which can be filed at any time, needs the debtor's signature, the name and address of the debtor and secured party, and a description of the collateral.

The security interest is perfected when two events have occurred:

1. The security interest "attaches"; that is, the goods are sold and the security agreement is executed.
2. The financing statement is filed.

If the seller delays filing the financing statement until after delivery of the goods to the buyer, the security interest is unperfected until the time of filing. Therefore, another security interest might attach to the property in the meantime.

Filing. Presentation of the filing statement to the filing officer with the fee, or that officer's acceptance of it, is a *filing*. When a debtor has met all obligations under the security agreement, a termination statement should be filed so that the secured party can no longer claim a security interest under the financing statement. If there is more than one perfected security interest in the same collateral, they rank according to priority in time of filing or perfection.

Rights of Unperfected Security Interests

Even if a security interest is not perfected, it is still good between the parties and against a third party who buys the goods from a person who deals in those goods. However, the secured party will be subordinate to the rights of the following persons:

1. One who then or later obtains a perfected security interest
2. A lien creditor, an assignee, a bankruptcy trustee, or a receiver
3. One who buys the property from a person who does not deal in that type of goods if that buyer does not know about the unperfected security interest

Default

Nonpayment is the most obvious form of default, but a security agreement may provide for other events to be considered defaults, such as failure to insure the collateral, the debtor's bankruptcy, loss or destruction of the collateral, or removing the collateral to another place. The following are the secured party's rights in the event of default:

1. *Suit on the underlying debt.* The secured party may proceed as though there were no security agreement and can sue the debtor on the note or obligation.

2. *Foreclosure.* The secured party can foreclose the debtor's interest in the collateral by retaining the collateral in full satisfaction of the debt or selling or leasing the collateral and applying the proceeds to satisfy the claim.

3. *Secured party's right to possession.* Unless the collateral is in the secured party's possession, that party has the right to regain possession through the courts or by other legally permissible means, such as lawful repossession.

4. *Retaining or selling the collateral.* The secured party's retention of the collateral in full satisfaction of the obligation may be advantageous to both parties.

5. *Disposition of the collateral.* If the secured party chooses or is required to sell or lease the collateral, this may be done at a public or a private sale with notification to the debtor. The purchaser at such a sale takes the goods free of the security interest and any subordinate security interests or liens.

The debtor or any other person subject to a security interest in the collateral may redeem the collateral at any time before it is sold by tendering full performance of the contract.

CONSUMER LAW

Consumer law includes federal and state legislation intended to assure fair treatment of consumers in dealings with suppliers of goods and services. Consumers have the protection of both fair trade and consumer credit laws.

Fair Trade Laws

Fair trade laws include the following:

1. The Federal Trade Commission Act
2. State unfair trade practice acts
3. State and federal consumer warranty laws

Federal Trade Commission Act. The *Federal Trade Commission (FTC) Act* of 1914[2] prevents unfair methods of competition and unfair or deceptive acts or practices in or affecting interstate commerce and does not apply to the insurance industry.

Federal *antitrust laws,* notably the *Sherman Act,*[3] protect commerce from unlawful restraints, price discrimination, price fixing, and unlawful monopolies. The FTC Act is not strictly an antitrust act, although it overlaps the Sherman Antitrust Act. For example, a restraint of trade, which is a violation of Sherman, is also an unfair method of competition. However, the FTC Act goes further and enjoins unfair or deceptive acts that have no relationship to competition. For example, price fixing is a violation of the Sherman Act and is also an unfair method of competition. However, misrepresentation is not usually a violation of the Sherman Act but is an unfair act affecting commerce within the meaning of the FTC Act.

The five-member Federal Trade Commission prevents unfair or deceptive practices in commerce in three ways:

1. *Cease and desist order.* The commission holds a hearing and issues a *cease and desist order* if it finds a violation of the FTC Act.

2. *Trade practice conference.* A *trade practice conference* deals with a subject, such as false and misleading advertising in a given industry, by devising a set of trade practice rules. In effect the industry has the opportunity to help write its own regulatory rules, which can deal with unfair methods of competition or with anticompetitive or unfair business practices.

3. *Informal settlements and consent orders.* The accused party, for settlement purposes, executes a stipulation agreeing to stop the challenged practice, a remedy usually employed when the transgression was unintentional. The consent order is used when a complaint and call for a formal hearing have been issued. In effect, the commission issues an order before the hearing is held, banning the alleged unlawful practice.

State Unfair Trade Practice Acts. In addition to federal laws, states have passed their own deceptive trade practice acts, insurance fair trade practice acts, and unfair claims settlement practices acts.

Deceptive Trade Practice Acts. Every state now has a *Deceptive Trade Practice Act (DTPA),* or "Little FTC Act." There are three variations of these laws, which include one or more of the following prohibited practices:

1. Unfair acts (oppressive or bad faith conduct)
2. Deceptive acts (fraud, deceit, and misrepresentation)
3. Unfair methods of competition (including antitrust violations such as price fixing and group boycotts)

These acts intend to compensate for perceived inadequacies in the FTC Act. For example, some of them permit private rights of action that the FTC Act does not permit. Many of these acts apply to insurance, unlike the FTC Act.

Insurance Fair Trade Practice Acts. Many states also have specific unfair trade practice acts that apply to insurance. They generally follow the model Insurance Fair Trade Practice Act. These acts generally prohibit anyone engaged in insurance from engaging in any unfair methods of competition or unfair and deceptive acts or practices, defined as follows:

1. Misrepresentation and false advertising of policies
2. Defamation of competitors
3. Boycott, coercion, and intimidation
4. False financial statements
5. Stock operations and advisory board contracts
6. Unfair discrimination (usually applicable only to life and accident and health insurance)
7. Rebates

The sixth item in the above list prohibits issuing capital stock, certificates, or securities or using advisory board or similar contracts that promise returns or profits as an inducement to the purchase of insurance, a sophisticated form of rebate.

Under the model act, a state commissioner who believes an act is unfair or deceptive under the law can call a hearing and has the power to order the person to cease from doing the act.

Consumer Warranties: Magnuson-Moss. The principal laws governing consumer warranties for many years were the U.C.C. provisions relating to express and implied warranties, which established implied warranties of merchantability and fitness for a particular purpose and described how express warranties are created. The problems with these warranties were that only a consumer could enforce them, and a consumer could also unwittingly waive them. Because of inadequate remedies, deception in product warranties became intolerable and resulted in the passage of the *Magnuson-Moss Act* in 1975,[4] which supplements the FTC Act and the antitrust laws. The FTC enforces Magnuson-Moss. Some states have also passed warranty laws, such as "lemon" laws applicable to cars.

Warranty Disclosures. Under Magnuson-Moss, a producer of goods need not give a warranty at all; but, if given, a written warranty must conform to certain standards. The law applies to consumer products, defined as tangible personal property for personal, family, or household use, including fixtures.

Under the regulations, the written warranty must disclose the following:

1. What it will and will not cover
2. When it expires
3. To whom it is given
4. What the warrantor will do if there is a malfunction
5. What service and parts are free
6. How to obtain redress under the warranty

Full or Limited Warranties. If the product costs more than $5, there must be a full and complete disclosure of the terms of the warranty. If the product costs more than $10, the warranty must be either "full" or "limited."

A *limited warranty* must contain the elements above, but it limits the consumer's rights in some other respects, such as by limiting the duration of the implied warranty of merchantability.

A *full warranty* has two important provisions:

1. The warrantor must remedy the product within a reasonable time and without charge.
2. It must have a "lemon" provision.

The *lemon provision* takes its name from slang describing a product that never seems to be right, no matter how often it is repaired. If repeated efforts to repair the product fail, the consumer must be given a choice of a full refund or a replacement without charge. Because of this provision, some manufacturers still call their warranties "limited" even though they probably otherwise constitute full warranties. For example, a car manufacturer may have a "twelve-month unlimited mileage" car warranty that it redesignates as a limited warranty to eliminate the possibility it might have to replace "lemons." A "lemon" law applies only to full warranties and is general in nature, thus limiting its application. Many states have adopted their own "lemon" laws.

The U.C.C. provides for implied warranties of merchantability and fitness for a particular purpose but permits a disclaimer of them. Under Magnuson-Moss, no disclaimer of implied warranties is permitted, but under a "limited" warranty the implied warranty may be limited to the same length of time as the express warranty. Under a "full" warranty, implied warranties cannot be limited in any way.

Consumer Credit Laws

Consumer credit laws include the federal Truth in Lending, Fair Credit Reporting, Fair Debt Collection Practices, and Equal Credit Opportunity Acts.

Truth in Lending Act. As credit transactions grew rapidly following World War II, it became apparent that consumers were overextending themselves and frequently did not know of the credit terms or the amount of interest charged. In an effort to correct this situation, Congress passed the Consumer Credit Protection Act of 1968, or *Truth in Lending Act.*[5] The federal act does not replace or preempt state credit disclosure acts unless they are clearly inconsistent with it, and then does so only to the extent of the inconsistency.

Application. The Truth in Lending Act applies only to credit for individuals and only to credit transactions for personal and real property purchased for personal, family, household, or agricultural purposes and not to business or commercial transactions.

The act applies to all persons who regularly extend credit or make a finance charge in connection with installment purchases and to situations in which the purchaser can pay for the item in more than four installments, whether or not there is credit or a finance charge. It is not applicable to the usual insurance installment payment plan under which credit is not actually extended, but it does apply to a premium financing plan through which the insured must pay a creditor for premium charges plus a finance charge or, if it is payable in more than four installments, regardless of charges.

Disclosure Requirements. The act does not control the terms of a credit transaction. Its purpose is to assure that the consumer will know what those terms are. Finance charges must be disclosed. Costs incidental to real estate transactions, such as the cost of title examination and title insurance, attorney's fees, escrow payments, appraisal fees, and credit report charges, are not finance charges. When in connection with the sale of personal property or with a consumer loan, however, loan fees, finders' fees, charges for credit reports, and service or carrying charges are considered finance charges. In all cases, interest or time-price differentials are finance charges.

Premiums for credit life or accident and health insurance are finance charges unless the debtor is informed in writing that the insurance is not a condition for obtaining credit and buys it voluntarily. Premiums for property or liability insurance are also finance charges, unless the debtor is informed in writing of the cost and is given the option to purchase it from a third party.

Ordinary Credit Transaction. In the ordinary credit transaction for the sale of goods, the seller must disclose all the finance charges, the cash price, the down payment (including any trade-in), other charges that are not part of the finance charge, and the annual percentage rate of interest charged. The seller must state the terms of payment clearly, including any charge for delinquent payments, and must give a description of any security interest in the goods sold.

Ordinary Consumer Loans, Open-End Consumer Credit Plans.   In a consumer loan with a definite amount and definite time of payment (a *close-end loan*), the same information must be given. In a "revolving" or continuous credit plan (an *open-end plan,* the usual department store charge card) the seller must state the conditions of making a charge, the method of calculating the balance due, the method of determining the amount of the finance charge, and any different rates for different balances. The seller must also disclose the conditions on which other charges may be made and under which the creditor retains a security interest. The debtor can request the average effective annual rate or a projected rate of return.

After the open-end plan account is opened, the creditor must furnish complete periodic statements that show the amount due at the beginning of the statement period, the amount and date of each additional extension of credit, the debtor's payment during the period, the finance charges added, the interest rate for the period, the annual percentage rate, and the outstanding balance at the end of the statement period and method of determination.

Credit Cards.   To control the proliferation of credit cards in the 1960s, including cards sent to people who did not request them, Congress amended the Truth in Lending Act in 1970 to cover the issuance and liability of credit card holders.

Today, no credit card may be issued without a request or application. One who holds a requested credit card is liable only for its authorized use. If it is lost or stolen and used without authority, the liability of the holder does not exceed $50. The buyer also has the right to withhold payment without incurring a finance charge until the settlement of disputes over the price or quality of goods purchased.

Under the *Fair Credit Billing Act,*[6] a person who has a problem with property or services purchased with a credit card has the right not to pay the remaining amount due if he or she first tries in good faith to return the property or give the merchant a chance to correct the problem. The credit card holder's bank usually charges the bill back to the bank servicing the merchant, who in turn charges the merchant, who must make good or sue for the bill.

Electronic Funds Transfer Systems.   *Electronic funds transfer (EFT) systems,* using what are known commonly as *debit cards,* have two features:

1. Using the card at point of purchase, the seller instantly transfers the sales amount to the seller's account from the buyer's account.
2. Most debit cards can also be used to make deposits and withdraw cash at automated teller machines. The rights and re-

sponsibilities of the parties are defined by the *Electronic Funds Transfer Act* of 1978[7] and Regulation E of the Federal Reserve Board. Valid cards can be issued only in response to specific requests. Liability in general is limited to $50 if the loss is reported within two business days.

Fair Debt Collection Practices Act. The *Fair Debt Collection Practices Act,*[8] an amendment to the Truth in Lending Act, prohibits unfair and oppressive collection practices by agencies specializing in debt collecting for others. The law eliminates such practices as using violent or criminal acts, using profane language, publishing lists of debtors, calling debtors repeatedly or in the middle of the night, threatening legal action with no intent to follow through, and contacting the debtor at work or at any unusual time or place except with the debtor's consent.

The act also prohibits contacting the debtor's employer, neighbors, or friends, except for the limited purpose of locating the debtor and without revealing any information concerning the agent's role in the collection process. The collection agency can send a written notice to the debtor. A debtor who wishes to prevent any further communications by the collection agency may indicate in writing the desire to stop all further contacts, in which case the collector must sue.

Fair Credit Reporting Act. The *Fair Credit Reporting Act*[9] attempts to insure that consumer reporting agencies exercise their responsibilities with fairness, impartiality, and a respect for consumers' rights. Improper use of consumer credit reports can result in both criminal and civil liability.

The basic premise of the act is that when a consumer is denied credit, insurance, or employment wholly or partly because of information in a credit report, the consumer should be notified and given an opportunity, in effect, to refute the information in the report.

Application. A consumer report is a consumer reporting agency's communication on the consumer's credit-worthiness, credit standing, and capacity, general reputation, personal character, or mode of living, to be used in whole or in part in establishing the consumer's eligibility for the following:

1. Credit or insurance to be used primarily for personal, family, or household purposes
2. Employment purposes
3. A legitimate business need for information in connection with a business transaction involving the consumer for personal, family, or household purposes

The act applies only to *consumer reporting agencies,* defined as any entity that, for money, or on a cooperative nonprofit basis, regularly assembles or evaluates consumer credit information or other information on consumers to furnish consumer reports to third parties.

Furnishing Reports. The agency can furnish a credit report only under the following circumstances:

1. In response to a court order
2. According to written instructions of the subject of the report
3. To a person who, it has reason to believe,
   * Intends to use the information in connection with a credit transaction
   * Intends to use it for employment purposes
   * Intends to use it in connection with insurance underwriting
   * Intends to use it to determine eligibility for a business license if the applicant's financial status is relevant
   * Otherwise has a legitimate business need for the information in connection with a business transaction

The law requires that the consumer be given notice whenever credit or insurance for personal, family, or household purposes or employment is denied. The consumer must also be advised of the consumer reporting agency's name and address.

The consumer has the right to obtain the information in the reporting agency's file, but not directly from the person who used the report. The consumer must also be advised of the identity of any other persons who have obtained consumer reports on him or her within the past six months and may take issue with any information in the report with which he or she does not agree. The agency must then reinvestigate and change its report if so indicated. The agency cannot issue any report containing adverse information that antedates the report by more than seven years, except that bankruptcies may be reported for a fourteen-year period.

Investigative Reports. An *investigative report* is a report in which a consumer reporting agency obtains information on a consumer's character, reputation, characteristics, or mode of living through personal interviews with neighbors, friends, or associates. The subject of an investigative report must be notified within three days of the ordering of the report.

Equal Credit Opportunity Act. The *Equal Credit Opportunity Act*[10] prohibits credit discrimination based on age, race, color, religion, national origin, or receipt of welfare benefits. It also prohibits treating married applicants more favorably than singles, such as by giving favored treatment to married men and women or failing to take alimony payments into consideration as income.

A lender who rejects an application or withholds credit must either give the applicant specific reasons or advise the applicant of the right to obtain specific reasons. Married persons can have their credit histories under the name of each spouse so that married women can develop credit histories and references under their own names, which is valuable if they become divorced, separated, or widowed.

BANKRUPTCY

Bankruptcy law adjusts the interests of insolvent debtors and their creditors, and the competing interests of those creditors, in the debtor's assets. Bankruptcy provides two avenues for relief:

1. Liquidation of the debtor's assets and distribution of the proceeds to the creditors
2. Reorganization of the debtor's affairs, free of claims of creditors during that process, and partial or full repayment of the debts

The federal *Bankruptcy Act*[11] and federal bankruptcy courts control bankruptcy in the United States, and states do not govern bankruptcy matters. Insurance companies, however, are unique in that they are not subject to federal bankruptcy law but are governed by state law when they become insolvent.

The Bankruptcy Act does not provide for relief of domestic or foreign insurance companies, or for banks, savings and loan associations, or other institutions engaged in aspects of banking, which are covered by other state and federal legislation. The act provides for reorganization, but not for liquidation, of municipalities and railroads. Liquidation and reorganization are available to individuals, married couples, corporations, and partnerships.

Many years ago, people in dire financial straits often went to prison. Today, however, most countries provide a legal process whereby a bankrupt person or organization either can reorganize operations to arrange for an orderly operation of business or payment of all or part of the debts or, if all else fails, can be relieved of debts and start anew.

Bankruptcy Act

The Bankruptcy Act has several chapters, with the most relevant for this discussion being Chapters 7, 11, 12, and 13.

Chapter 7. *Chapter 7* is the "last resort" chapter of the federal Bankruptcy Act. Under a successful Chapter 7 bankruptcy, the bankrupt's nonexempt assets are distributed to the bankrupt's various creditors, and the balance of the debtor's obligations are forgiven, or discharged.

Chapter 11. *Chapter 11* is the general reorganization chapter of the federal Bankruptcy Act. Under Chapter 11, most partnerships and corporations attempt to continue doing business and simply set up a payment plan for paying a portion or, possibly, all of the creditors of the ongoing business. This chapter permits the bankrupt to attempt to establish a plan of repayment and reorganization without the threat of litigation from creditors, which can involve multiple judgments and attachments of property or executions on property. In a successful Chapter 11 reorganization, the bankrupt continues business, and disruption is minimized. If the reorganization is unsuccessful, a Chapter 11 bankruptcy may turn into a Chapter 7 liquidation.

Chapter 12. *Chapter 12* is a special chapter aimed at farmers' special problems and is not intended to benefit large corporate farms. It provides for the same reorganization opportunities available under Chapter 11, except that the administration is geared specially to farm operations and is less complicated.

Chapter 13. *Chapter 13* provides for reorganization of individual bankrupts who are small business operators or wage earners.

Involuntary Bankruptcy

Any person or entity may apply voluntarily for Bankruptcy Act relief. If any creditors believe that a bankrupt person or organization favors other creditors or continues to dispute the remaining assets of a bankrupt estate, those creditors may petition the bankruptcy court for *involuntary bankruptcy* under any of the chapters discussed here.

The alleged bankrupt may contest an involuntary bankruptcy proceeding, and the bankruptcy court, after a hearing, determines whether to allow the bankruptcy action to proceed or to dismiss it. If a court dismisses the action in the debtor's favor, the debtor is also entitled to costs and expenses arising out of the court proceedings. The parties to the bankruptcy proceeding are the debtor, the creditors (both secured and unsecured), a trustee, a referee, and a bankruptcy judge. All parties may have legal representation.

The trustee must inventory the bankrupt's assets and, depending on the types of bankruptcy proceedings, either conserve them or dispose of them economically. The referee's job is to sort out the various creditor and trustee claims and to present what the referee believes to be the equitable payments under the law for the bankruptcy judge's approval.

Creditors may be numerous, often have representation by creditors' committees, and may have more than one committee for each type or class of creditor. Usually, secured creditors have priority interests in secured property up to the value of the security interest. If the debt exceeds the security, then the secured creditor is unsecured to that extent.

Assets Exempt From Bankruptcy

Federal law provides for a limited number of exemptions of the debtors' assets to keep those assets out of the bankruptcy estate. Exempt assets, such as tools of a trade, a limited homestead exemption, and life insurance, cannot be sold or dissipated in the bankruptcy proceedings.

Debtor's Good Faith Requirement

The bankruptcy system requires good faith on the debtor's part, and if the debtor "prefers" a creditor by paying him or her a disproportionate share of assets immediately before filing for bankruptcy, the court may avoid the preferred payment. The creditor must then repay the sum to the trustee. If the debtor hides assets, the bankruptcy court may rescind a discharge in bankruptcy.

Liquidation Proceedings

In a liquidation proceeding, there are usually not enough assets to pay all the creditors. Therefore, those creditors are prioritized into six main classes, as follows:

1. Administrative expenses of the bankruptcy proceeding
2. Unsecured business debts
3. A limited amount of wage claims
4. Contributions to employee benefits plans
5. Claims of unsecured individuals
6. Unsecured claims of governmental units

The goal of bankruptcy is eventually to discharge the debtor from all debts that arose before the date of the court's order for relief. In reorganization, full performance of the plan discharges the debtor. In liquidation, the court discharges an individual. Discharge is irrelevant to a corporation debtor in a liquidation proceeding because the corporation will not continue in business.

Some debts are not discharged:

1. Certain tax claims
2. Money, property, or services obtained by fraud
3. Claims for willful and malicious injury to persons or property
4. Alimony or support
5. Educational loans (unless five years before the bankruptcy filing)
6. Debts incurred in court actions arising from drunk driving

Discharge is not automatic. In general, a debtor who illegally and unjustifiably does not cooperate in a proceeding may not obtain discharge. The act speaks in grim terms about debtors who intentionally hinder, defraud, or delay creditors; who unjustifiably conceal, destroy, mutilate, falsify, or fail to keep or preserve records; or who knowingly and fraudulently make false oaths.

Prior bankruptcy within the previous six years will usually cause the denial of a discharge. A court may revoke a discharge in a later proceeding if the debtor obtained it by fraud or concealed property from the trustee.

SUMMARY

Article 2 of the U.C.C., the law of sales contracts, applies only to sales of goods. Although the general contract law rules apply to these sales, neither a stated price nor a formal acceptance is necessary in a sales contract. Consideration, however, is essential to sales contracts; and the general rules of fraud, mistake, duress, and undue influence are applicable.

Article 3 of the U.C.C. governs negotiable instruments, best exemplified by checks and promissory notes. To be negotiable, an instrument must meet the following requirements:

1. Signature by maker or drawer
2. Unconditional promise or order to pay a certain sum of money
3. Payable on demand or at a definite time
4. Payable to order or bearer

A holder in due course possesses a negotiable instrument and must have taken the instrument under the following circumstances:

1. For value
2. In good faith
3. Without notice that it is overdue or has been dishonored or of any defense against or claim to it on any person's part

U.C.C. Article 9 treats all security interests in personal property as secured transactions. When a buyer agrees to give a seller or lender a security interest in an article sold, the seller or lender (secured party) can take the goods (collateral) or otherwise prevent the buyer from disposing of them. A perfected security interest is superior to a later perfected security interest and to most subsequent lien creditors. There are three basic methods of perfecting a security interest:

1. Filing a financing statement
2. Transferring actual possession
3. Perfecting by attachment

Fair trade and consumer credit laws protect consumers in commercial transactions. Fair trade laws include the following:

1. The Federal Trade Commission Act (FTC Act)
2. State unfair trade practice acts
3. State and federal consumer warranty laws

The FTC Act prevents unfair competition and unfair or deceptive acts or practices affecting interstate commerce. State unfair trade practice acts also prevent such activities.

Insurance fair trade practice acts prevent unfair and deceptive activities in the insurance business. The Magnuson-Moss Act supplements the FTC Act and antitrust laws and applies to consumer products, regulating written warranty provisions by defining full and limited warranties.

Consumer credit laws include the following:

1. The Truth in Lending Act
2. The Fair Credit Reporting Act
3. The Fair Debt Collection Practices Act
4. The Equal Credit Opportunity Act

The Truth in Lending Act applies only to individual credit for personal and real property purchased for personal or agricultural purposes and does not control the terms of a credit transaction but assures that consumers have information about those terms. The Fair Credit Reporting Act requires that consumer reporting agencies exercise their responsibilities fairly by controlling reporting and investigation practices.

The Fair Debt Collection Practices Act prohibits unfair and oppressive collection practices by agencies specializing in debt collecting. The Equal Credit Opportunity Act prohibits credit discrimination on several grounds, such as sex, race, and national origin.

The federal Bankruptcy Act governs all bankruptcies, except those involving insurance companies, which are subject to state regulation, and contains the following chapters relevant to this course of study:

- Chapter 7—"Last resort" chapter by which bankrupt's non-exempt assets are distributed to creditors and the balance is discharged
- Chapter 11—General reorganization chapter under which most individuals and corporations attempt to continue doing business and set up payment plans for paying creditors
- Chapter 12—Section dealing with farmers' special problems
- Chapter 13—Reorganization of individual bankrupts who are small business operators or wage earners

Chapter Notes

1. U.C.C. § 2-106 (2).
2. 15 U.S.C. § 45.
3. 15 U.S.C. §§ 1-8.
4. 15 U.S.C. § 2312.
5. 15 U.S.C. § 1601.
6. 15 U.S.C. § 1681.
7. 15 U.S.C. § 1693.
8. 15 U.S.C. § 1692.
9. 15 U.S.C. § 1681.
10. 15 U.S.C. § 1691.
11. 11 U.S.C. § 101.

CHAPTER 7

Property Law

Property is anything one can possess exclusively. It involves ownership—the unrestricted and exclusive right to something. In American society the law views property as a bundle of legal rights or interests and protects those rights. Property rights are generally insurable. In some societies, such as the People's Republic of China, for example, the concept of private property ownership is not as significant as it is in the United States and many other countries. Property falls into two categories, real and personal property.

Real property refers to the rights in land and includes rights to water, minerals, and all things attached to land, such as buildings, trees, and fixtures that have become part of the realty. It also includes rights closely related to land, such as the right to pass over another person's land. *Personal property* includes all property other than interests in land. Some property, such as goods one may possess physically, is tangible. Other property, such as patents and insurance policies, represents intangible rights.

Although the law of real and personal property differs in many respects, many rules apply to both types of property. The methods of transferring property and the requirements of inheritance are examples of areas in which the "bundle of legal rights" a person has in property differs depending upon the nature of that property. The first part of this chapter discusses personal property, and the second part discusses real property.

PERSONAL PROPERTY

This section focuses on the law of tangible personal property. How does one come into possession and ownership of such property? What are the ways in which one may hold, use, and enjoy it? How may one give it away? What are the rights and duties of a person who holds property for someone else?

Ownership and Possession

Ownership is a relationship between the owner and the rest of society that includes (1) the right to exclude all others from use and enjoyment of the property owned, (2) the right to pass good title to the property, and (3) the obligation of ownership burdens, such as the duty to pay taxes and to use property so as not to interfere with the rights of others. Another term for legal ownership of property is *title*. Ownership is the highest right to property that a person can acquire.

Possession is the assertion of custody or control over property, and is not, of itself, ownership. A person can possess property without owning it. When a person possesses property, the law generally protects that possession against everyone except the true owner. When the owner grants possession, the possessor's rights to custody and control may be superior in some situations to the true owner's during the period of the agreement.

Methods of Obtaining Possession

One can acquire possession of and title to personal property in several ways. Creation of the property is one method. One may also obtain personal property through accession, confusion, bailments, or gifts, all of which are discussed below.

Intellectual Property. One may create property from one's own endeavors, such as writing a book or a song, inventing a device, or developing a process. The creative process results in *intellectual property rights,* which include copyrights and patents. Essentially, intellectual property rights protect the creations of a person's mind and talents. They are insurable property rights.

Copyrights. A *copyright* is a federally protected property right that gives authors the exclusive right to copy or otherwise reproduce the copyrighted material and to create additional works that derive from the original. The federal *Copyright Act of 1978*[1] permits the *fair use* by others of a copyrighted work for certain purposes such as teaching, research, criticism, or comment. What constitutes fair use is not precise and can cause problems in many cases. Courts consider the purpose of the use (commercial versus nonprofit education), the nature of the work, the amount and substantiality of the portion used, and the effect of the use on the value of the work.

The Copyright Act provides that an individual author's copyright is for the life of the author plus fifty years. If the copyright holder is a corporation or association, the copyright is for 100 years from the date of creation of the work or seventy-five years from the date of copyright, whichever expires first. Under prior law, if an author published a work without obtaining a copyright, the publication was a "dedication to the public," and anyone could copy or publish the work. A later copyright would not be possible. Under the new law, an author who publishes a work without obtaining a copyright may copyright a later printing. Copyrights apply to written works such as books and music, and also to computer software programs and the design of computer chips.

Patents. A *patent* is granted to one who has given physical expression to an idea. For example, an inventor imagines an invention, then physically creates it. The person obtaining the patent has the exclusive right to make, use, and sell the invention for seventeen years.

A patent is not renewable, and once the patent period elapses others may use the idea. To be patentable, an invention may be a new and useful device or machine or even a combination of known elements if they are combined to perform an additional or different purpose.

Accession. *Accession* is an increase or addition. Accession may be by natural accretion, as when an animal has offspring. It may result from a union of one thing with another, as a coat of paint applied to a house, or it may result from transformation of raw materials into a finished product, such as wooden barrels. The offspring of animals belong to the mother animal's owner. Thus, the owner of a cow is also the owner of each calf born to that cow.

Problems arise when one person adds value to another person's personal property without that person's consent. If a person knows that the owner has not consented and adds value anyway, payment is not necessary. Also, if a person wrongly takes another's property and then improves it, the wrongdoer does not acquire title to the finished product and is not entitled to payment for the improvements.

If, however, the original taking was innocent, as when one mistakenly cuts trees on another's land and transforms them into lumber, the *relative value test* may apply. Under this test, if the value of the finished product is greatly disproportionate to the value of the original goods, the innocent trespasser may retain title to the finished goods upon reimbursing the owner of the original goods for their reasonable value. When two innocent parties are involved, the law restores both parties to as nearly whole as possible.

Confusion. *Confusion* is the intermingling of goods of different owners. The problem usually arises when *fungible goods* in which each unit is identical to the others, such as wheat, are mixed so that it becomes impossible to identify and separate them. Courts consider whether the confusion resulted from willful misconduct or an innocent act. If the intermixture of goods was willful or fraudulent, the wrongdoer loses title to the goods, and the original owner has title.

When the confusion is innocent or accidental, the parties jointly own the entire mass in proportion to their respective interests. For example, a storm breaks down a fence between Bill's and George's pastures in which sheep that cannot be identified are grazing. Although Bill and George each know the number of sheep they had, they jointly own the sheep, having an interest in the mass of sheep in proportion to the original number owned. If the parties cannot determine the original numbers or amounts, they will each own a half interest in the mass. If, however, it is impossible to determine the original amounts contributed, the loss falls on the party who caused the intermixture. This could happen, for example, if either Bill or George were negligent, causing the fence to break down.

Bailments. Everyone becomes a bailor or bailee at some time. When one takes clothes to a cleaner or a car to a garage for repair, or lends a lawnmower to a neighbor, that person becomes a *bailor*. One who rents some tools, borrows a car, or undertakes to care for someone else's personal property becomes a *bailee*. The situation created is a *bailment*.

Elements. A bailment has three elements:

1. The transfer of possession of personal property without transfer of title
2. The acceptance of possession by the bailee
3. An express or implied agreement to redeliver the property to the bailor or to some third person whom the bailor designates

A bailment requires transfer of possession, which is something more than mere custody. In other words, when a shopkeeper hands an article to a customer to examine, the customer has only custody and is not a bailee. Similarly, an employee, such as a milk delivery person, is not a bailee of the company's milk, but has mere custody of the milk for delivery.

To be a bailee, one must accept delivery of the bailed property. If a person wants to return goods to a seller and, the goods not being accepted upon return, throws the goods on the floor, there is no bailment if the seller picks the goods up from the floor. Picking up the goods was for the purpose of getting them out of the way and not for the purpose of accepting responsibility for their care. Similarly, when one hangs one's coat on a coatrack in a restaurant, there is no bailment because there is no delivery to the owner. A bailment arises, however, if one leaves the coat with a cloakroom attendant. If, in parking a car in a parking lot, the car owner parks the car and takes the keys, there is no bailment, but merely a rental of space. If, however, the attendant parks the car and assumes control over the vehicle, there is a bailment, and a duty of care arises.

To be a bailee, one must also agree to redeliver the bailed goods to the bailor. If the bailee has the option to return other property in exchange for the goods, or to pay for the goods, no bailment exists.

Bailee's Duties and Rights. A bailee has possession only and cannot transfer title to a third party. If the bailee attempts to sell the bailed goods, the bailor may recover them from the third party unless the bailor has represented the bailee as the owner of the goods. The bailee must surrender the goods to the bailor upon request unless the bailment is for a term, such as a car rental, when the bailee may retain possession for that period. The bailee's possession is superior to any claims by third persons, and the bailee may sue third parties for damage to the bailed property.

Liens. A *possessory lien* is the bailee's right to retain possession of a bailor's property as security for the payment of a debt or performance of some other act. It is not an interest in the property itself. A lien may be nonpossessory, as a mortgage, in which the lienholder does not possess the property against which the lien is held. Most possessory liens arise from bailments of personal property. An example is an auto repair service, which can keep an auto until the owner pays the repair bill.

The lienholder is entitled to exclusive possession of the property until receipt of money owed. An owner of the property who wrongfully regains possession is liable to the lienholder.

The recovery is limited to the amount of money that the lien secures. The lienholder has the same right as any other bailee to hold third persons liable for damages to the property while it is in the lienholder's possession. The lienholder, as a bailee, must take reasonable care of the property, considering all circumstances. The duty of care includes making repairs and expenditures reasonably necessary to protect and preserve the property.

Bailee's Right To Use Property. To determine the extent of the bailee's right to use the bailed property, courts consider whether the bailment was for the bailee's sole benefit, for the bailor's sole benefit, or for the bailee's and bailor's mutual benefit. In a bailment for the bailee's sole benefit, as when a bailee borrows a bailor's car for personal use, the right to use the property is limited to the use the bailor contemplated. If the purpose is to travel between two points, any deviation from the route reasonably contemplated by the bailor might make the bailee liable for any loss that occurs during the deviation.

In a bailment for the bailor's sole benefit, the bailee may use or handle the property only to the extent necessary to preserve and protect it. For example, a bailee who accepts a watch for safekeeping should not wear it. In bailments for mutual benefit, the bailee may use the property within the agreement or contract. A leased car may be used according to the terms of the lease agreement. If the car is bailed for the purpose of storage or parking, the bailee may only store or park the vehicle and may not use it for other reasons.

Bailee's Right to Compensation. A bailment contract may require compensation. If not, a court will assume that the bailor intended to pay a reasonable value for the bailee's services if a reasonable person would have realized the services require payment. A bailment for the bailee's sole benefit does not imply a charge for services because it is not reasonable to assume that charges will be made. When compensation is expressed or implied, the bailee may assert a *lien,* which is a right to retain possession until paid against the goods for the value of the services performed in connection with the bailment.

A bailee may assert a lien only for charges due for the present transaction. A bailee who performs work or repairs on a vehicle, releases the vehicle to the bailor, and subsequently regains possession, may not assert a lien against the vehicle for the price of the original repairs, because the bailee loses the original right to assert a lien upon surrender of the vehicle. The bailee still has a right to compensation for the work but cannot assert a lien against the goods.

Bailee's Duties. The bailee must take reasonable care of the bailed goods. If the bailee exercises proper care, any loss or damage to the bailed property falls upon the bailor because he or she has title to it. Each type of bailment requires a different degree of care. In a bailment for the bailor's benefit, the bailee is gratuitously in charge of the goods and must use slight care only. Thus, if a bailor asks the bailee to care for the bailor's car, the bailee is liable for damage to the vehicle only if it was clear that the vehicle would be damaged and the bailee could have protected it without substantial trouble or expense.

When the bailment is for the bailee's sole benefit, as when the bailee borrows the bailor's car, the bailee must exercise an extraordinary degree of care. In bailments for mutual benefit, as when property is rented, the bailee must exercise the ordinary care of a reasonably prudent person under the circumstances.

Limiting Bailee Liability. By the contract of bailment, a bailee may extend or limit his or her liability for the bailed goods. The right to limit liability extends only to liability for ordinary negligence, not to willful or wanton misconduct.

Bailee's Insurable Interest. Because of the bailee's legal duty to care for the goods and to return them to the bailor, the bailee has an insurable interest in the goods and may obtain insurance to protect that interest. In the absence of a statute or specific contract requirement, however, the bailee has no duty to obtain insurance on the bailed goods. The bailee must hold insurance proceeds paid upon destruction of the bailed property in trust for the bailor, except for that amount representing the bailee's interest under the bailment agreement terms.

Bailor's Duties and Rights. In bailments for the bailor's sole benefit, the bailor is not entitled to compensation. In mutual benefit bailments and in bailments for the bailee's benefit, the bailor has a right to compensation according to the agreement.

If the bailed property is not returned at the end of the bailment term, the bailor may sue the bailee for refusal to surrender the goods. If the goods have been damaged, the bailor may sue either the bailee or a third person who damaged the property, whether negligently or willfully.

Bailor's Duties. In mutual benefit bailments, the bailor owes a duty to supply goods that are reasonably fit for the purpose the parties envision. The bailor must make a reasonable inspection of the goods to determine any defects.

The bailor implicitly warrants that the goods are in proper condition and is responsible for any damage the bailee suffers unless the bailee knows about the defects. In a bailment for the bailee's sole benefit, as when goods are lent to the bailee, the bailor must notify the bailee of known defects.

Bailor's Liability to Third Parties. A bailor is not usually liable for a bailee's negligent use of bailed property. For example, if one person borrows another's car and operates it negligently, the bailor is not negligent. Automobile liability insurance policies also cover permitted users of the vehicle insured. Because automobile bailees ordinarily have that protection, an injured third party has a source for recovery.

A bailor who negligently entrusts property to an incompetent bailee may be liable under the doctrine of *negligent entrustment* if injury results to third persons. For example, the owner who permits an unlicensed minor to operate the owner-bailor's car on the highway may be liable to third persons who sustain injuries as a result.

A bailor may also be held liable for injury to third persons if the bailed property is in a dangerous condition that is known or should be known to the bailor but is not known to the bailee.

Duty To Reimburse Bailee. The cost of repairs that are ordinary and incidental to the use of bailed goods under a rental contract is usually the bailee's responsibility. However, the cost of extensive repairs to the property must be paid by the bailor. For example, a bailee pays for repair of a flat tire but is not required to pay for new tires or an engine overhaul. The bailor must reimburse the bailee for repairs that the bailor should have made, such as installation of a new transmission in an automobile.

Termination of Bailment. A bailment for a specified period entitles the bailee to possession only for that period. If the bailment has no set time period, the bailor can terminate at any time and end the bailee's right to possession. The bailee must redeliver the goods within a reasonable time after the bailment period ends. An attempt by the bailee to sell the bailed goods, or to cause extensive damage to the goods, automatically terminates the bailment and entitles the bailor to recover the goods immediately.

Special Bailments. Special bailments include common carriers, hotelkeepers, warehouse operators, and factors. In these situations the bailees have unique obligations because they owe special duties of care to the bailors.

Common Carriers. A *common carrier* is any transporter that, by law, must carry all persons, or goods of all persons, who choose to use the carrier. Examples are public transit systems and airlines. Federal and state governments regulate common carriers' routes and rates. Carriage of goods is a mutual benefit bailment (that is, benefiting both the bailee and the bailor), but, because of the public interest involved, common carriers have a very high standard of care. A *shipper* is the party who owns or orders shipment of the goods.

A common carrier's liability to a shipper may be limited by contract between the parties. Statutes and administrative regulations create rules with which common carriers and shippers must comply to limit liability. It is against public policy to permit a common carrier to relieve itself entirely of liability for negligence.

The common carrier's liability arises at the time when it receives the goods. The common carrier's liability terminates either upon delivery of the goods to a freight terminal or when the recipient has had reasonable time to inspect and remove the goods from the carrier or terminal, depending upon the situation.

Hotelkeepers. A *hotelkeeper* offers lodging accommodations to transients. Like common carriers, the hotelkeeper insures the safety of a guest's personal belongings and goods. *Guests* are transients, not those who live permanently at a hotel. A hotelkeeper owes permanent residents, such as lodgers and boarders, the duty of reasonable care of their goods and personal effects. As a mutual benefit bailment, the hotelkeeper is liable only for failure to exercise reasonable care in protecting the property. A hotelkeeper's liability is limited if it provides a safe for storing guests' valuables.

Warehouse Operators. A public *warehouse* stores goods for the public. Warehouse operators can prescribe the type of goods they will accept for storage. The warehouse bailment is a bailment for mutual benefit, requiring a duty of reasonable care under the circumstances. The warehouse operator does not insure the stored goods. The warehouse operator issues a warehouse receipt for goods received, which may limit liability.

Factors. A *factor* is a person entrusted with possession of another's goods for sale on commission and is a special bailee who treats the goods as though he or she owns them. Although an ordinary bailee must return goods to a bailor, a factor can sell the goods. The factoring relationship is a bailment for mutual benefit. The factor must take reasonable care of the goods and return them in good condition if there is no sale.

Gifts. A *gift* is the voluntary and gratuitous transfer of property, without consideration. The giver is the *donor* and the recipient is the *donee*. A gift requires three elements:

1. Donative intent
2. Delivery
3. Acceptance by the donee

Donative Intent. A person may give away any or all of his or her property. Although the donor's subjective intent determines *donative intent,* objective manifestations such as the donor's comments and statements can help prove intent. Subjective intent is what the donor believes he or she is doing, and objective manifestations are what others might interpret as the donor's intent. The donor must intend to make a present gift, and a promise to make a future gift is not enforceable.

Delivery. *Delivery* of a gift may be actual physical transfer or may be *constructive,* which is implied delivery. In either case, the donor must give up all dominion over the article, and the donee must assume dominion over the article. If the donee already has the article, the donor need not repossess it and then return it to the donee. A donor handing car keys to a donee, for example, may establish constructive delivery of a car. When the tangible property is so extensive as to be incapable of physical delivery, a symbolic act is sufficient to accomplish delivery. A written document may prove delivery of an intangible item, such as a bank account.

Acceptance. Parties rarely dispute acceptance. When, however, a donee does not want the burdens of ownership, such as having to pay taxes, acceptance becomes important. One may not force a gift upon a donee, who must agree to accept the goods.

REAL PROPERTY

Real property is land and interests closely associated with land. Whether property is real or personal is important because the laws governing such matters as sales, mortgages, and transfers at death may differ when applied to each.

Real property includes the surface of the land and everything that is in, on, or above it, including oil, water, minerals, and gravel under the surface as well as trees, shrubs, and plants on the surface. It includes buildings permanently affixed to the land, as well as *fixtures,* which are personal property installed upon, attached to, or used with land or buildings in such a way as to become or be considered a part of the land.

Real Property Estates

Real property *estates* are various types of interest in land. An *interest* is a right, claim, or legal share of something. The total interest in real property consists of two elements:

1. Complete, outright, and full ownership (the quality)
2. Unlimited time (the duration)

Part of this total interest can be carved out to create lesser interests either as to the quality of the ownership or as to the length of time it exists.

Fee Simple Estate. A *fee simple estate* is complete ownership of property. The owner can leave the property to heirs and may sell, lease, or use it. When people say they "own land," they usually mean that they have a fee simple estate, which is an ancient English term.

Life Estate. A *life estate* lasts only until the life estate holder or another named person dies. For example, David grants land to Mary for the period of her life. Alternatively, David grants land to Mary for the period of Betty's life. In each case Mary is the *life tenant.*

The life tenant is entitled to exclusive possession of the land and to all income produced by it. If the life tenant sells the land, the buyer's interest lasts only as long as the life tenant lives. Therefore, a prospective buyer must be concerned with the life tenant's life expectancy.

Dower and Curtesy. *Dower* was the common law solution to a widow's need for support. At common law, a widow received, by law, a one-third interest for life in all real estate her husband had owned at any time during the marriage. The husband could not cut off the wife's right to dower without her consent. Dower rights took effect only when the husband died. Even today, a husband generally cannot disinherit a wife. If her husband's will gives a wife less than her dower portion, she may elect to receive the dower portion.

An important remnant of the common law is that a married man cannot transfer clear title to his real property without his wife's consent. If her husband attempts to sell real property without her consent and he dies before she does, his widow can sue a purchaser for the value of her interest. It is essential when obtaining a deed to real estate from a married man to make sure his wife signs the deed. A divorce bars the ex-wife's dower rights, but a mere separation does not. This consent requirement does not apply to personal property or to some real property situations.

Curtesy is the husband's equivalent of the dower right. At common law it was an interest in all the wife's real property owned during the marriage, for the husband's life, provided that a child was born of the marriage even if the child had died. Statutes have altered this right to grant the husband a certain minimum from his wife's property. When the wife sells her individually owned real estate, it is important for the buyer to obtain the husband's signature.

Both dower and curtesy differ among the states. Some state laws adhere much more closely to the common law than others, and it is always important to consult state law.

Concurrent Estates. It is common for two or more persons, particularly husband and wife, to own property concurrently. This ownership involves *concurrent estates,* which include joint tenancy, tenancy by the entireties, tenancy in common, community property, and cooperative and condominium ownership. In each of these situations the owners of the property may have interests they can insure even though they share the property with another person or other people. A *tenancy* is either a right to possession or ownership or both.

Joint Tenancy. *Joint tenancy* is probably the oldest form of concurrent ownership and is generally found today among members of the same family. The distinguishing feature of joint tenancy is that on the death of one joint tenant, the estate goes entirely to the other. If

David, Mary, and Betty are joint tenants, and David dies, his interest goes equally to Mary and Betty. If Mary then dies, the whole estate goes to Betty. If David is a married man, his wife has no dower interest in the property.

A joint tenancy must be created at one time, from one grantor, in equal shares. If there are two joint tenants, each must hold a one-half share, and so on. One of the joint tenants cannot be subject to a condition that does not apply to the others. They must all be named in the same deed.

Tenancy by the Entireties. A *tenancy by the entireties* is a special kind of joint tenancy created only between husband and wife. The usual form of deed is "to Husband and Wife, as tenants by the entireties." If the deed does not state "tenants by the entireties" explicitly, the law implies that phrase. Half of an estate may be taken as tenants by the entireties, and the other half by another person, as "to Husband and Wife, and Third Person."

A tenancy by the entireties is similar to a joint tenancy because the survivor takes the entire property. It differs from a joint tenancy in the following ways:

1. A sale or contract to sell does not sever the tenancy.
2. Individual creditors of either the husband or the wife cannot subject the property to a claim.
3. Neither party individually owns a portion that can be mortgaged.

Divorce ordinarily severs a tenancy by the entireties, which can also be terminated if both spouses join in a transfer of the property or if one spouse transfers his or her interest to the other.

Tenancy in Common. *Tenancy in common* differs from joint tenancy and tenancy by the entireties in the following ways:

1. It involves no survivorship.
2. The parties can own unequal shares.
3. They need not derive their interests in the same deed from the same grantor.

A will or deed may create a tenancy in common expressly, as when a deed is "to David and Mary, as tenants in common." More commonly it is created by operation of law. For example, if David dies intestate (without a will) and has three heirs, they will take David's real property as tenants in common.

Community Property. A few southern and western states follow the Spanish civil law theory that a husband and wife should share equally all property acquired during marriage by their communal efforts.

Under this *community property* concept, there are two types of property that may belong to a spouse—separate property and community property. The separate property of either spouse is that which the spouse owned at the time of marriage. It also includes any property that the spouse may acquire individually after marriage by gift or inheritance. Separate property is the sole property of the respective spouse because communal effort did not produce it, and it is free from all interest or control by the other spouse.

Under the community property concept, a husband and wife share equally in all community property, and the amount of their individual contribution to the joint effort does not change the equal interest. A gift to both spouses is community property.

Upon a spouse's death, the property is divided in half, with one-half going to the surviving spouse and the other half going to the deceased spouse's heirs, if any exist, unless more is given to the survivor by will. A spouse cannot, by will, dispose of more than one-half of community property, and there is neither dower nor curtesy in community property.

Cooperative Ownership. *Cooperative ownership* is not concurrent ownership in the strict sense of the term in that there is no unity of possession or an equal right to occupy the entire premises with all other tenants. However, it is closely akin to concurrent ownership and is a common method of owning real property, particularly apartments.

In cooperative ownership, a corporation holds title to the property. The participating cooperative owner purchases stock in the corporation and receives a long-term proprietary lease to a stipulated apartment. The lease sets forth the parties' rights and liabilities, including provisions for monthly payments. The number of shares in the corporation that each tenant owns may be equal or may vary according to the values of the apartments. For example, ten persons form a cooperative venture to construct ten apartments at a cost of $1 million. The five apartments on the ground floor are each valued at $120,000; the five on the second floor at $80,000. The corporation issues one hundred shares of $10,000 stock. Those desiring ground floor apartments purchase twelve shares, and those wanting the second floor purchase eight shares each.

The corporation ordinarily obtains a mortgage, constructs the building, and then operates it. Each tenant, as a shareholder in the corporation, has a proportional vote in its affairs based on the number of shares owned. The corporation levies monthly assessments to pay mortgage principal and interest, taxes, cost of operations, insurance on the structure in the name of the corporation, and other items.

Cooperative ownership provides for operation and maintenance by someone other than the tenant, while guaranteeing a right of occupancy for as long as desired. A disadvantage is the owner's limited control over external conditions, which may lead to a deterioration of the investment. It is sometimes difficult to find a purchaser for a premises, particularly if it is beginning to deteriorate. Also, if other tenants do not keep up their payments, and as a result the mortgage payments are not paid, the mortgagee may foreclose on the property. In that case all tenants may lose any equity they have built up in the property.

Condominium Ownership. *Condominium ownership,* like a cooperative, is similar to concurrent ownership. However, it is closer to a true concurrent ownership than the cooperative. Condominium ownership has two legal elements:

1. Individual ownership of a "unit," or separate, defined area
2. An undivided interest in common of public or common areas (common elements), which serve all individual units or areas

Unless both elements exist, there is no condominium interest, and the two elements cannot be separated. A unit owner cannot retain title to a unit and sell the undivided interest in the common element. Condominiums are usually multi-unit buildings, but sometimes groups of single-unit buildings qualify in this category.

The *common element* is essentially the land and the building, together with appurtenances, such as parking and storage areas, heating and cooling systems, and other building elements that serve two or more units. The unit an individual owns is just a "box of air."

A written declaration that details the number of units and the percentage interest that each unit has in the common elements creates a condominium. Bylaws usually govern day-to-day operations through an association established to run the common elements. All unit owners have interests as tenants in common in the common elements that may be, but usually are not, equal.

In contrast to cooperative ownership, the condominium owner, as a tenant in common, has a direct property interest in the land and buildings, rather than a secondary interest as a shareholder of a corporation. The individual can sell, transfer, mortgage, or leave to heirs his or her condominium interest.

Real Property Sales

Two basic documents establish most real property sales: contracts of sale and deeds.

Contracts of Sale. A contract of sale usually precedes a transfer of real property. The contract may be simple, but it must contain certain elements to be binding, and parties must be competent.

Vendor and Vendee. *Vendor* and *vendee* are the terms that apply, respectively, to the seller and purchaser of real property. After they execute the deed, they become the *grantor* and *grantee,* respectively.

Even if title is in the vendor's name only, if the vendor is married, the spouse should sign the contract of sale. The spouse's signature is necessary to transfer his or her interest to eliminate later claims for dower or curtesy, community property rights, or other rights.

Elements. A contract of sale for real property requires the following elements:

1. *Writing*—Under the Statute of Frauds, any agreement to transfer an interest in real property must be in writing and signed by the person to be bound. If the vendor attempts to enforce the contract against the vendee, the vendee must have signed it, and vice versa. The parties, however, may rescind a contract of sale orally because the rescission does not transfer an interest in real property and therefore need not be in writing. Any modification of the contract must be in writing.

2. *Essential Terms*—The contract must describe the premises to be sold and the price. The description need not be precise but must be sufficient to identify the property. Thus a reference to "1000 Park Avenue, to be sold for $100,000," would be sufficient.

3. *Unessential Terms*—Certain terms are not essential, but a complete contract of sale usually covers them. For example, the time of closing, if not stated, is to be within a reasonable time; payment usually occurs at closing.

Deeds. The instrument that actually transfers title to land is a *deed.* There are three principal types of deeds:

1. *Quit-Claim Deed*—The quit-claim deed merely transfers whatever title or interest, if any, the grantor may have in the land at the time of transfer. It contains no warranties, and if the land is encumbered by mortgages or liens, or has other claimants to it, they are the grantee's problems.

2. *Warranty Deed*—There are two types of warranty deeds, *general warranty* and *special warranty*. A general warranty deed, in addition to transferring whatever title the grantor has, contains the grantor's warranty that the title is free of all encumbrances (prior claims on the property), that the grantor has the title being transferred, and that no one else has a better title. In the event of breach of any of these warranties, also called

covenants, the grantee can sue the grantor. If there is an encumbrance, such as a mortgage on the property, the deed will say so. A special warranty deed contains warranties against only those encumbrances and defects in title that may have been created since the grantor took title. An insurance policy is even more important when a special warranty deed is used, because otherwise the grantee has no protection against earlier defects.

3. *Bargain-and-Sale Deed*—A bargain-and-sale deed is a special deed that transfers only the land and the grantor's interest but does not contain the warranties of title in the warranty deed. Frequently used by corporations, it transfers fee simple possession for a consideration.

It is more important for a deed to be absolutely accurate than the contract of sale because, if the two disagree, the deed prevails. The basic requirements of deeds are as follows:

- Under the Statute of Frauds, the deed must be in writing.
- The grantor must be legally competent, be named in the deed, and sign the deed.
- The deed must name the grantee.
- The deed must state the consideration.
- The deed must contain words that specifically state that a transfer of the property is taking place.
- The deed must contain a description of the property conveyed.
- The deed should be dated.
- The deed usually contains a paragraph reciting who transferred the property to the grantor, when it was transferred, and the place the recorded copy of that deed may be found.
- The grantor must sign the deed.
- A few states require the grantor's signature under seal.
- Several states require witnesses to the grantor's signature.
- The deed must be delivered to effect a transfer. Giving it to the grantee with an oral understanding that delivery is not to be effective until a stated condition is met is ineffective against an innocent third party.
- Most states require an acknowledgment, which is a formal, written statement by a public official, usually a notary public, that the grantor has appeared before the official and has declared that the instrument is his or her voluntary act and deed.

Recording and Priorities

Recording a deed means physically taking it to a local government office, usually known as the office of the recorder or register of deeds, and filing it along with all other local deeds. The purpose of recording is to give notice to the world that the transfer of real property has occurred, and the law assumes that the world knows of this or can know of it by checking at the recording office.

As between transfers of real property, the first transfer recorded prevails. If David sells land to Mary in 1970 and later sells the same land to Betty in 1976, under this rule Mary would prevail against Betty even though Betty knew nothing about the prior transaction.

To prevent such results, all states have recording acts. Under such an act any deed, mortgage, or other instrument affecting land is not valid against a subsequent purchaser for value without notice or knowledge unless the instrument has been recorded. For example, David sells land to Mary, who does not record the deed. David later sells the same land to Betty, who is unaware of the sale to Mary. Betty then records the deed. Betty's ownership takes priority over Mary's. An unrecorded document affecting property rights is effective between the immediate parties and persons who are not purchasers, such as donees and heirs, but not for subsequent purchasers for value without notice or knowledge.

Security Interests in Real Property

People have used real estate as collateral for loans for many centuries. Three principal types of contractual security devices apply to real property as security:

1. Mortgages
2. Trust deeds
3. Land contracts

Mortgages. The mortgage used in most states today is in the form of a deed or transfer of land by the borrower to the lender, with a statement of the debt and a provision that the mortgage shall be void upon the full payment of the debt. The *mortgagor* is the property owner who obtains the mortgage, and the *mortgagee* is the lender, such as a bank.

A real estate mortgage transfers an interest in real property and must be in writing and signed in the same manner as a deed. If not properly executed, it may not be eligible for recording. As between the parties, the validity of the mortgage does not depend on compliance with other formal requirements. Thus, if the parties intended the transaction as a loan and security type of transaction, it is a mortgage, regardless of the form of the contract. However, if a mortgagee with a warranty deed conveys the property to an innocent third party, the third party gets good title and the mortgagor can only recover damages from the mortgagee and cannot get the property back.

An unrecorded mortgage is not valid against good faith purchasers, subsequent mortgagees without knowledge, or creditors with liens on the property.

Mortgagor's Rights. As against most of the world, except the mortgagee, the mortgagor is the owner of the property. The mortgagor, who has the right to sell, lease, or even put another mortgage on property, is effectively the owner of the property as far as everyone else except the mortgagee is concerned. However, transactions after recording of a mortgage do not affect the mortgagee's rights.

Assume that David mortgages the land to Mary to secure a loan of $70,000 and records the mortgage properly. David then conveys the land to Betty. The sale is perfectly proper, but if David or Betty does not pay the loan when it falls due, Mary has a right to foreclose the mortgage and Betty's interest may be lost because it is subject to Mary's mortgage rights. If the proceeds of the sale are insufficient to satisfy the debt, the mortgagee has the right to obtain a deficiency judgment against the original mortgagor, and possibly against subsequent buyer, for the amount of the deficiency. If an excess is left after the sale, the surplus goes to the mortgagor or to a subsequent buyer.

Purchaser's Rights. Is a purchaser who takes property subject to an existing, properly recorded mortgage that is later defaulted liable to the mortgagee for a deficiency in payments after sale of the property to pay the debt? This depends upon the wording of the deed by which the buyer acquired the property.

If the deed states that the buyer takes the property "subject to" the mortgage, he or she is not liable for any deficiency in mortgage payments. If the deed states that the buyer "assumes and agrees to pay the mortgage debt," he or she then also becomes liable for any deficiency.

The original mortgagor who sells a property still remains liable on the original agreement to pay the debt and cannot be relieved of this liability without the consent of the mortgagee. In most states, the original mortgagor is a surety, or guarantor, for a buyer who assumes the debt. Therefore, if that buyer defaults in paying the mortgage and there is a deficiency in payments, the mortgagee can proceed against either the original mortgagor or the purchaser. However, an original mortgagor who pays may recover the amount paid from the purchaser, provided, of course, that the latter is solvent.

Mortgagee's Right To Assign. The mortgagee's interest in the property is assignable at any time, and the assignment must include the debt. If the debt is evidenced by a note, or series of notes, assignment is accomplished by negotiating the notes and making an outright assignment of the mortgage paper to the assignee. In most states, negotiation of the notes carries with it the right to the security, and their holder receives the benefits of the mortgage.

Foreclosure. Mortgage *foreclosure* is the mortgagee's remedy when the mortgagor defaults on mortgage payments, and foreclosure through public sale is the most common method of mortgage foreclosure. To foreclose, the mortgagee sues the mortgagor. Following trial, the court orders a judgment for the amount owed and orders a sale of the property. The proceeds of the sale first pay the judgment to the mortgagee. The surplus, if any, goes to the mortgagor. Generally, the mortgagor, or any other party claiming an interest in the property that may be cut off by foreclosure, may redeem the property after default and before expiration of a redemption period, usually six months or one year.

Trust Deeds. A regular mortgage has only two parties, the borrower (mortgagor) and the lender (mortgagee). The *trust deed,* also known as a deed of trust or trust indenture, has three parties. The borrower (*trustor*) transfers the land to a *trustee* for the benefit of the beneficiaries.

The trust deed is common in certain midwestern states and in California and is useful when large loans are involved. The trustee is in many respects a mortgagee, and the standard mortgage clause in an insurance policy usually refers not only to a mortgagee but also to a trustee.

Advantages. Trust deeds have three important advantages:

1. In several states, the trust deed can be foreclosed by a trustee's sale without any court proceedings, although some states treat it exactly like a mortgage and require court foreclosure.
2. The trust deed facilitates borrowing large amounts of money. For example, a company borrows a large sum from a bank and executes a trust deed on its property to the bank as trustee. The bank, in turn, sells a large number of notes or bonds authorized by the trust deed to investors who are secured by the trust deed, simplifying what might have been a very complicated mortgage procedure of separate notes and separate mortgages for each investor.
3. The holder of a bond secured by a trust deed can sell the bond with a minimum of expense and trouble. Sale of a note secured

by a mortgage requires an assignment of the mortgage, which is more complex.

Disadvantages. The principal disadvantage of trust deeds exists when the number of beneficiaries or bondholders is large. When the borrower pays off the trust deed, the trustee must be certain that all bondholders are paid. If not, the trustee is personally liable. Also, in a sale resulting from foreclosure, the trustee cannot purchase the property at foreclosure sale in most states, and a committee of bondholders must consummate the purchase.

Land Contracts. Under a *land contract,* the parties enter into an agreement of sale of property with a stipulation that the seller will not transfer title to the property until a certain percentage of the price, frequently 100 percent, has been paid. The percentage may be less than 100 percent, with the option to enter into a standard mortgage arrangement for the balance. Land contracts are frequently used when the buyer does not have a substantial credit rating or does not have enough money for a down payment.

The buyer takes possession of the land, pays all the taxes and assessments, insures the property, repairs it, and assumes all the obligations of an owner. In fact, the buyer is treated as the owner, and the seller has only the legal title. If the buyer defaults, the seller may declare the contract breached and repossess the property, treating the buyer as an ordinary tenant.

Mechanics' Liens on Real Property

A lien is a right that certain creditors have to obtain payment of debts owed to them from a debtor's real property, usually by a sale of the property. *Mechanics* and *material suppliers* are those who furnish labor and material for the construction of improvements on land. Because their contribution becomes part of the real property, they have security interests in the property, by statute, to ensure payment of their debts.

Any person whose labor and material contributes to the improvement of real property is entitled to a mechanic's lien on that property. Usually the work or material must become a permanent part of the real estate.

In some states, a lien claimant must show that the owner hired him or her to furnish work or material. In other states, a lien claimant may show that the owner consented to the work, even though another person, such as a tenant, ordered the work. Frequently, the owner cannot prevent a person from putting improvements on property. For example, a person who purchases land under a long-term contract orders the construction of improvements. The owner cannot object, but it is not fair for a lien to attach automatically. In these cases, some actual affirmative consent by the owner is necessary to bind the owner on a mechanic's lien.

Requirements for Obtaining a Lien. A general contractor who seeks to assert a lien must usually show substantial performance of the contract, the contract's improvement of a specific piece of property, and specific mention in the contract of the property to be improved.

State statutes usually require filing a notice of lien in some public office, such as the county clerk's office, within a period of time after completion of the work. Generally, the notice must state the amount claimed, the claimant's name and address, the type of improvement, a description of the land, and the owner's name. A mechanic's lien is usually for a specified time, and the lienholder must take steps to enforce or foreclose it within that time.

Priorities. There are four views among the states concerning when a mechanic's lien attaches to property and has priority over other secured interests:

1. In most states, mechanics' liens relate to the day the work started. A mortgage recorded on the following day is subordinate to the lien of a subcontractor who was not hired until later because that lien relates back to the start of the work. There are no priorities among lienholders.
2. The lien attaches when the mechanic who claims the lien commences work and cannot have priority over a mortgage recorded earlier.
3. The lien attaches on the date the mechanic makes the contract for improvement. This is called a *secret lien* because improvement contracts are usually not recorded, and even an inspection of the premises would not disclose that work is to be started later. Nevertheless, a mortgage recorded after the date of the improvement contract is subordinate to the mechanic's lien.
4. The lien attaches on the date notice is filed in the public office. A prior recorded mortgage, therefore, has priority.

Foreclosure. Foreclosing a mechanic's lien resembles foreclosing a mortgage. In some states, the lien attaches only to the building but not to the land, and in some places only to the additions or improvements themselves. Usually the materials furnished cannot be removed without injury to the property. Therefore, the courts frequently order the sale of the property and give the mechanic's lienholder a share of the proceeds.

Waiver of Lien. Parties may waive the right to a mechanic's lien in the contract for improvements. In some states, the provision is not valid unless the contract is filed. In some states, the waiver is valid against everybody, including subcontractors; in others it is valid only against the general contractor.

Another method of waiver is to obtain a partial waiver from the mechanic as work progresses and when the mechanic receives partial payments. The waiver usually recites that the mechanic waives all liens "for work and materials furnished" up to the date of the waiver. Any lien that is paid off is cleared from the public records by filing a *release of mechanic's lien* form in the office where the lien was filed.

Incidental Real Property Rights

This section discusses several important rights that are "incidental" to either possession or ownership of land:

1. Adverse possession
2. Rights under, above, and on the land's surface
3. Lateral and subjacent support
4. Water rights
5. Fixtures

Adverse Possession. A problem arises when one person who is in possession of land claims ownership, and another who is out of possession also claims ownership. The person who is not in possession, but who claims legal ownership, may sue the person in possession. The person who claims ownership by possession only is claiming *adverse possession,* which has four requisites:

1. The adverse party must have exclusive possession of the property and occupy it in the usual way, such as living in a residence.
2. Possession must be open and obvious.
3. Possession must be adverse, or *hostile,* and without the owner's permission.
4. Possession must be continuous for a period required by statute, which usually is a lengthy period of time.

Rights Under, Above, and on the Surface. Ownership of land includes the incidental rights of whatever is under, above, and on the surface.

Rights Under the Surface. Ownership of land includes ownership of everything below the surface, including such things as minerals, clay, stone, gravel, and sand. A transfer of land also transfers these materials, but one may reserve *mineral rights* in the deed. Oil and gas, on the other hand, flow freely under the surface, and no person owns them until he or she possesses them.

Rights Above the Surface. Ownership of the surface carries with it limited rights over the air space above the land. An owner can halt unauthorized intrusion into this air space, such as projections from an adjoining building or utility lines stretched across the air space. Generally planes may fly over land as long as they do not interfere unreasonably with the owner's use and enjoyment of the land.

Rights on the Surface. The property owner also has rights to products of the soil. Annual products, such as crops, are personal property. Permanent products, such as timber, can be real property.

Lateral and Subjacent Support. A landowner has the right to lateral and subjacent support systems that may not be on the landowner's property.

Lateral Support. The right of *lateral support* applies to land in its natural condition only. For example, David and Mary own adjoining vacant lots, and David excavates his land close to the property line, causing a part of Mary's land to fall into the excavation. David is liable to Mary for damages. However, if Mary's lot has a building on it, David is not liable because the duty extends only to land in its natural state. The right is only to support the land (not necessarily in the natural state), and if David builds a retaining wall to support Mary's land, that is sufficient.

If there is a building on Mary's land, David must give Mary reasonable notice of an intent to excavate, so that Mary can take steps to support the building, and David must excavate with reasonable care. If David fails to give notice and use reasonable care, he may be liable to Mary for damages should Mary's building fall over or collapse.

Subjacent Support. A party who sells a portion of the subsurface, such as the mineral rights, retains a natural right of *subjacent support* from the underlying mineral area, but for land in its natural state. If support is withdrawn and the surface subsides, the surface owner may recover damages without proving negligence by the subjacent owner. Also, as with lateral support, the subjacent owner may furnish artificial supports, such as columns or braces.

Water Rights. Another "incidental" land ownership right is water rights, including rights to both underground and surface waters.

Underground Water. An owner may remove underground waters that merely percolate through the soil and follow no defined course in such quantities as desired, even if it deprives other adjacent owners of water, so long as the owner uses it on the land and does not sell it at a distance, to the adjoining landowners' detriment. When water is scarce, an owner can use only a reasonable amount.

Surface Water. The discharge of surface water from one's land onto another's does not create a cause of action as long as the water is not collected by artificial means and discharged upon the adjoining land in new or concentrated channels so as to cause damage.

Streams. Streams may be property boundaries or may pass through part of the property. A person with a stream on or adjoining his or her property is a *riparian owner*. Water beneath the surface and flowing in a well-defined course, such as an underground river, is subject to the same rules as for surface streams.

A riparian owner may use as much water from the stream as needed for domestic purposes but must use only a reasonable amount for industrial purposes and consider downstream owners' needs. Riparian owners have a right to a pollution-free stream, and polluters are often liable to them in damages.

Fixtures. *Fixtures* are property installed upon, attached to, or used with land or buildings in such a way as to become real property themselves. Thus, if a tenant installs fixtures that were originally personal property, they become part of the realty and upon installation belong to the owner of the realty. Personal property that has become a fixture is transferred, without specific reference, along with the sale of land. Three tests help in determining whether an item is a fixture:

1. If an article cannot be removed from the realty without substantial injury to the realty, such as a fireplace, it is a fixture, even though the wall from which it is taken is rebuilt.

2. If an article is specially constructed or fitted for use in a building, or if the article was installed in the building to enable the building to be used for its purpose, it is a fixture. A heater and a door in a house are examples.

3. If the party who annexed the property intended an item to become part of the land, that item also is a fixture. This test must often be applied in conjunction with a fourth factor, which is the relationship of the parties to the property. An owner, for instance, who attaches to a wall a mirror that can be removed without substantial damage to the premises may intend that it be there permanently. A tenant, however, who attaches a similar mirror may intend to remove it at the end of the lease term.

Trade Fixtures. When a tenant rents a building to conduct a business, the test of intention applies in the tenant's favor. Between lessor and lessee, all structures attached for the purpose of trade during the tenancy, or *trade fixtures,* are removable, including such articles as heavy bakery ovens, stone piers for railroad trestles, brick tunnel kilns, and large steam boilers. So long as the article can be removed without permanent injury to the land or building, it may be removed if a tenant put it there solely for trade purposes, and it does not become part of the land.

Improvements and Betterments. The law of fixtures has a special insurance application in connection with covering *improvements and betterments.* Improvements and betterments are substantial alterations, additions, or changes to the premises made by a lessee beyond a simple repair job. For example, painting and papering as a part of a general plan of fixing up the premises for initial occupancy by the tenant is an improvement and not a repair and cannot be considered a fixture.

Land Use Restrictions

Just as incidental rights to possession and ownership can restrict an owner's otherwise absolute right to use land, other restrictions benefit either private parties or the public as a whole and include the following:

1. Incorporeal interests
2. Licenses
3. Legislative controls

Incorporeal Interests. Modern law recognizes four major *incorporeal interests,* which are nonmaterial interests, in real property:

1. Easements
2. Profits *à prendre*
3. Restrictions on land use
4. Rents

This section discusses the first three interests, and this chapter discusses lease situations, which include rents, in a later section.

Easements. An *easement* is the nonpossessory right to use another's real property for a particular purpose. It may be created expressly, by implication, or by prescription (adverse possession).

An easement may be created expressly by reserving it when the land to which it is to attach is sold. For example, David owns a piece of land fronting on a road. He subdivides the property into two lots. Lot 1 contains the family homestead and constitutes the back half of the property, away from the road. Lot 2 is the remaining half and has the entire road frontage. Lot 2 now cuts off Lot 1 from the road. David sells Lot 2 but expressly reserves a right of access across it from Lot 1 to the road. This is an expressly created easement applicable to Lot 2 in David's favor, even though David no longer owns the land.

An easement may also be created by implication. In the previous example, if David sells Lot 2 without expressly reserving an easement, the easement, in such a case called an easement by necessity, would probably be created by implication, particularly if the only means of access to Lot 1 is a well-defined roadway running across Lot 2 to Lot 1.

Profits à Prendre. *Profits à prendre* differ from regular easements. The usual easement must benefit adjacent land and be next to that land. Profits *à prendre* may be next to the land, but they are independent of the ownership of any other land.

A profit *à prendre* is one person's right to take a part of the soil belonging to another person, or the product of that soil. For example, the rights to mine coal, remove sand and gravel, cut down trees, and remove similar materials are profits *à prendre* rights. Rights to water or oil are not profits *à prendre* because the term applies only to a part of the land that is subject to ownership. Liquids are not the subject of ownership until removed and reduced to possession because they flow freely under the land and are not in a fixed position.

The profits *à prendre* right includes the right to do anything reasonably necessary to obtain the materials. Thus, it includes the right to enter upon the land, dig holes to get to the substances, and perform related acts.

Restrictions on Land Use. In selling real property, an owner may restrict its use. A restriction may be to preserve or enhance the value of land retained by the seller, or it may be for the benefit of the land sold.

Examples of legally valid restrictions are agreements on the minimum cost of homes, the minimum size of buildings, and the types of construction. Discriminatory agreements prohibiting sale to certain racial or ethnic groups, on the other hand, are unenforceable. Some states expressly limit restrictions on land use to a statutory period of thirty or forty years. Changed conditions, such as economic conditions in the area, may make restrictions unenforceable.

Licenses. A *license,* as distinguished from an easement, is merely permission to do something on someone else's property that otherwise would be a trespass or another illegal act. Permission to hunt or fish on another's land, a ticket for a seat in a theater, and the renting of a hotel room are typical licenses.

The license gives no interest in the land but is mere permission to use it in some way. A license can be oral, written, or implied. For example, by implication the public has a license to use the public halls in an office building.

Government Controls.   Government, like some private parties, has certain powers over the use of land on behalf of the public as a whole. The law in this area is evolving constantly, and what may have been an unreasonable governmental restraint years ago may not be considered so today. The government, under the guise of protecting the public, cannot interfere arbitrarily with the lawful use of land or impose unreasonable and unnecessary restrictions upon it. An example of the lawful exercise of government's power is the regulation of the number of wells that may be drilled and the flow of oil and gas from those wells on the grounds of protecting against waste, in which not only adjoining landowners but also the public at large has an interest. The condemnation and destruction of diseased trees or plants is another example.

Zoning, building codes, and eminent domain are the most frequent methods governments employ to restrict land use.

Zoning.   *Zoning* is government's regulation of building construction and occupancy and land use according to a comprehensive plan.

A zoning ordinance must provide a comprehensive general plan for the entire community and must be uniform for each class or kind of occupancy or use of land within a given district. Requirements may vary from district to district, but, within limits, all property in like circumstances must be treated the same. Matters affected by zoning laws include lot size, minimum size of buildings, number of families to reside in the buildings, maximum height of each building, and parking areas.

A zoning ordinance cannot single out a small area of land for a use classification that is totally different from that of the surrounding area when the result benefits the owner of the particular area to the neighbors' detriment. Such a permitted use is *spot zoning.* Zoning that restricts land use either by prohibiting additional building or by requiring high standards, such as five-acre lots or single-family dwellings, is *exclusionary zoning.* Two ways to relieve a property from compliance with a restrictive ordinance are *special exceptions* and *variances.*

Special Exceptions.   A special exception is a use explicitly permitted by the zoning ordinance but subject to certain limitations. Exceptions are special uses considered desirable for the general welfare, but only when controlled, such as the building of a school or a church in a residential zone. The use will be permitted by an ordinance, but only if approved by the government.

Variances.   A variance is relief from the strict application of an ordinance to permit a use that is not permitted otherwise. There are two types of variances. The first, a *hardship variance,* applies to situations in which, because of size, topography, or other physical limitations, a given lot in a division does not conform to the ordinance requirements. If strict application of the requirements were to result in peculiar and exceptional difficulties or undue hardship on the owner, the government may grant a variance.

The second group is called *use variances.* In particular cases and for special reasons, the government may grant a use variance to permit an otherwise prohibited use within the zone. An example of a "special reason" is a use that benefits the general welfare.

To avoid the constitutional prohibition against taking property without due process, any *nonconforming use* existing at the time an ordinance is passed is permitted to continue. The use must exist at the time and not just be permitted. Such a use may not be enlarged and can be terminated by total destruction of the structure, by abandonment of the use, or by a change in use.

Building Codes.   Many cities and states have adopted *building codes,* which may overlap zoning ordinances. However, they address the more technical details of construction, electrical wiring, heating, and similar matters. Owners must submit building plans to a building department for examination to see whether they conform to the code. If they do, a building permit is issued. After the structure is completed, a final inspection occurs before anyone can occupy the structure, and the government must issue a certificate of occupancy.

Eminent Domain.   Another method by which government controls the use of private property is the exercise of *eminent domain,* by which the government seizes the property for use to benefit the public at large. Eminent domain usually requires a *condemnation proceeding,* by which the condemnor files a petition in court stating the exact property desired and the public use involved. There are two conditions for granting the petition:

1.   The land must be taken for public use.
2.   Just compensation must be paid to the owner. Just compensation is the fair market value at the time of the taking.

Landlord and Tenant

Landlord and tenant law governs lease interests in real property, which are limited interests of limited duration. State laws vary significantly with regard to many of the principles discussed in this section.

Types of Estates.   The three types of landlord and tenant estates are estates for years, tenancy at will, and periodic tenancy.

Estates for Years. *Estates for years* are created for a definite number of years, such as a tenancy for twenty years, or, for shorter periods, such as three months.

Tenancies at Will. *Tenancy at will* is merely permission to occupy a premises at the landlord's will. Under a tenancy at will, the landlord can put the tenant out at any time the landlord pleases without advance notice.

Periodic Tenancies. A *periodic tenancy* is a variation of tenancy for years, because it does not have a fixed termination date but runs for a period of time, such as one year, with a provision for automatic renewal for similar periods until one of the parties gives notice of intent to terminate.

A periodic tenancy may be created by an express agreement, usually called a "tenancy from year to year" or "from month to month." It may also be created by implication. For example, a lease has no expiration date but states that the rental is $10,000 per year, payable one-twelfth each month. This implies a tenancy from year to year, based on the periodic rent payments. Such a tenancy may also arise by implication of law. This occurs when one is a *holdover tenant,* who has a lease for a number of years and at the expiration of that lease continues to occupy the premises. The tenant becomes what is called a *tenant at sufferance,* who, if the landlord does not acquiesce in the occupancy, may be ejected. However, if the landlord expressly approves the occupancy or accepts rent, then by implication of law a periodic tenancy arises.

The periodic tenancy maybe from month to month or year to year, depending on the terms of the prior tenancy. By statute in some states, it is a month-to-month tenancy unless the parties otherwise agree. The other terms of the prior lease continue to apply. The notice period is usually one lease period, but if the period is a year or longer, most states require three-to-six months' notice.

Landlord's Rights and Duties. The landlord's primary duty is to deliver possession of the premises to the tenant on the inception date of the lease. The landlord's primary rights are to receive the rent when due and to recover the premises at the end of the lease in the same condition in which they were leased, except for reasonable wear and tear.

If the tenant defaults, the landlord is under no duty to lessen the financial loss by trying to find another tenant. If a tenant abandons the property, the landlord may treat abandonment as an anticipatory breach and receive as damages the amount of the remaining rent payments. In these cases, the landlord must mitigate, or lessen, the loss. Many long-term leases provide that in event of default the landlord may accelerate the payments, reenter the premises, act as the tenant's agent to sublet, and sue the tenant for any resulting losses.

Many landlords require *security deposits,* which are either a percentage of the rent or equivalent to a specified period of rent. The lease usually provides that, in case of default, the security deposit represents damages that the landlord may retain. Some statutes provide that the security deposit is the tenant's property, that the landlord must keep it in a bank escrow account, and that the landlord must return it to the tenant after termination of the lease.

Landlord's Remedies. When a tenant remains in possession at the termination of the lease, or the tenant owes rent or has breached the lease, the landlord may evict the tenant with or without court assistance. In a so-called "self-help" eviction, the landlord may remove the tenant's possessions from the premises and bar the tenant from reentering the premises by changing door locks or by other peaceful means. The landlord must demand rent from the tenant, or correction of other breaches, to make the tenant a tenant at sufferance. If the landlord uses force or a threat of force, the eviction is unlawful and the tenant is entitled not only to reenter but also to recover damages.

The landlord may also apply to the courts for help. Many states provide for a *summary eviction proceedings* to apply when the lease is terminated and the tenant refuses to move, or during the lease term if there is a default in rent. The landlord must send the tenant a written notice that terminates the tenancy and demands possession. After a period of time, the landlord serves a summons and complaint, followed by a court hearing. If the landlord establishes a right to possession, the court enters an order of repossession followed by a warrant of removal. The tenant has only two defenses:

1. The rent has been paid.
2. The rent is not legally due.

In the latter case, the tenant may demonstrate that the landlord has not evicted the tenant through legal procedures but has effectively "driven out" the tenant by rendering the premises uninhabitable. Otherwise, there is usually no defense to eviction by a landlord, and the landlord need give no reason for the termination.

Eviction may be either actual or constructive. Actual eviction from the whole or even a part of the premises ends the obligation to pay rent. *Constructive eviction* occurs when conditions arise that prevent the tenant's enjoyment of a substantial or integral part of the premises. Examples include inadequate heat or hot water, leaky plumbing, serious disturbances by other tenants, and infestation by bugs or rodents.

When the tenant is in default on rent, the landlord may seize possession of the tenant's property and hold it for the rent. This is called *distraint*. The landlord must seize the goods peacefully and sell them at a public sale. Distraint and self-help are very similar, particularly if the landlord removes the tenant's property from the premises in the self-help proceedings.

In addition to distraint, a landlord also has a nonpossessory lien on the tenant's property for rent due. This lien applies frequently to commercial leases, when the tenant becomes insolvent. The lien attaches merely by declaring that the goods on the premises are subject to the lien and by notifying the defaulting tenant of the lien. Any purchaser of the goods, or creditor of the tenant, who takes the goods with notice of the lien is liable for damages.

Tenant's Rights and Duties. The tenant's rights and duties exactly complement those of the landlord. Thus, the tenant must pay rent and leave the premises in the condition in which they were received, except for reasonable wear and tear. The tenant has a right to occupy the premises, and upon eviction, the obligation to pay rent may end.

The tenant is relieved of responsibility to pay rent only if (1) demand is made on the landlord to correct the situation, (2) the landlord does not do so within a reasonable time, and (3) the tenant leaves the premises at the end of that reasonable time. Staying at the premises may constitute a waiver. The tenant has a right to vacate the premises and escape liability for rent but does not have an action for damages. However, if an express covenant in the lease requires the landlord to make repairs, there may be damages for breach of contract.

Liability of Parties. As a general rule, the landlord is liable to third parties for injuries sustained on the premises to the same extent he or she would be liable to the tenant. Thus, liability is restricted to the landlord's negligent acts or latent defects on the premises.

In many states, the landlord may escape liability to the tenant by an exculpatory clause in the lease whereby the tenant relieves, or excuses, the landlord of any liability. This does not affect the landlord's liability to third persons. If the defective condition arises after the inception of the lease and there is no lease requirement that the landlord keep the premises in repair, the landlord is usually not liable even to third parties. However, if the condition continues and exists at the time the lease is renewed, the landlord becomes liable on the theory of a continuing nuisance of which he or she had notice at time of renewal.

The tenant is liable to third parties for injuries caused by any acts he or she causes. The tenant is liable when he or she has sole possession of the premises, and the landlord has no obligation to repair. A single policy of insurance may protect both the landlord and the tenant. The tenant is also liable to the landlord for any damages to the premises exceeding ordinary wear and tear. Here again, there may be a clause exculpating the tenant from liability.

SUMMARY

Real property is land, buildings, and things attached to land or buildings. Personal property is everything else one can own. The first part of this chapter examined personal property, beginning with intellectual property. One may obtain personal property through creation of property, accession, confusion, bailments, or gifts.

One can create property rights in intellectual property and therefore have a copyright or a patent right. Accession is an increase or addition. Confusion is the intermingling of goods of different owners.

In bailments, a bailor leaves personal property with a bailee for safekeeping or repair. A bailment requires three elements:

1. The transfer of possession without transfer of title
2. The bailee's acceptance of possession
3. An express or implied agreement to redeliver the property to the bailor or to a third person whom the bailor designates

A bailee has possession only and cannot transfer title to the property but may have a right to use the property. Special bailments involve common carriers, hotelkeepers, warehouse operators, and factors. Each type of bailment requires a different degree of care.

A possessory lien is the right to retain possession of personal property as security for the payment of a debt or performance of an act and is not an interest in property. A gift of personal property is the donor's voluntary transfer of property to a donee without consideration and requires three elements:

1. Donative intent
2. Delivery
3. Donee's acceptance

The second part of the chapter discusses real property total interest, which consists of two elements:

1. Complete, outright, and full ownership (quality)
2. Unlimited time (duration)

A fee simple estate is complete ownership of real property. Parts of this total interest can be carved out to create lesser interests, either as to the quality of the ownership or the length of time it exists. Examples are life estates and dower and curtesy rights.

Concurrent estates include the following:

1. Joint tenancy
2. Tenancy by the entireties
3. Tenancy in common
4. Community property
5. Cooperative ownership
6. Condominium ownership

Upon one joint tenant's death, the estate goes entirely to the other. A tenancy by the entireties is a joint tenancy created between husband and wife, and the survivor takes possession of the entire property. Tenancy in common involves no survivorship, and parties can own unequal shares. Community property provides that a husband and wife share equally all property acquired during marriage by their communal efforts.

In cooperative ownership, a corporation holds title to the property, and the participating cooperative owner purchases stock in the corporation and receives a long-term proprietary lease to an apartment. Condominium ownership involves individual ownership of a unit and an undivided interest in the common elements.

A real property sale involves a contract of sale and a deed, both of which, under the Statute of Frauds, must be in writing. Recording of real estate transfer documents protects buyers against subsequent purchasers. Security interests in real property include mortgages, trust deeds, and land contracts. Mechanics' liens give certain creditors rights to have their debts paid out of debtors' property, usually by sale.

Incidental real property rights include adverse possession claims; rights under, above, and on the land's surface; the right to lateral and subjacent support; water rights; and the right to fixtures. Land use restrictions include easements, profits *à prendre,* restrictions on land use, rents, licenses, zoning, building codes, and eminent domain.

Landlord-tenant law governs lease interests in real property, which are limited interests of limited duration. A landlord's primary duty is to deliver possession of the premises to the tenant at the inception of the lease. The tenant must pay rent and leave the premises in the condition in which they were received, except for reasonable wear and tear. The landlord is liable to third parties for injuries sustained on the premises to the same extent he or she would be liable to the tenant, and the tenant is liable to third parties for injuries caused by any acts he or she causes.

Chapter Note

1. 17 U.S.C. § 101.

APPENDIX

CONSTITUTION OF THE UNITED STATES

Proposed by Convention September 17, 1787
Effective March 4, 1789

WE the people of the United States, in order to form a more perfect union, establish justice, insure domestic tranquility, provide for the common defense, promote the general welfare, and secure the blessings of liberty to ourselves and our posterity, do ordain and establish this Constitution for the United States of America.

ARTICLE I

SECTION 1.   All legislative powers herein granted shall be vested in a Congress of the United States, which shall consist of a Senate and House of Representatives.

SECTION 2.   1. The House of Representatives shall be composed of members chosen every second year by the people of the several States, and the electors in each State shall have the qualifications requisite for electors of the most numerous branch of the State legislature.

2.   No person shall be a representative who shall not have attained to the age of twenty-five years, and been seven years a citizen of the United States, and who shall not, when elected, be an inhabitant of that State in which he shall be chosen.

3.   Representatives [and direct taxes]* shall be apportioned among the several States which may be included within this Union, according to

* See the 16th Amendment.

their respective numbers, [which shall be determined by adding to the whole number of free persons, including those bound to service for a term of years, and excluding Indians not taxed, three fifths of all other persons.]* The actual enumeration shall be made within three years after the first meeting of the Congress of the United States, and within every subsequent term of ten years, in such manner as they shall by law direct. The number of representatives shall not exceed one for every thirty thousand, but each State shall have at least one representative; and until such enumeration shall be made, the State of New Hampshire shall be entitled to choose three, Massachusetts eight, Rhode Island and Providence Plantations one, Connecticut five, New York six, New Jersey four, Pennsylvania eight, Delaware one, Maryland six, Virginia ten, North Carolina five, South Carolina five, and Georgia three.

4. When vacancies happen in the representation from any State, the executive authority thereof shall issue writs of election to fill such vacancies.

5. The House of Representatives shall choose their speaker and other officers; and shall have the sole power of impeachment.

Section 3.   1. The Senate of the United States shall be composed of two senators from each State, [chosen by the legislature thereof,]† for six years; and each senator shall have one vote.

2. Immediately after they shall be assembled in consequence of the first election, they shall be divided as equally as may be into three classes. The seats of the senators of the first class shall be vacated at the expiration of the second year, of the second class at the expiration of the fourth year, and of the third class at the expiration of the sixth year, so that one third may be chosen every second year; and if vacancies happen by resignation, or otherwise, during the recess of the legislature of any State, the executive thereof may make temporary appointments until the next meeting of the legislature, which shall then fill such vacancies.†

3. No person shall be a senator who shall not have attained to the age of thirty years, and been nine years a citizen of the United States, and who shall not, when elected, be an inhabitant of that State for which he shall be chosen.

4. The Vice President of the United States shall be President of the Senate, but shall have no vote, unless they be equally divided.

5. The Senate shall choose their other officers, and also a president *pro tempore,* in the absence of the Vice President, or when he shall exercise the office of the President of the United States.

6. The Senate shall have the sole power to try all impeachments. When sitting for that purpose, they shall be on oath or affirmation. When the

* See the 14th Amendment.
† See the 17th Amendment.

President of the United States is tried, the chief justice shall preside: and no person shall be convicted without the concurrence of two thirds of the members present.

7. Judgment in cases of impeachment shall not extend further than to removal from office, and disqualifications to hold and enjoy any office of honor, trust or profit under the United States: but the party convicted shall nevertheless be liable and subject to indictment, trial, judgment and punishment, according to law.

SECTION 4. 1. The times, places, and manner of holding elections for senators and representatives, shall be prescribed in each State by the legislature thereof; but the Congress may at any time by law make or alter such regulations, except as to the places of choosing senators.

2. The Congress shall assemble at least once in every year, and such meeting shall be on the first Monday in December,* unless they shall by law appoint a different day.

SECTION 5. 1. Each House shall be the judge of the elections, returns and qualifications of its own members, and a majority of each shall constitute a quorum to do business; but a smaller number may adjourn from day to day, and may be authorized to compel the attendance of absent members, in such manner, and under such penalties as each House may provide.

2. Each House may determine the rules of its proceedings, punish its members for disorderly behavior, and, with the concurrence of two thirds, expel a member.

3. Each House shall keep a journal of its proceedings, and from time to time publish the same, excepting such parts as may in their judgment require secrecy; and the yeas and nays of the members of either House on any question shall, at the desire of one fifth of those present, be entered on the journal.

4. Neither House, during the session of Congress, shall, without the consent of the other, adjourn for more than three days, nor to any other place than that in which the two Houses shall be sitting.

SECTION 6. 1. The senators and representatives shall receive a compensation for their services, to be ascertained by law, and paid out of the Treasury of the United States. They shall in all cases, except treason, felony, and breach of the peace, be privileged from arrest during their attendance at the session of their respective Houses, and in going to and returning from the same; and for any speech or debate in either House, they shall not be questioned in any other place.

2. No senator or representative shall, during the time for which he was elected, be appointed to any civil office under the authority of the

* Modified by the 20th Amendment.

United States, which shall have been created, or the emoluments whereof shall have been increased during such time; and no person holding any office under the United States shall be a member of either House during his continuance in office.

SECTION 7.   1. All bills for raising revenue shall originate in the House of Representatives; but the Senate may propose or concur with amendments as on other bills.

2.   Every bill which shall have passed the House of Representatives and the Senate, shall, before it becomes a law, be presented to the President of the United States; if he approves he shall sign it, but if not he shall return it, with his objections to that House in which it shall have originated, who shall enter the objections at large on their journal, and proceed to reconsider it. If after such reconsideration two thirds of that House shall agree to pass the bill, it shall be sent, together with the objections, to the other House, by which it shall likewise be reconsidered, and if approved by two thirds of that House, it shall become a law. But in all such cases the votes of both Houses shall be determined by yeas and nays, and the names of the persons voting for and against the bill shall be entered on the journal of each House respectively. If any bill shall not be returned by the President within ten days (Sundays excepted) after it shall have been presented to him, the same shall be a law, in like manner as if he had signed it, unless the Congress by their adjournment prevent its return, in which case it shall not be a law.

3.   Every order, resolution, or vote to which the concurrence of the Senate and the House of Representatives may be necessary (except on a question of adjournment) shall be presented to the President of the United States; and before the same shall take effect, shall be approved by him, or being disapproved by him, shall be repassed by two thirds of the Senate and House of Representatives, according to the rules and limitations prescribed in the case of a bill.

SECTION 8.   The Congress shall have the power

1.   To lay and collect taxes, duties, imposts, and excises, to pay the debts and provide for the common defense and general welfare of the United States; but all duties, imposts, and excises shall be uniform throughout the United States;

2.   To borrow money on the credit of the United States;

3.   To regulate commerce with foreign nations, and among the several States, and with the Indian tribes;

4.   To establish a uniform rule of naturalization, and uniform laws on the subject of bankruptcies throughout the United States;

5.   To coin money, regulate the value thereof, and of foreign coin, and fix the standard of weights and measures;

6. To provide for the punishment of counterfeiting the securities and current coin of the United States;

7. To establish post offices and post roads;

8. To promote the progress of science and useful arts, by securing for limited times to authors and inventors the exclusive right to their respective writings and discoveries;

9. To constitute tribunals inferior to the Supreme Court;

10. To define and punish piracies and felonies committed on the high seas, and offenses against the law of nations;

11. To declare war, grant letters of marque and reprisal, and make rules concerning captures on land and water;

12. To raise and support armies, but no appropriation of money to that use shall be for a longer term than two years;

13. To provide and maintain a navy;

14. To make rules for the government and regulation of the land and naval forces;

15. To provide for calling forth the militia to execute the laws of the Union, suppress insurrections and repel invasions;

16. To provide for organizing, arming, and disciplining the militia, and for governing such part of them as may be employed in the service of the United States, reserving to the States respectively, the appointment of the officers, and the authority of training the militia according to the discipline prescribed by Congress;

17. To exercise exclusive legislation in all cases whatsoever, over such district (not exceeding ten miles square) as may, by cession of particular States, and the acceptance of Congress, become the seat of the government of the United States, and to exercise like authority over all places purchased by the consent of the legislature of the State in which the same shall be, for the erection of forts, magazines, arsenals, dockyards, and other needful buildings; and

18. To make all laws which shall be necessary and proper for carrying into execution the foregoing powers, and all other powers vested by this Constitution in the government of the United Stales, or in any department or officer thereof.

SECTION 9.   1. The migration or importation of such persons as any of the States now existing shall think proper to admit, shall not be prohibited by the Congress prior to the year one thousand eight hundred and eight, but a tax or duty may be imposed on such importation, not exceeding ten dollars for each person.

2. The privilege of the writ of *habeas corpus* shall not be suspended, unless when in cases of rebellion or invasion the public safety may require it.

3. No bill of attainder or *ex post facto* law shall be passed.

4. No capitation, or other direct, tax shall be laid unless in proportion to the census or enumeration hereinbefore directed to be taken.*

5. No tax or duty shall be laid on articles exported from any State.

6. No preference shall be given by any regulation of commerce or revenue to the ports of one State over those of another: nor shall vessels bound to, or from, one State be obliged to enter, clear, or pay duties in another.

7. No money shall be drawn from the treasury, but in consequence of appropriations made by law; and a regular statement and account of the receipts and expenditures of all public money shall be published from time to time.

8. No title of nobility shall be granted by the United States: and no person holding any office of profit or trust under them, shall, without the consent of the Congress, accept of any present, emolument, office, or title, of any kind whatever, from any king, prince, or foreign State.

Section 10. 1. No State shall enter into any treaty, alliance, or confederation; grant letters of marque and reprisal; coin money; emit bills of credit; make anything but gold and silver coin a tender in payment of debts; pass any bill of attainder, *ex post facto* law, or law impairing the obligation of contracts, or grant any title of nobility.

2. No State shall, without the consent of the Congress, lay any imposts or duties on imports or exports, except what may be absolutely necessary for executing its inspection laws; and the net produce of all duties and imposts laid by any State on imports or exports, shall be for the use of the treasury of the United States; and all such laws shall be subject to the revision and control of the Congress.

3. No State shall, without the consent of the Congress, lay any duty of tonnage, keep troops, or ships of war in time of peace, enter into any agreement or compact with another State, or with a foreign power, or engage in war, unless actually invaded, or in such imminent danger as will not admit of delay.

ARTICLE II

Section 1. 1. The executive power shall be vested in a President of the United States of America. He shall hold his office during the term of four years, and, together with the Vice President, chosen for the same term, be elected as follows:

*See the 16th Amendment.

2. Each State* shall appoint, in such manner as the legislature thereof may direct, a number of electors, equal to the whole number of senators and representatives to which the State may be entitled in the Congress: but no senator or representative, or person holding an office of trust or profit under the United States, shall be appointed an elector.

The electors shall meet in their respective States, and vote by ballot for two persons, of whom one at least shall not be an inhabitant of the same State with themselves. And they shall make a list of all the persons voted for, and of the number of votes for each; which list they shall sign and certify, and transmit sealed to the seat of the government of the United States, directed to the president of the Senate. The president of the Senate shall, in the presence of the Senate and House of Representatives, open all the certificates, and the votes shall then be counted. The person having the greatest number of votes shall be the President, if such number be a majority of the whole number of electors appointed; and if there be more than one who have such majority, and have an equal number of votes, then the House of Representatives shall immediately choose by ballot one of them for President; and if no person have a majority, then from the five highest on the list the said House shall in like manner choose the President. But in choosing the President, the votes shall be taken by States, the representation from each state having one vote; a quorum for this purpose shall consist of a member or members from two thirds of the States, and a majority of all the States shall be necessary to a choice. In every case, after the choice of the President, the person having the greatest number of votes of the electors shall be the Vice President. But if there should remain two or more who have equal votes, the Senate shall choose from them by ballot the Vice President.†

3. The Congress may determine the time of choosing the electors, and the day on which they shall give their votes; which day shall be the same throughout the United States.

4. No person except a natural born citizen, or a citizen of the United States, at the time of the adoption of this Constitution, shall be eligible to the office of President; neither shall any person be eligible to that office who shall not have attained to the age of thirty-five years, and been fourteen years a resident within the United States.

5. In case of the removal of the President from office, or of his death, resignation, or inability to discharge the powers and duties of the said office, the same shall devolve on the Vice President, and the Congress may by law provide for the case of removal, death, resignation, or inability, both of the President and Vice President, declaring what officer shall then

* See 23rd Amendment.
† This paragraph was superseded by the 12th Amendment.

act as President, and such officer shall act accordingly, until the disability be removed, or a President shall be elected.*

6. The President shall, at stated times, receive for his services a compensation, which shall neither be increased nor diminished during the period for which he shall have been elected, and he shall not receive within that period any other emolument from the United States, or any of them.

7. Before he enter on the execution of his office, he shall take the following oath or affirmation:—"I do solemnly swear (or affirm) that I will faithfully execute the office of President of the United States, and will to the best of my ability, preserve, protect and defend the Constitution of the United States."

Section 2.   1. The President shall be commander in chief of the army and navy of the United States, and of the militia of the several States, when called into the actual service of the United States; he may require the opinion, in writing, of the principal officer in each of the executive departments, upon any subject relating to the duties of their respective offices, and he shall have power to grant reprieves and pardons for offenses against the United States, except in cases of impeachment.

2. He shall have power, by and with the advice and consent of the Senate, to make treaties, provided two thirds of the senators present concur; and he shall nominate, and by and with the advice and consent of the Senate, shall appoint ambassadors, other public ministers and consuls, judges of the Supreme Court, and all other officers of the United States, whose appointments are not herein otherwise provided for, and which shall be established by law: but the Congress may by law vest the appointment of such inferior officers, as they think proper, in the President alone, in the courts of law, or in the heads of departments.

3. The President shall have power to fill up all vacancies that may happen during the recess of the Senate, by granting commissions which shall expire at the end of their next session.

Section 3.   He shall from time to time give to the Congress information of the state of the Union, and recommend to their consideration such measures as he shall judge necessary and expedient; he may, on extraordinary occasions, convene both Houses, or either of them, and in case of disagreement between them with respect to the time of adjournment, he may adjourn them to such time as he shall think proper; he shall receive ambassadors and other public ministers; he shall take care that the laws be faithfully executed, and shall commission all the officers of the United States.

Section 4.   The President, Vice President, and all civil officers of the

* See the 25th Amendment.

United States, shall be removed from office on impeachment for and conviction of, treason, bribery, or other high crimes and misdemeanors.

ARTICLE III

SECTION 1.   The judicial power of the United States shall be vested in one Supreme Court, and in such inferior courts as the Congress may from time to time ordain and establish. The judges, both of the Supreme and inferior courts, shall hold their offices during good behavior, and shall, at stated times, receive for their services, a compensation, which shall not be diminished during their continuance in office.

SECTION 2.   1. The judicial power shall extend to all cases, in law and equity, arising under this Constitution, the laws of the United States, and treaties made, or which shall be made, under their authority;—to all cases affecting ambassadors, other public ministers and consuls;—to all cases of admiralty and maritime jurisdiction;—to controversies to which the United States shall be a party;—to controversies between two or more States; —between a State and citizens of another State;—between citizens of different States;*—between citizens of the same State claiming lands under grants of different States, and between a State, or the citizens thereof, and foreign States, citizens or subjects.

2.   In all cases affecting ambassadors, other public ministers and consuls, and those in which a State shall be party, the Supreme Court shall have original jurisdiction. In all the other cases before mentioned, the Supreme Court shall have appellate jurisdiction, both as to law and to fact, with such exceptions, and under such regulations as the Congress shall make.

3.   The trial of all crimes, except in cases of impeachment, shall be by jury; and such trial shall be held in the State where the said crimes shall have been committed; but when not committed within any State, the trial shall be at such place or places as the Congress may by law have directed.

SECTION 3.   1. Treason against the United States shall consist only in levying war against them, or in adhering to their enemies, giving them aid and comfort. No person shall be convicted of treason unless on the testimony of two witnesses to the same overt act, or on confession in open court.

2.   The Congress shall have power to declare the punishment of treason, but no attainder of treason shall work corruption of blood, or forfeiture except during the life of the person attained.

* See the 11th Amendment.

ARTICLE IV

SECTION 1.   Full faith and credit shall be given in each State to the public acts, records, and judicial proceedings of every other State. And the Congress may by general laws prescribe the manner in which such acts, records and proceedings shall be proved, and the effect thereof.

SECTION 2.   1. The citizens of each State shall be entitled to all privileges and immunities of citizens in the several States.*

2. A person charged in any State with treason, felony, or other crime, who shall flee from justice, and be found in another State, shall on demand of the executive authority of the State from which he fled, be delivered up to be removed to the State having jurisdiction of the crime.

3. No person held to service or labor in one State under the laws thereof, escaping into another, shall, in consequence of any law or regulation therein, be discharged from such service or labor, but shall be delivered up on claim of the party to whom such service or labor may be due.†

SECTION 3.   1. New States may be admitted by the Congress into this Union; but no new State shall be formed or erected within the jurisdiction of any other State; nor any State be formed by the junction of two or more States, or parts of States, without the consent of the legislatures of the States concerned as well as of the Congress.

2. The Congress shall have power to dispose of and make all needful rules and regulations respecting the territory or other property belonging to the United States; and nothing in this Constitution shall be so construed as to prejudice any claims of the United States, or of any particular State.

SECTION 4.   The United States shall guarantee to every State in this Union a republican form of government, and shall protect each of them against invasion; and on application of the legislature, or of the executive (when the legislature cannot be convened) against domestic violence.

ARTICLE V

The Congress, whenever two thirds of both Houses shall deem it necessary, shall propose amendments to this Constitution, or, on the application of the legislatures of two thirds of the several States, shall call a

* See the 14th Amendment, Sec. 1.
† See the 13th Amendment.

convention for proposing amendments, which in either case, shall be valid to all intents and purposes, as part of this Constitution when ratified by the legislatures of three fourths of the several States, or by conventions in three fourths thereof, as the one or the other mode of ratification may be proposed by the Congress; Provided that no amendment which may be made prior to the year one thousand eight hundred and eight shall in any manner affect the first and fourth clauses in the ninth section of the first article; and that no State, without its consent, shall be deprived of its equal suffrage in the Senate.

ARTICLE VI

1. All debts contracted and engagements entered into, before the adoption of this Constitution, shall be as valid against the United States under this Constitution, as under the Confederation.

2. This Constitution, and the laws of the United States which shall bemade in pursuance thereof; and all treaties made, or which shall be made, under the authority of the United States, shall be the supreme law of the land; and the Judges in every State shall be bound thereby, anything in the Constitution or laws of any State to the contrary notwithstanding.

3. The senators and representatives before mentioned, and the members of the several State legislatures, and all executive and judicial officers, both of the United States and of the several States, shall be bound by oath or affirmation to support this Constitution; but no religious test shall ever be required as a qualification to any office or public trust under the United States.

ARTICLE VII

The ratification of the conventions of nine States shall be sufficient for the establishment of this Constitution between the States so ratifying the same.

Done in Convention by the unanimous consent of the States present the seventeenth day of September in the year of our Lord one thousand seven hundred and eighty-seven, and of the independence of the United States of America the twelfth. In witness whereof we have hereunto subscribed our names. [Names omitted]

[Articles in addition to, and amendment of, the Constitution of the United States of America, proposed by Congress, and ratified by the legislatures of the several States pursuant to the fifth article of the original Constitution.]

AMENDMENTS

First ten amendments (Bill of Rights) passed by Congress Sept. 25, 1789. Ratified by three-fourths of the States December 15, 1791.

ARTICLE I

Congress shall make no law respecting an establishment of religion, or prohibiting the free exercise thereof; or abridging the freedom of speech, or of the press; or the right of the people peaceably to assemble, and to petition the government for a redress of grievances.

ARTICLE II

A well regulated militia, being necessary to the security of a free State, the tight of the people to keep and bear arms, shall not be infringed.

ARTICLE III

No soldier shall, in time of peace be quartered in any house, without the consent of the owner, nor in time of war, but in a manner to be prescribed by law.

ARTICLE IV

The right of the people to be secure in their persons, houses, papers, and effects, against unreasonable searches and seizures, shall not be violated, and no warrants shall issue, but upon probable cause, supported by oath or affirmation, and particularly describing the place to be searched, and the persons or things to be seized.

ARTICLE V

No person shall be held to answer for a capital, or otherwise infamous crime, unless on a presentment or indictment of a grand jury, except in cases arising in the land or naval forces, or in the militia, when in actual service in time of war or public danger; nor shall any person be subject for the same offense to be twice put in jeopardy of life or limb; nor shall be compelled in any criminal case to be a witness against himself, nor be deprived of life, liberty, or property, without due process of law; nor shall private property be taken for public use without just compensation.

ARTICLE VI

In all criminal prosecutions, the accused shall enjoy the right to a speedy and public trial, by an impartial jury of the State and district wherein the crime shall have been committed, which district shall have been previously ascertained by law, and to be informed of the nature and cause of the accusation; to be confronted with the witnesses against him; to have compulsory process for obtaining witnesses in his favor, and to have the assistance of counsel for his defense.

ARTICLE VII

In suits at common law, where the value in controversy shall exceed twenty dollars, the right of trial by jury shall be preserved, and no fact tried by a jury shall be otherwise reexamined in any court of the United States, than according to the rules of the common law.

ARTICLE VIII

Excessive bail shall not be required, nor excessive fines imposed, nor cruel and unusual punishments inflicted.

ARTICLE IX

The enumeration in the Constitution of certain rights shall not be construed to deny or disparage others retained by the people.

ARTICLE X

The powers not delegated to the United States by the Constitution, nor prohibited by it to the States, are reserved to the States respectively, or to the people.

ARTICLE XI

Passed by Congress March 4, 1794. Ratified February 7, 1795.

The judicial power of the United States shall not be construed to extend to any suit in law or equity, commenced or prosecuted against one of the United States by citizens of another State, or by citizens or subjects of any foreign State.

ARTICLE XII

Passed by Congress December 9, 1803. Ratified July 27, 1804.

The electors shall meet in their respective States, and vote by ballot for President and Vice President, one of whom, at least, shall not be an inhabitant of the same State with themselves; they shall name in their ballots the person voted for as President, and in distinct ballots, the person voted for as Vice President, and they shall make distinct lists of all persons voted for as President and of all persons voted for as Vice President, and of the number of votes for each, which lists they shall sign and certify, and transmit sealed to the seat of the government of the United States, directed to the President of the Senate;—The President of the Senate shall, in the presence of the Senate and House of Representatives, open all the certificates and the votes shall then be counted;—The person having the greatest number of votes for President, shall be the President, if such number be a majority of the whole number of electors appointed; and if no person have such majority, then from the persons having the highest numbers not exceeding three on the list of those voted for as President, the House of Representatives shall choose immediately, by ballot, the President. But in choosing the President, the votes shall be taken by States, the representation from each State having one vote; a quorum for this purpose shall consist of a member or members from two thirds of the States, and a majority of all the States shall be necessary to a choice. And if the House of Representatives shall not choose a President whenever the right of choice shall devolve upon them, before the fourth day of March*

* See 20th Amendment

next following, then the Vice President shall act as President, as in the case of the death or other constitutional disability of the President. The person having the greatest number of votes as Vice President shall be the Vice President, if such number be a majority of the whole number of electors appointed, and if no person have a majority, then from the two highest numbers on the list, the Senate shall choose the Vice President; a quorum for the purpose shall consist of two thirds of the whole number of Senators, and a majority of the whole number shall be necessary to a choice. But no person constitutionally ineligible to the office of President shall be eligible to that of Vice President of the United States.

ARTICLE XIII

Passed by Congress January 31, 1865. Ratified December 6, 1865.

SECTION 1.   Neither slavery nor involuntary servitude, except as punishment for crime whereof the party shall have been duly convicted, shall exist within the United States, or any place subject to their jurisdiction.

SECTION 2.   Congress shall have power to enforce this article by appropriate legislation.

ARTICLE XIV

Passed by Congress June 13, 1866. Ratified July 9, 1868.

SECTION 1.   All persons born or naturalized in the United States, and subject to the jurisdiction thereof, are citizens of the United States and of the State wherein they reside. No State shall make or enforce any law which shall abridge the privileges or immunities of citizens of the United States; nor shall any State deprive any person of life, liberty, or property, without due process of law; nor deny to any person within its jurisdiction the equal protection of the laws.

SECTION 2.   Representatives shall be apportioned among the several States according to their respective numbers, counting the whole number of persons in each State, excluding Indians not taxed. But when the right to vote at any election for the choice of electors for President and Vice President of the United States, representatives in Congress, the executive and judicial officers of a State, or the members of the legislature thereof, is denied to any of the male inhabitants of such State, being twenty-one years of age, and citizens of the United States, or in any way abridged, except for participation in rebellion, or other crime, the basis of representation therein shall be reduced in the proportion which the number of such male citizens shall bear to the whole number of male citizens twenty-one years of age in such State.

SECTION 3.　　No person shall be a senator or representative in Congress, or elector of President and Vice President, or hold any office, civil or military, under the United States, or under any State, who having previously taken an oath, as a member of Congress, or as an officer of the United States, or as a member of any State legislature, or as an executive or judicial officer of any State, to support the Constitution of the United States, shall have engaged in insurrection or rebellion against the same, or given aid or comfort to the enemies thereof. But Congress may by a vote of two thirds of each House, remove such disability. ˙

SECTION 4.　　The validity of the public debt of the United States, authorized by law, including debts incurred for payment of pensions and bounties for services in suppressing insurrection or rebellion, shall not be questioned. But neither the United States nor any State shall assume or pay any debt or obligation incurred in aid of insurrection or rebellion against the United States, or any claim for the loss or emancipation of any slave; but all such debts, obligations, and claims shall be held illegal and void.

SECTION 5.　　The Congress shall have power to enforce, by appropriate legislation, the provisions of this article.

ARTICLE XV

Passed by Congress February 26, 1869 Ratified February 3, 1870.

SECTION 1.　　The right of citizens of the United States to vote shall not be denied or abridged by the United States or by any State on account of race, color, or previous condition of servitude.

SECTION 2.　　The Congress shall have power to enforce this article by appropriate legislation.

ARTICLE XVI

Passed by Congress July 2, 1909. Ratified February 3, 1913.

The Congress shall have power to lay and collect taxes on incomes, from whatever source derived, without apportionment among the several States, and without regard to any census or enumeration.

ARTICLE XVII

Passed by Congress May 13, 1912. Ratified April 8, 1913.

The Senate of the United States-shall be composed of two senators from each state, elected by the people thereof, for six years; and each senator shall have one vote. The electors in each State shall have the qualifications requisite for electors of the most numerous branch of the State legislature.

When vacancies happen in the representation of any State in the Senate, the executive authority of such State shall issue writs of election to fill such vacancies: *Provided,* That the legislature of any State may empower the executive thereof to make temporary appointments until the people fill the vacancies by election as the legislature may direct.

This amendment shall not be so construed as to affect the election or term of any senator chosen before it becomes valid as part of the Constitution.

ARTICLE XVIII*

Passed by Congress December 18, 1917. Ratified January 16, 1919.

After one year from the ratification of this article, the manufacture, sale, or transportation of intoxicating liquors within, the importation thereof into, or the exportation thereof from the United States and all territory subject to the jurisdiction thereof for beverage purposes is hereby prohibited.

The Congress and the several States shall have concurrent power to enforce this article by appropriate legislation.

This article shall be inoperative unless it shall have been ratified as an amendment to the Constitution by the legislatures of the several States, as provided in the Constitution, within seven years from the date of the submission hereof to the states by Congress.

ARTICLE XIX

Passed by Congress June 4, 1919. Ratified August 18, 1920.

The right of citizens of the United States to vote shall not be denied or abridged by the United States or by any State on account of sex.

The Congress shall have power by appropriate legislation to enforce the provisions of this article.

* Repealed by the 21st Amendment.

ARTICLE XX

Passed by Congress March 2, 1932. Ratified January 23, 1933.

SECTION 1.   The terms of the President and Vice President shall end at noon on the 20th day of January, and the terms of Senators and Representatives at noon on the 3d day of January, of the years in which such terms would have ended if this article had not been ratified; and the terms of their successors shall then begin.

SECTION 2.   The Congress shall assemble at least once in every year, and such meeting shall begin at noon on the 3d day of January, unless they shall by law appoint a different day.

SECTION 3.   If, at the time fixed for the beginning of the term of the President, the President-elect shall have died, the Vice President-elect shall become President. If a President shall not have been chosen before the time fixed for the beginning of his term, or if the President-elect shall have failed to qualify, then the Vice President-elect shall act as President until a President shall have qualified; and the Congress may by law provide for the case wherein neither a President-elect nor a Vice President-elect shall have qualified, declaring who shall then act as President, or the manner in which one who is to act shall be selected, and such person shall act accordingly until a President or Vice President shall have qualified.

SECTION 4.   The Congress may by law provide for the case of the death of any of the persons from whom the House of Representatives may choose a President whenever the right of choice shall have devolved upon them, and for the case of the death of any of the persons from whom the Senate may choose a Vice President whenever the right of choice shall have devolved upon them.

SECTION 5.   Sections 1 and 2 shall take effect on the 15th day of October following the ratification of this article.

SECTION 6.   This article shall be inoperative unless it shall have been ratified as an amendment to the Constitution by the legislatures of three-fourths of the several States within seven years from the date of its submission.

ARTICLE XXI

Passed by Congress February 20, 1933. Ratified December 5, 1933.

SECTION 1.   The Eighteenth Article of amendment to the Constitution of the United States is hereby repealed.

SECTION 2.   The transportation or importation into any State, Territory, or possession of the United States for delivery or use therein of intoxicating liquors in violation of the laws thereof, is hereby prohibited.

SECTION 3.   This article shall be inoperative unless it shall have been ratified as an amendment to the Constitution by conventions in the several States, as provided in the Constitution, within seven years from the date of the submission thereof to the States by the Congress.

ARTICLE XXII

Passed by Congress March 21, 1947. Ratified February 27, 1951.

No person shall be elected to the office of the President more than twice, and no person who has held the office of President, or acted as President, for more than two years of a term to which some other person was elected President shall be elected to the office of the President more than once.

But this article shall not apply to any person holding the office of President when this article was proposed by the Congress, and shall not prevent any person who may be holding the office of President, or acting as President, during the term within which this article becomes operative from holding the office of President or acting as President during the remainder of such term.

This article shall be inoperative unless it shall have been ratified as an amendment to the Constitution by the legislatures of three-fourths of the several states within seven years from the date of its submission to the states by the Congress.

ARTICLE XXIII

Passed by Congress June 16, 1960. Ratified March 29, 1961.

SECTION 1.   The District constituting the seat of Government of the United States shall appoint in such manner as the Congress may direct:

A number of electors of President and Vice President equal to the whole number of Senators and Representatives in Congress to which the District would be entitled if it were a State, but in no event more than the least populous state; they shall be in addition to those appointed by the states, but shall be considered, for the purpose of the election of President and Vice President, to be electors appointed by a state; and they shall meet in the District and perform such duties as provided by the twelfth article of amendment.

SECTION 2.   The Congress shall have power to enforce this article by appropriate legislation.

ARTICLE XXIV

Passed by Congress August 27, 1962. Ratified January 23, 1964.

SECTION 1.   The right of citizens of the United States to vote in any primary or other election for President or Vice President, for electors for President or Vice President, or for Senator or Representative in Congress, shall not be denied or abridged by the United States or any State by reason of failure to pay any poll tax or other tax.

SECTION 2.   The Congress shall have the power to enforce this article by appropriate legislation.

ARTICLE XXV

Passed by Congress July 6, 1965. Ratified February 10, 1967.

SECTION 1.   In case of the removal of the President from office or his death or resignation, the Vice President shall become President.

SECTION 2.   Whenever there is a vacancy in the office of the Vice President, the President shall nominate a Vice President who shall take the office upon confirmation by a majority vote of both houses of Congress.

SECTION 3.   Whenever the President transmits to the President pro tempore of the Senate and the Speaker of the House of Representatives his written declaration that he is unable to discharge the powers and duties of his office, and until he transmits to them a written declaration to the contrary, such powers and duties shall be discharged by the Vice President as Acting President.

SECTION 4.   Whenever the Vice President and a majority of either the principal officers of the executive departments, or of such other body as Congress may by law provide, transmit to the President pro tempore of the Senate and the Speaker of the House of Representatives their written declaration that the President is unable to discharge the powers and duties of his office, the Vice President shall immediately assume the powers and duties of the office of Acting President.

Thereafter, when the President transmits to the President pro tempore of the Senate and the Speaker of the House of Representative his written declaration that no inability exists, he shall resume the powers and duties of his office unless the Vice President and a majority of either the principal officers of the executive department, or of such other body as Congress may by law provide, transmit within four days to the President pro tempore of the Senate and the Speaker of the House of Representatives their written declaration that the President is unable to discharge the powers and duties of his office. Thereupon Congress shall decide the issue, assembling within 48 hours for that purpose if not in session. If the Congress, within 21 days after receipt of the latter written declaration, or, if Congress is not in session, within 21 days after Congress is required to assemble, determines by two thirds vote of both houses that the President is unable to discharge the powers and duties of his office, the Vice President shall continue to discharge the same as Acting President; otherwise, the President shall resume the powers and duties of his office.

ARTICLE XXVI

Passed by Congress March 23, 1971. Ratified June 30, 1971.

SECTION 1.   The right of citizens of the United States, who are eighteen years of age or older, to vote shall not be denied or abridged by the United States or any state on account of age.

SECTION 2.   The Congress shall have the power to enforce this article by appropriate legislation.

ARTICLE XXVII

Proposed by Congress September 25, 1989.
Ratified May 7, 1992.

No law, varying the compensation for the services of the Senators and Representatives, shall take effect, until an election of Representatives shall have intervened.

Index

I

M

N

Q

R

S